MW01617137

ATLANTIS

THE LOST CITY IS IN JAVA SEA

ATLANTIS

THE LOST CITY IS IN JAVA SEA

DHANI IRWANTO

INDONESIA HYDRO® MEDIA
BOGOR, INDONESIA

FOR MY CHILDREN

HANGGARA SURYA DEWANGGA
HANGGITA INDRASARI DEWI

First published in Indonesia in 2015
by INDONESIA HYDRO® MEDIA

© 2015 Dhani Irwanto

All rights reserved. No part of this publication may be
reproduced, stored in a retrieval system, or transmitted
in any form or by any means, electronic, mechanical,
photocopying, recording, or otherwise, without the prior
permission of the copyright owner.

Dhani Irwanto has asserted his right to be
identified as the author of this work.

A CIP catalogue record for this book is available
from the National Library of Indonesia

Website: atlantisjavasea.com

ISBN 978-602-72449-1-7

Printed and bound in Indonesia by
INDONESIA HYDRO® MEDIA
Bukit Golf, Riverside II Block B01 No 46
Gunungputri, Bogor Regency
West Java 16963
Indonesia

CONTENTS

***

INTRODUCTION

After thousands of years, so many of us still search for the answer to the mystery of Atlantis. From time to time, archaeologists and historians locate evidence. There have been many locations proposed for the location of Atlantis. Some are more or less serious attempts at legitimate scholarly or archaeological works; others have been made by psychic or other pseudoscientific means. Ever since the first recorded history of Atlantis, written by the Greek philosopher Plato over 2,300 years ago, debate has raged as to whether or not Atlantis ever really existed. The existence of Atlantis is still not proven and most people regard it as a fairy tale.

Plato describes Atlantis as a land larger than Libya and Asia Minor put together, located just beyond the Pillars of Heracles. Atlantis was an extraordinary utopian society, thriving around 9,600 BC, which valued peace, art and wisdom, possessed advanced technological knowledge for the time, and enjoyed riches beyond that of any subsequent civilization. The land was said to have been very fertile, with abundant food, water, animals, wood, and flowers. It was protected by the god Poseidon, who made his son Atlas king and namesake of the land Atlantis. As the Atlanteans grew powerful, their ethics declined. Their armies eventually conquered Africa as far as Egypt and Europe as far as Tyrrhenia before being driven back by an Athenian-led alliance. Later, by way of divine punishment, violent and devastating earthquakes and the resulting waves and floods destroyed the Athenian army as well as the entire island continent of Atlantis, submerging it beneath the sea "in a single day and night".

Plato's writings pertaining to Atlantis are the *Timaeus* and the *Critias*, written in *ca* 360 BC, at which time Plato would have been aged about 67 or 68. These are the earliest known written records about the lost continent of Atlantis, all other written references to Atlantis have been written since, and have been based on these writings by Plato. The *Timaeus* includes only a passing reference to Atlantis but the second writing, the *Critias*, has a much more in depth descriptions of Atlantis leading up to its downfall.

The *Timaeus* and the *Critias* are actually written in the form of dialogues among four main characters: Socrates (Greek philosopher and Plato's teacher), Critias (a poet and historian, Plato's great grandfather), Timaeus (an Italian astronomer) and Hermocrates (a statesman and soldier from Syracuse). All were real people.

1

The story of Atlantis as told by the Egyptian priest is probably ever really existed but Plato had been distorting the facts in order to support his ideology of an ideal state as in *The Republic*, or he added some embellishments of his own or aspects drawn from other legends. He embodied Athens as part of the story to show the greatest and noblest action of Ancient Athens, which was probably another state in the myth told by the Egyptian priest.

The existence of Atlantis is supported by the fact that it is described in great details, mainly in *Critias*. In additions, various conditions, events and goods like the two-season climate, flood (tsunami), *orichalcum*, geographical features, buffalo and many fruits unknown to Plato are also described in detailed and lengthy words. The recent knowledge of late glacial and postglacial sea level rise and land subsidence that occurred almost precisely at the time described by Plato also becomes strong evidence to the truth of the story.

The author agrees to the statement of the late Professor Santos that Atlantis could not be found because everyone had been looking in the wrong place and that Plato's work on the subject had been misunderstood. The true location of Atlantis was in Indonesia and the neighboring lands that man, after emigrating from the semi-deserted savannas of Africa, first found the ideal climatic conditions for development, and it was there that he invented agriculture and civilization. During the Pleistocene and, more exactly, during the glacial episodes that happened at intervals of about 20 thousand years, sea level was about 100 – 150 meters below the present value. With this, a large coastal strip – the so-called Continental Platform – became exposed, forming land bridges that interconnected many islands and regions. The most dramatic of such exposures took place in the region of Indonesia, precisely the spot where humanity first flourished. It is known as Sundaland, a biogeographical region of Southeast Asia which encompasses the Sunda Shelf, the part of the Asian continental shelf that was exposed during the last glacial period, popularly known as the Ice Age.

As stated by Professor Oppenheimer, as the Ice Age ended, there were three catastrophic and rapid rises in sea level. The last of these, which finished shortly before the start of civilization in Mesopotamia, may have been the one that was remembered. These three floods drowned the coastal cultures and all the flat continental shelves of Southeast Asia. As the sea rolled in, there was a mass emigration from the sinking continent. These flood-driven refugees carried their domestic animals with them in large ocean-going canoes in all directions. The networks of sea trade, created by their settlements around the Indian Ocean, fertilized the Neolithic cultures of China, India, Mesopotamia and Egypt. The most solid facts come from oceanographic research of the last decades. It now appears that the great rise in sea level after the last Ice Age, known about for many years, was not gradual; three sudden ice-melts, the last of which was only 8,000 years ago, had catastrophic effects on tropical coasts with flat continental shelves. Rapid land loss was compounded by super waves, set off by cracks in the earth's crust as the weight of ice shifted to the seas.

The Younger Dryas stadial, also referred to as the Big Freeze, was a geologically brief (1,300 ± 70 years) period of cold climatic conditions and drought which occurred between approximately 12,800 and 11,500 years BP. The sea surface temperature in Sundaland region during the Younger Dryas period was approximately 1 °C below the present-day temperature, and the sea level was approximately 60 meters below the present-day sea level. The Sundaland vegetation during the Last Glacial Maximum consist of mainly tropical rainforest, tropical grasslands, monsoon or dry forest and a few tropical semi deserts.

As described by Plato, the state of Atlantis was larger than Libya and Asia Minor put together, the way to other islands, and might pass to the whole of the opposite continent which encompasses the true ocean. Sundaland during the Ice Age fits those descriptions. It was the way to other islands like Nusatenggara Islands, Sulawesi, Maluku Islands, Mindanau and Luzon. Passing through these islands, one might reach the opposite continent, *ie* the large "Sahul Continent" combining the Australian Continent, Papua and the land connecting them, which encompassed Pacific and Indian Oceans.

Also, as described by Plato, Atlantis and the surrounding regions reaped the benefit of the annual rainfall, abundance of water, had an excellently attempered two-season climate, very lofty and precipitous. These are strongly interpreted as characteristics of a tropical climate where Sundaland is located. Atlantis was full of rich earth, abundance of wood, cultivated by true husbandment, had the noble nature, had the best soil in the world, abundance of animals including elephants; roots, herbage, woods or essences which distil from fruit and flower; and two harvests each year of cultivation fed by rains and irrigation canals. These are also the characteristics of Sundaland which is a major global key producer of a wide variety of agricultural tropical products, has high levels of biodiversity and endemicity of flora and fauna, has dense tropical forest, and has rice cultivation cultures.

Minerals were explored in Atlantis: gold, *orichalcum*, silver, tin, brass and stone. Sundaland, until today, is the producer of various minerals with relatively large quantities due to its geological and tectonic conditions that favor the formation of the mineral resources.

The Atlantis Island was situated in front of a strait, which was called (by the Athens) the Pillars of Heracles, surrounded by a real sea and there was a harbor inside having a narrow entrance. The surrounding land may be most truly called a boundless continent. The boundless continent is the main land of Sundaland attached to the Asian Continent, and the only sea surrounded by it was in those days the ancient Java Sea. Therefore, the author hypothesizes that the Atlantis Island is located in Java Sea. The Atlantis Island was an island located near the main land identified from the elevation grids. The island was situated in front of a strait separating the island and the main land. There was a relatively flat plain on the north; part of it is now the southern part of Kalimantan Island.

The whole country of Atlantis had a level, smooth and even plain descended towards the sea, surrounded by mountains celebrated for their number, size and beauty, looked towards the south and sheltered from the north. There was a relatively flat plain on the north of ancient Java Sea; part of it is now the southern part of Kalimantan Island. The slope of the ground surface of southern Kalimantan is mostly less than 1% declining southward towards the Java Sea and no visible mound on the whole plain. One may consider this as a very flat plain. The present-day conditions of the plain above the sea water level consist of swampy areas, tidal swamp irrigation practices, housing over water, water transportation, mangroves and peat land. There are two mountainous areas around the northern part of the plain, Muller-Schwaner and Meratus Mountains. These mountains are mostly covered by primary forest, inhabited by enormous kinds of animals and as the inhabitations of the native Dayak tribes.

Plato describes the state of Atlantis in great details, mainly in *Critias*. These become the subjects of the author to hypothesize that the lost city of Atlantis is in Java Sea. The subjects of the hypotheses include comprehensive studies of topography, bathymetry, geology, hydrology, climatology, oceanography, geophysics, hydraulics, metallurgy, agriculture, biology, civilization, mythology, folklore, culture, linguistics, history and archaeology of the Sundaland and other related regions in the world. These include over 5-year research and analysis of textbooks, papers, internet sites and digital data collected by the author as well as some site observations.

***

4

PLATO'S ATLANTIS

The story of Atlantis comes to us from *Timaeus* and *Critias*, Socratic dialogues, written in about 360 BC by Plato. There are four people at this meeting who had met the previous day to hear Socrates describes the ideal state. Socrates wants Timaeus of Locri, Hermocrates, and Critias to tell him stories about Athens interacting with other states. The first is Critias, who talks about his great grandfather's meeting with Solon, one of the seven sages, an Athenian poet and famous lawgiver. Solon had been to Egypt where priests had compared Egypt and Athens and talked about the gods and legends of both lands. One such Egyptian story is about Atlantis.

Atlantis, a likely legendary land nation mentioned in Plato's dialogues *Timaeus* and *Critias*, has been an object of fascination among western philosophers and historians for nearly 2,400 years. Plato (*ca* 424 – *ca* 328 BC) describes it as a powerful and advanced kingdom that sank, in a night and a day, into the ocean around 9,600 BC.

Plato (through the character Critias in his dialogues) describes Atlantis as a land larger than Libya and Asia Minor put together, located just beyond the Pillars of Heracles. Its culture was advanced and it had a constitution suspiciously similar to the one outlined in Plato's *Republic*. It was protected by the god Poseidon, who made his son Atlas king and namesake of the land Atlantis. As the Atlanteans grew powerful, their ethics declined. Their armies eventually conquered Africa as far as Egypt and Europe as far as Tyrrhenia (modern Lebanon) before being driven back by an Athenian-led alliance. Later, by way of divine punishment, the island was beset by an earthquake and a flood, and sank into a muddy sea.

ORIGINS

In Plato's *Timaeus* and *Critias*, Critias said he heard the story of Atlantis from his grandfather, Critias (the same name). Critias the elder was told by his father, Dropides, who had heard it from the Athenian statesman Solon (300 years before Plato's time), who had learned it from an Egyptian priest, who said it had happened 9,000 years before that.

THE STORY

When Poseidon fell in love with a mortal woman, Cleito, he created a dwelling at the top of a hill near the middle of an island and surrounded the dwelling with rings of water and land to protect her. Cleito gave birth to five sets of twin boys who became the first rulers of Atlantis. The land of Atlantis was divided among the brothers with the eldest, Atlas, first king of Atlantis, being given control over the central hill and surrounding areas.

To facilitate travel and trade, the zones of water were then bridged over, and water canals through the rings of land and from the outermost ring of water to the sea were cut. The city of Atlantis sat just outside the outer ring of water and spread across the land. This was a densely populated area where the majority of the population lived.

At the top of the central hill, a temple was built to honor Poseidon which housed a giant gold statue of Poseidon riding a chariot pulled by winged horses. It was here that the rulers of Atlantis would come to discuss laws, pass judgments and pay tribute to Poseidon.

Beyond the city lay a fertile plain looked toward the south and sheltered from the north surrounded by a perimeter canal used to collect water from the rivers and streams of the mountains. Surrounding the plain to the north were mountains which soared to the skies. Villages, lakes, rivers, and meadows dotted the mountains. Inland canals and transverse passages were cut on the plain.

The climate was such that two harvests were possible each year, one in the winter fed by the rains and one in the summer fed by irrigation from the canal. Besides the harvests, the island provided all kinds of herbs, fruits, and nuts. An abundance of animals, including elephants, roamed the island.

For generations the Atlanteans lived simple, virtuous lives. But slowly they began to change. Greed and power began to corrupt them. When Zeus saw the immorality of the Atlanteans he gathered the other gods to determine a suitable punishment. Soon, in one violent surge it was gone. The island of Atlantis, its people, and its memory were swallowed by the sea.

Some writers debate the English translation of the dialogues written in Ancient Greek. Some of them like "in front of the straits" can be "beyond the straits" or "ahead of the straits"; "pillars" can be "walls", "stone blocks" or "columns"; "islands" can be "continents" or "lands", or vice versa; "seas" can be "oceans" or "waters", or vice versa; and "fruits" can be "crops", "groceries" or "produces". The author prefers to use the translation made by Benjamin Jowett*, though others also used as references.

PLATO

Plato was a student of Socrates until the latter's death in *ca* 399 BC at the hands of the Athenian authorities. After his teacher's death, Plato traveled extensively, including journeys in Egypt.

In 387 BC he returned to Athens and founded an academy, a school of science and philosophy that became the model for the modern university. Perhaps the most famous student of the academy was Aristotle whose teachings have had tremendous impact on philosophy through today.

Due to the academy's safekeeping, many of Plato's works have survived. His extant writings are in the form of letters and dialogues, the most famous of which is probably *The Republic*. His writings cover subjects ranging from knowledge to happiness to politics to nature.

Two of his dialogues, *Timaeus* and *Critias*, hold the only known original references to the Atlantis.

TIMAEUS AND *CRITIAS*

Timaeus and *Critias*, two of Plato's dialogues, are the only existing written records which specifically refer to Atlantis. The dialogues are conversations between Socrates, Hermocrates, Timaeus, and Critias. Apparently in response to a prior talk by Socrates about ideal societies, Timaeus and Critias agree to entertain Socrates with a tale that is "not a fiction but a true story".

The story is about the conflict between the ancient Athenians and the Atlanteans 9,000 years before their time. Knowledge of the distant past apparently forgotten to the Athenians of Plato's day, the story of Atlantis was conveyed to Solon by Egyptian priests. Solon passed the tale to Dropides, the great grandfather of Critias. Critias learned of it from his grandfather also named Critias, son of Dropides.

---

* Benjamin Jowett (15 April 1817 – 1 October 1893) was renowned as an influential tutor and administrative reformer in the University of Oxford, a theologian and translator of Plato. He was Master of Balliol College, Oxford.

All of the men, except for Timaeus, who take part in or are mentioned in *Timaeus* and *Critias* are known to have actually existed in ancient Greece. Records of their lives and deeds have been recorded in other writings from the time period.

There are two people named Critias related to the story of Atlantis and this can lead to some confusion. There is the Critias who actually takes part in the dialogues. He is the one who tells the story of Atlantis to Socrates. Then there is Critias who was the grandfather of the Critias of the dialogues. This elder Critias told the story of Atlantis to his grandson, Critias, who then conveyed the story to Socrates in the dialogues.

Those who actually take part in the dialogues:

1. Timaeus – there is no historical record of him.
2. Critias – Plato's great grandfather.
3. Socrates – Plato's mentor and teacher. He was condemned to death by authorities in Athens for "corrupting the moral of Athenian youth"; he lived from *ca* 469 to *ca* 399 BC.
4. Hermocrates – statesman and soldier from Syracuse.

Those whom mentioned in the dialogues:

1. Solon – Athenian traveler, poet, and lawgiver who lived from approximately *ca* 638 to *ca* 559 BC. According to Plato it was he who learned of the story of Atlantis from an Egyptian priest.
2. Dropides – Critias' great grandfather who was told the story of Atlantis by Solon, a distant relative and close friend.
3. Critias – Son of Dropides and grandfather of Critias who takes part in the dialogues. It was he who related the story of Atlantis to the Critias of the dialogues.

SHORT DESCRIPTIONS OF ATLANTIS

FROM *TIMAEUS*

1. Beyond the Pillars of Heracles
2. The "Atlantic" was then navigable
3. Larger than Libya and Asia Minor combined
4. The way to the other islands
5. Might pass to the opposite continent encompasses true ocean

FROM *CRITIAS*

CANAL FROM SEA

1. 300 feet wide and 100 feet deep
2. 50 stadia (9,250 meters) long beginning from the sea to the rings of water and land

CENTER LAND

1. 5 stadia (925 meters) in diameter
2. A temple was built to honor Poseidon which housed a giant gold statue of Poseidon riding a chariot pulled by winged horses
3. Surrounded by a wall covered with *orichalcum*
4. Surrounded by a ring of water 1 stadium (185 meters) wide

INNER-RING LAND

1. 2 stadia (370 m) wide
2. Surrounded by a wall covered with tin
3. Surrounded by a ring of water 2 stadia (370 meters) wide

OUTER-RING LAND

1. Ring closest to sea and 3 stadia (555 meters) in width
2. Contained horse racing track
3. Surrounded by a wall covered with brass
4. Surrounded by a ring of water 3 stadia (555 meters) wide

PLAIN

1. Rectangular and oblong, 3,000 stadia (555 kilometers) long, 2,000 stadia (370 kilometers) wide
2. Open to the sea on the south (where the canal exited to the sea)
3. Surrounded by mountains to the north
4. Abundant timber, meadows, marshes, swamps, rivers, mountains, plains

DITCHES

1. Perimeter ditch: 100 feet deep, 1 stadium (185 meters) wide and 10,000 stadia (1850 kilometers) long surrounding the whole plain
2. Artificial, received streams from the mountain, winding around the plain, meeting at the city and let off into the sea
3. Further inland, straight canals of 100 feet wide and 100 stadia (1850 meters) interval let off into the perimeter ditch
4. Transfer passages canals from one canal into another and to the city

5. Conveyed the wood from the mountain and produces in ships (boats, vessels)

PRODUCES

1. Two harvests each year, in the winter fed by the rains and in the summer fed by irrigation from the canals
2. Abundance of animals, including elephants, horses and bulls
3. Roots, herbage, woods and essences distilled from fruit and flower
4. Fruit admits of cultivation, both the dry sort, for nourishment and any other which use for food – common name pulse
5. Fruits having a hard rind, affording drinks, meats and ointments
6. Chestnuts and the like, which furnish pleasure and amusement
7. Fruits spoil with keeping, the pleasant kinds of dessert, console after dinner

MILITARY

1. Plain consisted of 10-square-stadium (3.4-square-kilometer) lots
2. For total of 60,000 lots
3. Each lot supplied 1/6 of a war chariot, 2 horses and riders, one pair of chariot horses, a horseman, and a charioteer; 2 heavily armed soldiers, 2 slingers, 3 stone shooters, 3 javelin men and 4 sailors (for fleet of 1,200 ships)

MISCELLANEOUS

1. 5 sets of twins – Atlas was first king
2. Names of the ten kings of Atlantis: Atlas, Gadeirus, Ampheres, Evaemon, Mneseos, Autochthon, Elasippus, Mestor, Azaes and Diaprepes
3. They governed other land as far as Egypt and Tyrrhenia
4. *Orichalcum*, a metal unknown to Plato was mined in quantities – second in value to gold
5. Two-season climate, very lofty and precipitous, abundance of water, excellently attempered climate, hot and cold springs suitable in summer and in winter
6. Stone was white, black and red – excavated from center island and land rings to form covered docking areas
7. Sank, in a night and a day, into the ocean around 9,600 BC or 11,600 BP

***

EXISTING LOCATION HYPOTHESES OF ATLANTIS*

The ancient Greeks were divided as to whether Plato's story was to be taken as history or mere metaphor. Since the 19th century there has been renewed interest in linking Plato's Atlantis to historical locations.

The historicity of Plato's tale was controversial in ancient times – his follower Crantor is said to have believed it, while Strabo (writing a few centuries later) records Aristotle's joke about Plato's ability to conjure nations out of thin air and then destroy them.

In the first centuries of the Christian era, Aristotle was taken at his word and Atlantis was little discussed. In 1627, the English philosopher and scientist Francis Bacon published a utopian novel titled *The New Atlantis*, depicting, like Plato before him, a politically and scientifically advanced society on a previously unknown oceanic island. In 1882, former US Congressman Ignatious L Donnelly published *Atlantis: The Antediluvian World*, which touched off a frenzy of works attempting to locate and learn from a historical Atlantis. Donnelly hypothesized an advanced civilization whose immigrants had populated much of ancient Europe, Africa and the Americas, and whose heroes had inspired Greek, Hindu and Scandinavian mythology. Donnelley's theories were popularized and elaborated by turn-of-the-20th-century theosophists and are often incorporated into contemporary New Age beliefs.

From time to time, archaeologists and historians locate evidence. There have been many locations proposed for the location of Atlantis. Some are more or less serious attempts at legitimate scholarly or archaeological works; others have been made by psychic or other pseudoscientific means. Many of the proposed sites share some of the characteristics of the Atlantis story (water, catastrophic end, relevant time period), but none have been proven conclusively to be the historical Atlantis.

Most of the historically proposed locations are in or near the Mediterranean Sea, either islands such as Sardinia, Crete and Santorini, Cyprus, Malta, and Ponza or as land based cities or states such as Troy, Tartessos or Tantalus (in the province

---

* Cited from Wikipedia® with some replenishment

11

of Manisa), Turkey, and the new theory of Israel-Sinai or Canaan as possible locations.

The massive Thera eruption, dated either to the 17th or the 15th century BC, caused a massive tsunami that experts hypothesize devastated the Minoan civilization on the nearby island of Crete, further leading some to believe that this may have been the catastrophe which inspired the story.

Locations as far-flung as Antarctica, Indonesia and the Caribbean have been proposed as the true site of Atlantis. The submerged island of Spartel near the Strait of Gibraltar would coincide with some elements of Plato's account, matching both the location and the date of submersion given in the *Critias*.

In the area of the Black Sea at least three locations have been proposed: Bosporus, Sinop and Ancomah (a legendary place near Trabzon).

The nearby Sea of Azov was proposed as another site in 2003. Various islands or island groups in the Atlantic Ocean were also identified as possible locations, notably the Azores (Mid-Atlantic islands which are a territory of Portugal), and several Caribbean islands.

In Northern Europe, Sweden (by Olof Rudbeck in *Atland*, 1672 – 1702), Ireland, and the North Sea have been proposed (Swedish geographer Ulf Erlingsson combines the North Sea and Ireland in a comprehensive hypothesis).

Areas in the Pacific and Indian Ocean have also been proposed including Indonesia, Malaysia or both (*ie* Sundaland) and stories of a lost continent off India named "Kumari Kandam" have drawn parallels to Atlantis. Even Cuba has been suggested.

The Canary Islands have also been identified as a possible location, west of the Straits of Gibraltar but in close proximity to the Mediterranean Sea. Some believe that Atlantis stretched from the tip of Spain to Central America.

Indonesia in recent years have seen an increasing number of supporters for the idea of Atlantis being located in the vicinity of today's archipelago, prior to the ending of the last Ice Age, on the submerged continental shelf now frequently referred to as Sundaland.

AROUND EGYPT

THERA (SANTORINI)

The theory that Thera was the site of the capital of Atlantis was suggested by Angelos Galanopoulos in 1960.

Soon after the discovery of the Minoan civilization at Knossos on Crete by Sir Arthur Evans in 1900, theories linking the disappearance of this advanced empire with the destruction of Atlantis were proposed by KT Frost in 1913 and ES Balch in 1917. This theory was revived by Spyridon Marinatos in 1950 and PBS Andrews in 1967. More recent archaeological, seismological, and volcanological evidence (recent arguments for Akrotiri being Atlantis have been popularized on television in shows such as The History Channel show *Lost Worlds* episode "Atlantis") has expanded the asserted connection of Crete, the island of Santorini, and the Minoan civilization with Plato's description of Atlantis. Evidence said to advance this idea includes:

1. The Minoan palace and buildings discovered at the digs at Knossos on Crete and at Akrotiri on the island of Thera have revealed that the Minoans possessed advanced engineering knowledge enabling the construction of three- and four-story buildings with intricate water piping systems, advanced air-flow management, and earthquake-resistant wood and masonry walls. This level of technology was, it is said, far ahead of that found on mainland Greece at the time.

2. Thera (also called Santorini) is the site of a massive volcanic caldera with an island at its center. Volcanologists have determined that the island was engulfed by a volcanic eruption, the Thera eruption, around 1,600 BC. The event, referred to as the Minoan eruption, was among the most powerful eruptions occurring in the history of civilization, ejecting approximately 60 km³ of material, leaving a layer of pumice and ash 10 to 80 meters thick for 20 to 30 km in all directions and having widespread effects across the eastern Mediterranean region. Volcanic events of this magnitude are known to generate tsunamis and archaeological evidence suggests that such a tsunami may have devastated the coastal Minoan settlements on Crete. Plato did not describe a volcanic eruption, although the events he described as "sunk by an earthquake" or "violent earthquakes, and only a flood (in singular)", could perhaps be interpreted as consistent with such an eruption and the resulting tsunami.

3. Plato described quarries on Atlantis where "one kind of stone was white, another black, and a third red", writing that these stones were quarried from the island and used in the construction. Rocks like this are found on Santorini.

4. The center of the metropolis of Atlantis was described as being laid out in circular manner, surrounded by three circular concentric pits of seawater and two earth-rings, each connected to the sea by a deep canal. Docks for a large number of ships, with a causeway, were also mentioned. Scientists reconstructing the shape of the island prior to the eruption have concluded that there was a ring configuration with only one narrow entrance to a larger lagoon with islands inside, much as Plato described. One fresco in the ruins of Akrotiri is believed to be a landscape of the city. It shows a large city in an island in the center of the caldera lagoon.

5. The ancient Greek for "between" and "larger" are easily confused in transcription and translation, so "larger than Asia and Libya", might have originally read "between Asia and Libya", which is how Classical Greeks would have described Thera and Crete.

NEAR CYPRUS

It has been argued by Robert Sarmast, an American architect, that the lost city of Atlantis lies at the bottom of the eastern Mediterranean within the Cyprus Basin. In his book and on his web site, he argues that images prepared from sonar data of the sea bottom of the Cyprus Basin southeast of Cyprus show features resembling man-made structures on it at depths of 1,500 meters. He interprets these features as being artificial structures that are part of the lost city of Atlantis as described by Plato. According to his ideas, several characteristics of Cyprus, including the presence of copper and extinct Cyprus Dwarf Elephants and local place names and festivals (Kataklysmos), support his identification of Cyprus as once being part of Atlantis. As with many other theories concerning the location of Atlantis, Sarmast speculates that its destruction by catastrophic flooding is reflected in the story of Noah's Flood in Genesis.

In part, Sarmast bases his claim that Atlantis can be found offshore of Cyprus beneath 0.9 mile (1.5 km) of water on an abundance of evidence that the Mediterranean Sea dried up during the Messinian Salinity Crisis when its level dropped by 3.2 to 4.9 km below the level of the Atlantic Ocean as the result of tectonic uplift blocking the inflow of water through Strait of Gibraltar.

Separated from the Atlantic Ocean, the Mediterranean Sea either partly or completely dried up as the result of evaporation. As a result, its formerly submerged bottom turned into a desert with large saline and brackish lakes. This area all was flooded when a ridge collapsed allowing the catastrophic flooding through the Straits of Gibraltar. However, Sarmast disagrees with mainstream geologists, oceanographers, and paleontologists in arguing that the closing of the Straits of Gibraltar; the desiccation and subaerial exposure of the floor of the Mediterranean Sea; and its catastrophic flooding has occurred "forty times or more times in its long and turbulent existence" and that "the age of each of these events is unknown". In the same interview, he also contradicts what mainstream geologists, oceanographers, and paleontologists argue in claiming that "Scientists know that roughly 18,000 years ago, there was not just one Mediterranean Sea, but three." However, he does not specify who these scientists are; nor does he cite peer-reviewed scientific literature that supports this claim.

Marine and other geologists, who have also studied the bottom of the Cyprus basin, and professional archaeologists completely disagree with his interpretations. Investigations by Dr C Hübscher of the Institut für Geophysik, Universität Hamburg, Germany, and others of the salt tectonics and mud volcanism within the Cyprus Basin, eastern Mediterranean Sea, demonstrated that the features which Sarmast interprets to be Atlantis consist only of a natural compressional fold caused by local salt tectonics and a slide scar with surficial compressional folds at the downslope end and sides of the slide. This research collaborate seismic data shown and discussed in the *Atlantis: New Revelations 2-hour Special episode of Digging for the Truth*, a History Channel documentary television series. Using reflection seismology, this documentary demonstrated techniques that what Sarmast interpreted to be artificial walls are natural tectonic landforms.

Furthermore, the interpretation of the age and stratigraphy of sediments blanketing the bottom of the Cyprus Basin from sea bottom cores containing Pleistocene and older marine sediments and thousands of kilometers of seismic lines from the Cyprus and adjacent basins clearly demonstrates that the Mediterranean Sea last dried up during the Messinian Salinity Crisis between 5.59 and 5.33 million years ago. For example, research conducted south of Cyprus as part of Leg 160 of the Ocean Drilling Project recovered from Sites 963, 965, and 966 cores of sediments underlying the bottom of the Mediterranean Sea at depths as shallow as 470, 1506, and 1044 meters below sea level. Thus, these cores came from parts of sea bottom of the eastern Mediterranean Sea that either lie above or at the depth of Sarmast's Atlantis, which lies at depths between 1460 and 1510 meters below mean sea level. These cores provide a detailed and continuous record of sea level that demonstrates that for millions of years at least during the entire Pliocene, Pleistocene, and Holocene epochs that the feature that Sarmast interprets to be Atlantis and its adjacent sea bottom were always submerged below sea level. Therefore, the entire Cyprus Basin, including the ridge where Sarmast claims that Atlantis is located, has been submerged beneath the Mediterranean Sea for millions of years. Since its formation, the sea bottom feature identified by Sarmast as "Atlantis" has always been submerged beneath over a kilometer of water.

HELIKE

A Giovannini has argued that the submergence of the Greek city of Helike in 373 BC, *ie* while Plato was alive, may have been the inspiration for a totally fictional story about Atlantis. The claim that Helike is the inspiration for Plato's Atlantis is also supported by Dora Katsonopoulou and Steven Soter.

SARDINIA

In 2002 the Italian journalist Sergio Frau published a book, *Le colonne d'Ercole* ("Pillars of Hercules"), in which he states that before Eratosthenes, all the ancient Greek writers located the Pillars of Hercules on the Strait of Sicily between Sicily and Tunisia, while only Alexander the Great's conquest of the east obliged Eratosthenes to move the pillars at Gibraltar in his description of the world.

According to his thesis, the Atlantis described by Plato could be identified with Sardinia. He argues that a tsunami once hit Sardinia which destroyed the enigmatic Nuragic civilization and that the survivors migrated to the Italian peninsula, founding the Etruscan civilization (which is now thought to have come from the Eastern Mediterranean).

In April 2005, Sergio Frau's theories were debated at a conference organized by UNESCO in Paris. At the same time, an exposition of his findings was on display in the UNESCO building.

SICILY

The concept of the identification of Atlantis with the island of Sicily is the idea that the Italians were involved in the Sea Peoples movement (a similar story to

Plato's account), that the name "Atlas" may have been derived from "Italos" via the Middle Egyptian language, and Plato's descriptions of the island and the city of Atlantis share several traits with Sicily and its Bronze Age culture.

MALTA

Malta, being situated in the dividing line between the western and eastern Mediterranean Sea, and being home to some of the oldest man-made structures in the world, is considered a possible location of Atlantis both by some current researchers and by Maltese amateur enthusiasts.

In *Malta: Echoes of Plato's Island* (2000), Anton Mifsud, Simon Mifsud, Chris Agius Sultana and Charles Savona Ventura catalogues the many archaeological sites and ancient remains in Malta that could be related to Atlantis.

In *Malta fdal Atlantis* (Maltese remains of Atlantis) (2002), Francis Galea writes about several older studies and hypotheses, particularly that of Maltese architect Giorgio Grongnet, who in 1854 claimed that the Maltese Islands are the remnants of Atlantis. Already 1828, the same Giorgo Grongnet was involved in a scandal concerning forged findings which were intended to provide a "proof" for the claim that Malta was Atlantis.

MIDDLE EAST

Jaime Manuschevich argues that the real place of the mythical civilization is the territory that today corresponds to Israel and Sinai, and that this region was an island in the Great Rift Valley, surrounded by the Jezreel Valley on the north, the Dead Sea and Red Sea on the east and the Gulf of Suez and the Mediterranean on the west until *ca* 5,600 BC. In addition, Manuschevich proposes that Atlantean civilization corresponds to the Natufian peoples, the first food-producing people, whose main political and harbor center was Jericho. These people lived in the region in the dates established by Plato (*ca* 11,600 BC).

TURKEY

Peter James, in his book *The Sunken Kingdom*, identifies Atlantis with the kingdom of Zippasla. He argues that Solon did indeed gather the story on his travels, but in Libya, not Egypt as Plato states; that Atlantis is identical with Tantalis, the city of Tantalus in Asia Minor which was (in a similar tradition known to the Greeks) said to have been destroyed by an earthquake. The legend of Atlantis' conquests in the Mediterranean is based on the revolt by King

Madduwattas of Zippasla against Hittite rule. Zippasla is identical with Sipylus, where Greek tradition placed Tantalis and that the now vanished lake to the north of Mount Sipylus was the site of the city.

TROY

The geoarchaeologist Eberhard Zangger has proposed the hypothesis that Atlantis was in fact the city state of Troy. He both agrees and disagrees with Rainer W Kühne: "He too believes that the Trojans-Atlanteans were the sea peoples, but only a minor part of them." He proposes that all Greek speaking city states of the Aegean civilization or Mycenae constituted the sea peoples and that they destroyed each other's economies in a series of semi-fratricidal wars lasting several decades.

BLACK SEA

German researchers Siegfried and Christian Schoppe locate Atlantis in the Black Sea. Before *ca* 5,500 BC, a great plain lay in the northwest at a former freshwater-lake. In *ca* 5,510 BC, rising sea level topped the barrier at today's Bosporus. They identify the Pillars of Hercules with the Strait of Bosporus. They gave no explanation how the ships of the merchants coming from all over the world had arrived at the harbor of Atlantis when it was 100 meters below global sea-level.

They claim Oreichalcos means the obsidian stone that used to be a cash-equivalent at that time and was replaced by the spondylus shell around 5,500 BC, which would suit the red, white, black motif. The geocatastrophic event led to the Neolithic diaspora in Europe, also beginning *ca* 5,500 BC.

In 2000, the Guardian reported that Robert Ballard, in a small submarine, found remains of human habitation around 100 meters underwater in the Black Sea off the north coast of Turkey. The area flooded around 5,000 BC. This flood is also believed to have inspired the Biblical story of Noah's Ark known as the Black Sea deluge theory.

Another candidate bordering the Black Sea, suggested by Hasan Umur in the 1940s, would be Ancomah, a legendary place near Trabzon.

AROUND GIBRALTAR

ANDALUSIA

Andalusia is a region in modern day southern Spain which once included the "lost" city of Tartessos, which disappeared in the 6th century BC. The Tartessians were traders known to the Ancient Greeks who knew of their legendary king Arganthonios. The Andalusian hypothesis was originally developed by the Spanish author Juan de Mariana and the Dutch author Johannes van Gorp (Goropius Becanus), both of the 16th century, later by Jose Pellicer de Ossau y Tovar in 1673, who suggested that the metropolis of Atlantis was between the islands Mayor and Menor, located almost in the center of the Doñana Marshes, and expanded upon by Juan Fernández Amador y de los Ríos in 1919, who suggested that the metropolis of Atlantis was located precisely where today are the "Marismas de Hinojo". These claims were made again in 1922 by the German author Adolf Schulten, and further propagated by Otto Jessen, Richard Hennig, Victor Berard, and Elena Wishaw in the 1920s. The suggested locations in Andalusia lie outside the Pillars of Hercules, and therefore beyond but close to the Mediterranean itself.

In 2005, based upon the work of Adolf Schulten, the German teacher Werner Wickboldt also claimed this to be the location of Atlantis. Wickboldt suggested that the war of the Atlanteans refers to the war of the Sea Peoples who attacked the Eastern Mediterranean countries around 1,200 BC and that the Iron Age city of Tartessos may have been built at the site of the ruined Atlantis. In 2000, Georgeos Diaz-Montexano published an article explaining his belief that Atlantis was located somewhere between Andalusia and Morocco. An Andalusian location was also supported by Rainer W Kühne in his article that appeared in the journal *Antiquity*. Kühne's theory says: "Good fiction imitates facts. Plato declared that his Atlantis tale is philosophical fiction invented to describe his fictitious ideal state in the case of war. Kühne suggests that Plato has used three historical elements for this tale. (i) Greek tradition on Mycenaean Athens for the description of ancient Athens, (ii) Egyptian records on the wars of the Sea Peoples for the description of the war of the Atlanteans, and (iii) oral tradition from Syracuse about Tartessos for the description of the city and geography of Atlantis." According to Wickboldt, satellite images show two rectangular shapes on the tops of two small elevations inside the marsh of Doñana which he hypothesizes are the "temple of Poseidon" and "the temple of Cleito and Poseidon." On satellite images parts of several "rings" are recognizable, similar in their proportion with the ring system by Plato. It is not known if any of these shapes are natural or manmade and archaeological excavations are planned. Geologists have shown that the Doñana National Park experienced intense erosion from *ca* 4,000 BC until 9th century AD, where it became a marine environment. For thousands of years until the Medieval Age, all that occupied the area of the modern Marshes Doñana was a gulf or inland sea-arm, but there was not even a small island with sufficient space to house a small village.

In 2011, a team led by Richard Freund claimed to have found strong evidence for the location in Doñana National Park based on underground and underwater surveys, and the existence of what they characterized as "memorial cities" rebuilt in Atlantis' image. Spanish scientists have dismissed Freund's claims claiming that he was sensationalizing their work. The anthropologist Juan Villarías-Robles, who works with the Spanish National Research Council, said "Richard Freund was a newcomer to our project and appeared to be involved in his own very controversial issue concerning King Solomon's search for ivory and gold in Tartessos, the well documented settlement in the Donaña area established in the first millennium BC" and described his claims as "fanciful".

Simcha Jacobovici, involved in the production of a documentary on Freund's work for the National Geographic Channel, stated that the biblical Tarshish (which he believes is the same as Tartessos) was Atlantis, and that "Atlantis was hiding in the Tanach". Aren Maeir, a professor of archeology at Bar-Ilan University said "a lot of people have made many crazy claims about Atlantis – it's one of those classic places where you have a lunatic fringe looking for all types of things. And Richard Freund is known as someone who makes 'sensational' finds. I would say that I am exceptionally skeptical about the thing, but I wouldn't discount it 100% until I see the details, which haven't been published as far as I know... every few years we hear something like this from him... And the fact that it's on National Geographic doesn't mean much. Unfortunately, over the past years they've had many questionable programs."

SPARTEL BANK

Two hypotheses have put Spartel Bank, a submerged former island in the Strait of Gibraltar, as the location of Atlantis. The more well-known hypothesis was proposed in a September 2001 issue of *Comptes Rendus de l'academie des Sciences* by French geologist Jacques Collina-Girard. The lesser-known hypothesis was first published by Spanish-Cuban investigator Georgeos Díaz-Montexano in an April 2000 issue of Spanish magazine *Más Allá de la Ciencia* (Beyond Science), and later in August 2001 issues of Spanish magazines *El Museo* (The Museum) and *Año Cero* (Year Zero). The origin of Collina-Girard's hypothesis is disputed, with Díaz-Montexano claiming it as plagiarism of his own earlier hypothesis, and Collina-Girard denying any plagiarism. Both individuals claim the other's hypothesis is pseudoscience.

Collina-Girard's hypothesis states that during the most recent Glacial Maximum of the Ice Age sea level was 135 m below its current level, narrowing the Gibraltar Strait and creating a small half-enclosed sea measuring 70 km by 20 km between the Mediterranean and Atlantic Ocean. The Spartel Bank formed an archipelago in this small sea with the largest island measuring about 10 to 12 kilometers across. With rising ocean levels the island began to slowly shrink, but then at around 9,400 BC (11,400 years ago) there was an accelerated sea level rise of 4 meters per century known as Meltwater Pulse 1A, which drowned the top of the main island. The occurrence of a great earthquake and tsunami in this region, similar to the 1755 Lisbon earthquake (magnitude 8.5 – 9) was proposed by marine geophysicist Marc-Andrè Gutscher as offering a possible explanation for the described catastrophic destruction. Collina-Girard proposes that the disappearance of this island was recorded in prehistoric Egyptian tradition for 5,000 years until it was written down by the first Egyptian scribes around 4,000 – 3,000 BC, and the story then subsequently inspired Plato to write a fictionalized version interpreted to illustrate his own principles.

A detailed review in the Bryn Mawr Classical Review comments on the discrepancies in Collina-Girard's dates and use of coincidences, concluding that he "has certainly succeeded in throwing some light upon some momentous developments in human prehistory in the area west of Gibraltar. Just as certainly, however, he has not found Plato's Atlantis".

MOROCCO

According to Michael Hübner, Atlantis core region was located in South-West Morocco at the Atlantic Ocean. In his papers an approach to the analysis of Plato's dialogues *Timaeus* and *Critias* is described. By means of a hierarchical constraint satisfaction procedure, a variety of geographically relevant indications from Plato's accounts are used to infer the most probable location of Plato's Atlantis Nesos. The outcome of this is the Souss-Massa plain in today's South-West Morocco. This plain is surrounded by the High Atlas, the Anti-Atlas, the Sea of Atlas (Atlantis Thalassa, today's Atlantic Ocean). Because of this isolated position, Hübner argued, this plain was called Atlantis Nesos, the Island of Atlas by ancient Greeks before the Greek Dark Ages. The Amazigh (Berber) people actually call the Souss-Massa plain island. Of major archaeological interest is the fact that in the North-West of the Souss-Massa plain a large annular caldera-like geomorphologic structure was discovered. This structure has almost the dimensions of Plato's capital of Atlantis and is covered with hundreds of large and small prehistoric ruins of different types. These ruins were made out of rocks colored red, white and black. Hübner also shows possible harbor remains, an unusually geomorphological structure, which applies to Plato's description of roofed over docks, which were cut into red, white and black bedrock. These 'docks' are located close to the annular geomorphological structure and close to Cape Ghir, which was named Cape Heracles in antiquity. Hübner also argued, that Agadir is etymologically related to the Semitic g-d-r and probably to Plato's Gadir. The Semitic g-d-r means enclosure, fortification and sheep fold. The meaning of enclosure, sheep fold corresponds to the Greek translation of the name Gadeiros which is Eumelos = Rich in Sheep.

Hübner's above-the-waves hypothesis is what author Mark Adams calls "the most convincing on paper" of the handful of theories he chased down in his book *Meet Me in Atlantis* published in 2015.

ATLANTIC OCEAN

AZORES ISLANDS

One of the suggested places for Atlantis is around the Azores Islands, a group of islands belonging to Portugal located about 1,500 km west of the Portuguese coast. Some people believe the islands could be the mountain tops of Atlantis. Ignatius L Donnelly, an American congressman, was perhaps the first one to talk about this possible location in his book *Atlantis: The Antediluvian World*. Ignatius L Donnelly also makes a connection to the mythical Aztlán.

The Azores are steep-sided volcanic seamounts that drop rapidly 1,000 meters to a plateau. Cores taken from the plateau and other evidence shows that this area has been an undersea plateau for millions of years. Ancient indicators, *ie* relict beaches, marine deposits, and wave cut-terraces, of Pleistocene shorelines and sea level show that the Azores Islands have not subsided to any significant degree. Instead, they demonstrate that some of these islands have actually risen during the Late and Middle Pleistocene. This is evidenced by relict, Pleistocene wave-cut platforms and beach sediments that now lie well above current sea level. For example, they have been found on Flores Island at elevations of 15 – 20, 35 – 45, ~100, and ~250 meters above current sea level.

CANARY ISLANDS, MADEIRA AND CAPE VERDE

The Canary Islands have been identified as remnants of Atlantis by numerous authors. For example in 1803, Bory de Saint-Vincent in his *Essai sur les îles fortunées et l'antique Atlantide* proposed that the Canary Islands, along with the Madeira, and Azores, are what remained after Atlantis broke up. Many later authors, *ie* Lewis Spence in his *The Problem of Atlantis*, also identified the Canary Islands as part of Atlantis leftover from when it catastrophically sank.

Detailed geomorphic and geologic studies of the Canary Islands clearly demonstrate that over the last 4 million years, they have been steadily uplifted, without any significant periods of subsidence, by geologic processes such as erosional unloading, gravitational unloading, lithospheric flexure induced by adjacent islands, and volcanic underplating. For example, Pliocene pillow lavas, which solidified underwater and now exposed on the northeast flanks of Gran Canaria, have been uplifted between 46 and 143 meters above sea level. Also, marine deposits associated with lavas dated as being 4.1 and 9.3 million years old in Gran Canaria, *ca* 4.8 million years old in Fuerteventura, and *ca* 9.8 million years old in Lanzarote demonstrate that the Canary Islands have for millions of years undergone long term uplift without any significant, much less catastrophic, subsidence. A series of raised, Pleistocene marine terraces, which become progressively older with age, on Fuerteventura indicate that it has risen in elevation at about 1.7 cm per thousand years for the past one million years. The elevation of the marine terrace for the highstand of sea level for the last interglacial period shows that this island has experienced neither subsidence nor significant uplift for the past 125,000 years. Within the Cape Verde Islands, the detailed mapping and dating of 16 Pleistocene marine terraces and Pliocene marine conglomerate found that they have been uplifted throughout most of the Pleistocene and remained relatively stable without any significant subsidence since the last interglacial period. Finally, detailed studies of the sedimentary deposits surrounding the Canary Islands have demonstrated, except for a narrow rim around each island exposed during glacial lowstands of sea level, a complete lack of any evidence for the ocean floor surrounding the Canary Islands having ever been above water.

NORTHERN SPAIN

According to Jorge Maria Ribero-Meneses, Atlantis was in northern Spain. He specifically argues that Atlantis is the underwater plateau, known internationally as "Le Danois Bank" and locally as "The Cachucho". It is located about 25 kilometers from the continental shelf and about 60 km off the coast of Asturias, and Lastres between Ribadesella. Its top is now 425 meters below the sea. It is 50 kilometers from east to west and 18 km from north to south. Ribero-Meneses hypothesized that is part of the continental margin that broke off at least 12,000 years ago as the result of tectonic processes that occurred at the end of the last ice age. He argues that they created a tsunami with waves with heights of hundreds of meters and that the few survivors had to start virtually from scratch.

Detailed studies of the geology of the Le Danois Bank region have refuted the hypothesis proposed by Jorge Maria Ribero-Meneses that the Le Danois Bank was created by the collapse of the northern Cantabrian continental margin about 12,000 years ago. The Le Danois Bank represents part of the continental margin that have been uplifted by thrust faulting when the continental margin overrode oceanic crust during the Paleogene and Neogene periods. Along the northern edge of the Le Danois Bank, Precambrian granulite and Mesozoic sedimentary rocks have been thrust northward over Miocene and Oligocene marine sediments. The basin separating the Le Danois Bank from the Cantabrian continental margin to the south is a graben that simultaneously formed as a result of normal faulting associated with the thrust faulting. In addition, marine sediments that range in age from lower Pliocene to Pleistocene, cover large parts of Le Danois Bank, and fill the basin separating it from the Cantabrian continental margin demonstrate that this bank has been submerged beneath the Bay of Biscay for millions of years.

IRISH SEA

In his book *Atlantis of the West: The Case for Britain's Drowned Megalithic Civilization* (2003), Paul Dunbavin argues that a large island once existed in the Irish Sea and that this island was Atlantis. He argues that this Neolithic civilization in Europe was partially drowned by rising sea levels caused by a comet impact that caused a pole shift and changed the earth's axis around 3,100 BC. Such changes would be readily detectable to modern science, however, and Dunbavin's claims are considered pseudo-scientific at best within the scientific community.

GREAT BRITAIN

William Comyns Beaumont believed that Great Britain was the location of Atlantis and the Scottish journalist Lewis Spence claimed that the ancient traditions of Britain and Ireland contain memories of Atlantis.

On December 29, 1997, the BBC reported that a team of Russian scientists believed they found Atlantis in the ocean 100 miles off of Land's End, Cornwall, Britain. The BBC stated that Little Sole Bank, a relatively shallow area, was believed by the team to be the capital of Atlantis. This may have been based on the myth of Lionesses.

IRELAND

The idea of Atlantis being located in Ireland was presented in the book Atlantis from a Geographer's Perspective: *Mapping the Fairy Land* (2004) by Swedish geographer Dr Ulf Erlingsson from Uppsala University. It hypothesized that the empire of Atlantis refers to the Neolithic Megalithic tomb culture, based on their similar geographic extent, and deduced that the island of Atlantis then must correspond to Ireland. Erlingsson found the similarities of size and landscape to be statistically significant, while he rejected his null hypothesis that Plato invented Atlantis as fiction.

Based on this result, the speculation was made that the capital of Atlantis could be connected with Newgrange, Knowth, and Tara, Ireland. As regards the sinking of Atlantis, it was suggested that it is a memory from another time and place, notably the Dogger Bank area. It was an island that sank in the North Sea about 6,100 BC. While the world sea level rose gradually as the Ice Age ice sheets melted, there was a sudden sea level rise at this time due to the final drainage of Lake Agassiz. At about the same time a tsunami from the Storegga Slide is believed to have devastated the island in the manner described by Plato. (See also entry on North Sea below.)

Other hypotheses place the location of Atlantis between Britain and France on the Celtic Shelf. This hypothesis was first developed by Lewis Spence and has been recently revived by some oceanographers.

NORTH SEA

The North Sea is known to contain lands that were once above water; the medieval town of Dunwich in East Anglia, for example, crumbled into the sea. The land area known as "Doggerland", between England and Denmark, was inundated by a tsunami around 8,200 BP (6,200 BC), caused by a submarine landslide off the coast of Norway known as the Storegga Slide, and prehistoric human remains have been dredged up from the Dogger Bank. Atlantis itself has been identified besides Heligoland off the north-west German coast by the author Jürgen Spanuth, who postulates that it was destroyed during the Bronze Age around 1,200 BC, only to partially re-emerge during the Iron Age. Ulf Erlingsson hypothesized that the island that sank referred to Dogger Bank, and the city itself referred to the Silverpit crater at the base of Dogger Bank. A book allegedly by Oera Linda claims that a land called Atland once existed in the North Sea, but was destroyed in 2,194 BC.

DENMARK

In his book *The Celts: The People Who Came Out of the Darkness* (1975), author Gerhard Herm links the origins of the Atlanteans to end of the ice age and the flooding of eastern coastal Denmark.

FINLAND

Finnish eccentric Ior Bock located Atlantis in the Baltic Sea, at southern part of Finland where he claimed a small community of people lived during the Ice Age. According to Bock, this was possible due to Gulf Stream which brought warm water to the Finnish coast. This is a small part of a large saga that he claimed had been told in his family through the ages, dating back to the development of language itself. The family saga tells the name Atlantis comes from Swedish words allt-land-is ("all-land-ice") and refers to the last Ice-Age. Thus in the Bock family saga it's more a time period than an exact geographical place. According to this the Atlantis disappeared in 8,016 BC when the Ice-Age ended in Finland and the ice melted away.

SWEDEN

In 1679 Olaus Rudbeck wrote *Atland (Atlantica)*, where he argues that Scandinavia, specifically Sweden, is identical with Atlantis. According to Rudbeck the capital city of Atlantis was identical to the ancient burial site of Swedish kings Gamla Uppsala.

AMERICAS

When Columbus returned from his voyage to the west, some historians of the period such as Francisco López de Gómara, writing in 1552 thought that what Columbus had discovered was the Atlantic Island of Plato.

In 1556 Agustín de Zárate stated that the Americas was Atlantis which at one time began from the straits of Gibraltar and extended westwards to include North and South America and that it was as a result of Plato that the new continent was discovered. He also said it had all the attributes of the continent described by Plato yet at the same time mentioned that the ancient peoples crossed over by a route from the island of Atlantis. Zarate also mentions that the 9,000 "years" of Plato were 9,000 "months" (750 years). This was also repeated and clarified by historian Pedro Sarmiento de Gamboa in 1572 in his *History of the Incas*, who by calculation of longitude stated that Atlantis must have stretched from within two leagues of the strait of Gibraltar westwards to include "all the rest of the land from the mouth of the Marañon (Amazon River) and Brazil to the South Sea, which is what they now call America". He thought the sunken part to be now in the Atlantic Ocean but that it was from this sunken part that the original Indians had come to populate Peru via one continuous land mass. He says that South America was also known by the name of the *Isla Atlanticus*.

It first appeared as the Atlantic Island (*Insula Atlantica*) on a map of the New World by cartographer Sebastian Münster in 1540 and again on the map titled *Atlantis Insula* by Nicolas Sanson and son (1669) which identified both North and South America as "Atlantis Insula", the eastern part of the Atlantic Ocean as "Oceanus Atlanticus" and the western part of the Atlantic Ocean plus the Pacific Ocean as "Atlanticum Pelagus". This edition was further embellished with features from the Atlantis legend by his son Guillaume Sanson including the names of the ten kings of Atlantis with Atlas' portion being in Mexico. Sanson's map supposedly showed what the earth looked like 200,000 years before there were any humans on it.

SOUTH AMERICA

A hypothesis by author Jim Allen argues that Plato's description exactly fits South America with the island capital in what is now Bolivia because he describes a level rectangular-shaped plain which he said lay in the center of the continent, next to the sea and midway along the longest side of the continent. He also described the capital city of Atlantis which was built on a small volcanic island and also called Atlantis. The city lay on the level rectangular plain, five miles from the sea and according to Plato the whole region was high above the level of the ocean sea, rising sheer out of the ocean sea to a great height on that side of the continent. Allen contends that the Altiplano region of Bolivia meets these characteristics.

CUBA

Author Andrew Collins has advocated a Cuban connection to Atlantis in his book Gateway to Atlantis: *The Search for the Source of a Lost Civilization*. Collins supports his hypothesis with indirect historical and geographical evidence. He suggests Isle of Youth and the shallow sea bottom that surrounds it as a possible location for Atlantis.

Sonar images suggested to be a complex of submerged structures or a Cuban underwater city were recorded off the coast of the Guanahacabibes peninsula near the Pinar del Río Province in 2001.

SOUTH AND NORTH POLES

ANTARCTICA

The theory that Antarctica was Atlantis was particularly fashionable during the 1960s and 1970s, spurred on partly both by the isolation of the continent, and also the Piri Reis map, which purportedly shows Antarctica as it would be ice free, suggesting human knowledge of that period. Flavio Barbiero, Charles Berlitz, Erich Von Däniken and Peter Kolosimo are some of the popular authors who made this proposal.

More recently Rose and Rand Flem-Ath have proposed this in their book, *When the Sky Fell*; the theory was revised and made more specific in Rand's work with author Colin Wilson, in *The Atlantis Blueprint* (published in 2002). The second work theorized that Atlantis was to be found in Lesser Antarctica, near the coast of the Ross Ice Shelf. A geological theory known as "Earth Crust Displacement" forms the basis of their work. *The Atlantis Blueprint* uses both scientific and pseudoscientific (such as mere speculation and assumptions) means to back up the theory.

Charles Hapgood came up with the "Earth Crustal Displacement" theory. Hapgood's theory suggests that Earth's outer crust is able to move upon the upper mantle layer rapidly up to a distance of 2,000 miles, placing Atlantis in Antarctica, when considering the movements of the crust in the past. It is to be noted that Albert Einstein was one of the few voices to answer Hapgood's theory. Einstein wrote a preface for Hapgood's book Earth's shifting crust, published in 1958. This theory is particularly popular with Hollow Earthers, and can be seen as a mirror of the Hyperborean identification. In his book *Fingerprints of the Gods*, author Graham Hancock argues for the Earth Crustal

Displacement theory in general, and the Atlantis/Antarctica connection specifically, then goes on to propose archaeological exploration of Antarctica in search of Atlantis.

What is now known about the Quaternary and Holocene history of Antarctica completely discredits any hypothesis about it being the location of Atlantis. Mapping and dating of the edges of the Antarctic ice sheet during the Last Glacial Maximum; mapping and dating of glacial erratics, tills, and striations within now ice-free areas; microfossils from post-glacial lake deposits; coring and analysis of glacial tills and marine sediments underlying the Ross and Wedell seas; coring and analysis of ice cores; and other research has accumulated an enormous amount of data that has disproved the various hypotheses that any sizable part of Antarctica was sufficiently ice-free and temperate in climate during the last 100,000 years and earlier to have supported any civilization. This research soundly refutes Flem-Ath's proposal that lesser (West) Antarctica was ice-free and temperate prior to 9,600 BC (11,600 BP).

NORTH POLE

The professor of systematic theology at Boston University William Fairfield Warren (1833 – 1929) wrote a book promoting his belief that the original center of mankind once sat at the North Pole entitled *Paradise Found: The Cradle of the Human Race at the North Pole* (1885). In this work Warren placed Atlantis at the North Pole, as well as the Garden of Eden, Mount Meru, Avalon and Hyperborea. Warren believed all these mythical lands were folk memories of a former inhabited far northern seat where man was originally created.

Warren's identification of Atlantis with the North Pole was maintained by positioning Atlas in the far north by mapping out ancient Greek cosmology. Warren equated the primordial Titan Atlas of Greek mythology who supported the Heavens on his shoulders (or supported the earth on a pillar) to the Atlas described in Plato's dialogue *Critias* as the first ruler of Atlantis. In Warren's view, all the axis mundi or cosmic-axis of ancient legends (Yggdrasil, Irminsul and Atlas' pillar) had to be in the far north "at the top of the world":

> *...To locate these in right mutual relations, one must begin by representing to himself the earth as a sphere or spheroid, and as situated within, and concentric with, the starry sphere, each having its axis perpendicular, and its north pole at the top. The pole-star is thus in the true zenith, and the heavenly heights centering about it are the abode of the supreme god or gods.*

Warren noted how Homer, Virgil and Hesiod all placed Atlas or his world pillar at the "ends of the earth", meaning in his view the far northern arctic regions, while Euripides related Atlas to the Pole Star, so as he concluded:

> *......in oldest Greek thought Atlas belongs at the North Pole, and it is only reasonable to locate the kingdom of Atlas in the same locality.*

Therefore in Warren's view Atlantis sat in the far north, at the North Pole, since the Atlas in his ancient Greek cosmological mapping stood in the far northern zenith, under the Pole Star.

INDONESIA/SUNDALAND

The South China Sea north of Indonesia and the Java Sea has been advocated as a site for Atlantis. Key to this argument that Sundaland was the location of Atlantis is that the Ocean of Atlantis refers to the ocean which encircles Eurasia and Africa, which was the historical understanding until the time of Christopher Columbus. Proponents of this idea claim that natives of Sundaland who fled the rising waters or volcanic explosions eventually had contact with Ancient Egyptians, who later passed the story onto Plato who gets some but not all of the details correct, including location and time period.

The first suggested linkage between Atlantis and Indonesia came from the leading Theosophist, CW Leadbeater (1854 – 1934 AD). In a booklet, *The Occult History of Java*, published in 1951 he proposed that Java had been an Atlantean colony.

One of the first researchers to Atlantis there (mid-1990s) have located, is the American polymath William Lauritzen, in about the same time Arysio Nunes dos Santos (1937 – 2005 AD), a former professor of nuclear energy technology at the Brazilian Federal University of Minas Gerais, who also made the Sundaland internationally known hypothesis.

Zia Abbas, a computer scientist, in his book *Atlantis: The Final Solution* claims to prove that Plato's Atlantis is to be found in the South China Sea. Other high-profile representative of this Atlantis-localization is Sunil Prasannan, a molecular biologist who has worked among others at Imperial College London.

The atlantology of Sundaland hypothesis is also flanked by the studies of the geologist and geophysicist Robert M Schoch from the College of General Studies at Boston University. Together with Robert Aquinas McNally in 2003 published a book in which to express the two authors have reasons to suspect the concept of pyramid construction had been developed by a lost civilization, which formerly existed in Sundaland.

In 2013, joined also the Indonesian geologist Danny Hilman Natawidjaja after its discovery that Gunung Padang in the province of Cianjur, West Java, was apparently brought by people in pyramid form about 13,000 years ago, the adoption of Atlantis was in the greater of the present-day Indonesia located.

The concept of a Sundaland connection was given a huge boost by the publication of the late Brazilian professor of nuclear physics Arysio Nunes dos Santos' book *Atlantis: The Lost Continent Finally Found*. During the Last Glacial Maximum, what is now known as the Sunda Shelf was the location of a large sub aerial coastal plain that was part of Sundaland. During the Last Glacial Maximum, Sundaland extended northward from Indonesia to Kalimantan and northwestward to the coast of Southeast Asia. Sundaland is quite tectonically stable lacking any known prehistory of any significant, much less cataclysmic, tectonic subsidence. Numerous studies by petroleum and Quaternary geologists have found a complete lack of any evidence for any Neogene and Quaternary volcanic activity within the Sunda Shelf despite its proximity to Indonesia.

Detailed studies of late glacial and postglacial sea level rise for this part of the Sunda Shelf demonstrates that the first significant submergence of Sundaland by rising sea level occurred between 14,000 and 15,000 years ago. Periods of abrupt rise in sea level submerged a significant part of Sundaland beneath the South China Sea between 13,000 and 14,000 years ago. Between 14,300 and 14,600 years ago, a period of 300 years, sea level rose 16 m. Between 12,000 and 13,000 years ago, the submergence of Sundaland by rising sea level was relatively minor. A final period of rapid flooding of Sundaland by the South China Sea occurred between 11,000 to 12,000 years ago. The submergence of Sundaland during this period was minor in extent relative to the area submerged between 13,000 and 14,000 years ago. Evidence for any significant or cataclysmic submergence of Sundaland as the result of tectonic processes is completely lacking.

The idea was given a boost in February 2012 when it was reported by a somewhat incredulous Jakarta Post that the Indonesian president Susilo Bambang Yudoyono had given his support to a search for an ancient sunken civilization in Indonesian waters following meetings with researchers including British author Stephen Oppenheimer.

Danny Hilman Natawidjaja claims that Atlantis was part of prehistoric Indonesia. In the book, entitled *Penemuan Atlantis Nusantara* (The Discovery of Atlantis in the Archipelago) he claimed to base his theory on Plato's text. Natawidjaja also claims that a site at Gunung Padang, 120 kilometers southwest of Jakarta may be more than 9,000 years old. Graham Hancock has expanded on this claim.

Zia Abbas, a computer scientist and works as a freelance software engineer and consultant for many companies, is the author of *Atlantis: The Final Solution* in which he claims to prove that Plato's Atlantis is to be found in the South China Sea. The core proposal of this book is that Atlantis was located on the continental shelf in the South China Sea, known as Sundaland, which was exposed before the end of the last Ice Age, when it was inundated as the glaciers retreated. According to Zia Abbas, this large landmass contained the original Atlantis and was known as Idress. It is quite probable that early urban settlements did exist along the coast and at the river mouths of Sundaland, and were subsequently flooded.

The prehistoric flooding of the Sundaland region is covered extensively in Stephen Oppenheimer's *Eden in the East*.

Sunil Prasannan, a molecular biologist who has worked at the Department of Biological Sciences, Imperial College London, has contributed to a number of internet forums relating to Atlantis. On balance he believes that Plato's description best fits the Sundaland hypothesis.

***

CITED THEORIES

The Sundaland or specifically Indonesia has been advocated as a site for Atlantis. Key to this argument is that the Ocean of Atlantis refers to the ocean which encircles Eurasia and Africa, which was the historical understanding until the time of Christopher Columbus. Proponents of this idea claim that natives of Sundaland who fled the rising waters or volcanic explosions eventually had contact with Ancient Egyptians, who later passed the story onto Plato who gets some but not all of the details correct, including location and time period.

The first suggested linkage between Atlantis and Indonesia came from the leading Theosophist, CW Leadbeater (1854 – 1934 AD), in a booklet, *The Occult History of Java*, published in 1951. An American polymath William Lauritzen and about the same time Arysio Nunes dos Santos (1937 – 2005 AD) also made the Sundaland internationally known hypothesis. Zia Abbas, a computer scientist, claims to prove that Plato's Atlantis is to be found in the South China Sea. Other high-profile representative of this Atlantis-localization is Sunil Prasannan, a molecular biologist who has worked among others at Imperial College London.

The atlantology of Sundaland hypothesis is also flanked by the studies of the geologist and geophysicist Robert M Schoch from the College of General Studies at Boston University, together with Robert Aquinas McNally, in 2003 published a book in which to express the two authors have reasons to suspect the concept of pyramid construction had been developed by a lost civilization, which formerly existed in Sundaland. In 2013, joined also the Indonesian geologist Danny Hilman Natawidjaja after its discovery that the Mount Padang in the province of Cianjur, West Java, was apparently brought by people in pyramid form about 13,000 years ago, the adoption of Atlantis was in the greater of the present-day Indonesia located.

ARYSIO NUNES DOS SANTOS

Arysio Nunes dos Santos (1937 – 2005 AD), was a highly qualified engineer with many patents to his credit. He was Professor of Nuclear Engineering at the Federal University of Minas Gerais in Brazil, and had also worked as a geologist and climatologist. He was also an amateur linguist who had mastered Greek and Sanskrit among others. Apart from his professional interests, Santos has written on a diverse range of subjects including Symbolism, Alchemy, the Holy Grail and Comparative Mythology and Religion. His studies led him to conclude that

Atlantis and the biblical Eden were the same and more controversially that it had been located in the area of the Indian Ocean and the South China Sea.

Professor Santos explains his theory on Atlantis using infinitude of arguments, which range from the strictly scientific (such as geology, linguistics, and anthropology) to the more arcane and occult ones. Being the first one to ever link the catastrophic events of the end of the last Ice Age (11,600 years ago) with the world-wide traditions of the universal flood and the destruction of Atlantis, Professor Santos managed to find a perfect site for the location of the Lost Continent. Such site strives unrivaled as being the most logical one ever proposed, matching all the features mentioned by the Greek philosopher Plato, as well as those cited by other sources.

Much exactly like Plato indicated, Atlantis was a real story. Plato's Atlantis description and its history were based on facts. Professor Santos studies involved the production of a great number of articles and books that may shed some light to the scientists and scholars that become interested in the "occult" story of Atlantis. Before taken as a legend, for the most sure, being a very real story.

There is an interesting website promoting his theories and in 2005 his ideas were published in book form titled *Atlantis: The Lost Continent Finally Found*. Professor Santos passed away just weeks after it was launched. Since then his work has been championed by his son Antonio Roberto dos Santos and Frank Joseph Hoff, who had done research for Santos over a number of years.

Professor Santos had a completely new theory that Atlantis could not be found because everyone had been looking in the wrong place and that Plato's work on the subject had been misunderstood. He claims that the true location of Atlantis was in the area of the Indian Ocean and the South China Sea. The Indonesian islands are all that is left of it.

It was in Indonesia and the neighboring lands that man, after emigrating from the semi-deserted savannas of Africa, first found the ideal climatic conditions for development, and it was there that he invented agriculture and civilization. All this took place during the Pleistocene, the last of the geological eras, which ended a scant 11,600 years ago. Though long by human standards, this is but a brief moment in geological terms.

The Pleistocene – a name which is Greek for "most recent" – is also called Anthropozoic Era or Quaternary Era or, yet, the Ice Age. During the Pleistocene and, more exactly, during the glacial episodes that happened at intervals of about 20 thousand years, sea level was about 100 – 150 meters below the present value. With this, a large coastal strip – the so-called Continental Platform (with a width of about 200 kilometers) – became exposed, forming land bridges that interconnected many islands and regions.

The most dramatic of such exposures took place in the region of Indonesia, precisely the spot where humanity first flourished. The vast expansion of the South China Sea then formed an immense continent, indeed "larger than Asia Minor and Libya put together". This is, as we shall see, precisely what Plato affirms in his discourse on Atlantis, the *Critias*.

With the end of the Pleistocene Ice Age, the immense glaciers that covered the whole of the northern half of North America and Eurasia melted away. Their waters drained to the sea, whose level rose by the estimated amount of about 100 – 150 meters quoted above. With this rise, Atlantis sunk away and disappeared for good, along with most of its population, which we estimate, based on Plato's data, at about 20 million people, huge for the epoch in question.

India was one of its nearest and many colonies and that the holy books known as the Vedas and the Hindu religion are based on and in Atlantis. Many other religious ceremonies such as baptism and the others among the seven sacraments of Christianity were memories of Atlantis and how it perished under the seas.

Guanche language was derived from Dravidian and set out a very good case proving this by comparing Dravidian words with those of the Guanche tongue – many are nearly identical. Professor Santos had also written on *The Mysterious Origin of the Guanches*.

The "Golden Age", the "Garden of Eden" and the "Paradise" were all memories of Atlantis as it once was and that after its destruction the survivors had to begin again and had lost all their technological advances and were reduced to a very primitive way of living. Atlantis was destroyed following a cataclysmic volcanic eruption and tsunami that shook the entire world.

Table 1 – The Atlantis locations checklist

FEATURE	Plato et al	Thera/Crete	Incas of Peru	Mayas of Mexico	Sunken Atlantic Island	Antarctica	Scandinavia and North Sea	Troy (Hissarlik)	Celtiberia	Northwest Africa	Tartessos	The East Indies
Atlantic Location	✓	✗	✗	✓	✓	✓	✓	✓	✓	✓	✓	✓
Navigation/Irrigation Canals	✓	✗	?	✓	✗	?	?	✗	✗	✗	✓	✓
Elephants (Mammoths?)	✓	✗	?	✓	?	✗	?	✗	?	✓	?	✓
Continental Size	✓	✗	✓	✓	✗	✓	✗	✗	✗	✓	✓	✓
Tropical Climate	✓	✗	✓	✓	?	✗	✗	✗	✗	✓	✗	✓
Coconuts/Pineapples	✓	✗	✓	✓	?	✗	✗	✗	✗	✗	✗	✓
Perfumes and Incenses	✓	✗	✓	✓	✗	✗	✗	✗	✗	✗	✗	✓
Large Population	✓	✗	✗	✓	✗	✗	✗	✗	✗	✗	✗	✓
Horses and War Chariots	✓	?	✗	✗	✗	✗	✗	✓	?	✗	?	✓
Human Presence at the Epoch	✓	✗	✗	✗	✗	✗	✗	✗	✓	?	✓	✓
Megalithic Construction	✓	✗	✓	✓	?	✗	✓	✗	✓	✓	✗	✓
Volcanism and Earthquakes	✓	✓	✓	✓	✗	✗	✗	✗	✗	✓	✗	✓
Sunken Continent	✓	✗	✗	✗	✗	?	✗	✗	✗	✗	✗	✓
Innavigable Seas	✓	✗	✗	✗	✗	?	?	✗	✗	✗	✗	✓
Beyond Pillars of Hercules	✓	✗	✗	✓	✓	✓	✓	✗	✓	✓	✓	✓
Outer Continents Beyond	✓	✓	?	?	✓	?	✓	✗	✓	✓	✓	✓
Many Islands Beyond	✓	✓	✓	✗	✗	✓	✓	✗	✓	✓	✓	✓
Site of Paradise (Eden)	✓	✗	✓	✗	✓	✗	✓	?	✗	✓	✗	✓
Evidences of Cataclysm	✓	✓	✓	?	?	✗	✗	✗	✓	✗	✗	✓
Pyramid Cult	✓	✗	✓	✓	?	✗	✗	✗	✗	✗	✗	✓
Sargasso Sea Beyond	✓	✗	✗	✓	✓	✗	✗	✗	✗	✗	✓	✓
Transoceanic Commerce	✓	✓	✓	✗	✗	✗	✓	✓	✗	✓	✓	✓
Riches in Metals	✓	✗	✓	?	?	✗	✗	✗	✓	✗	✓	✓
Superior Technology	✓	✗	✓	✓	?	✗	✗	✗	✗	✗	✓	✓
Terraced Mountain Cultivation	✓	✗	✓	?	✗	✗	✗	✗	✗	✗	✗	✓
Sacred Geometry	✓	✓	✓	✓	?	✓	?	✗	✓	✗	?	✓
Holy Mountain and Volcanoes	✓	✓	✓	✓	?	?	✓	✗	✗	✗	✗	✓
Date Compatible	✓	✗	?	?	?	?	✗	✗	✗	✗	✗	✓
Two Crops a Year	✓	✗	✗	✗	?	?	✗	✗	✗	✗	✗	✓
Metals	✓	✓	✓	✓	?	?	✓	✓	✓	✓	✓	✓
O-Blood Group	?	?	✓	✓	?	?	✓	✗	✓	✓	?	✓
Writing/Alphabet	✓	?	✓	✓	?	?	✓	?	✓	?	?	✓
Scores (% Right)	97	25	59	56	16	13	38	13	38	41	38	100

The East Indies here refers to Indonesia. The Atlantic Ocean was seen by the Greeks as all the water surrounding the continents, which is true. The Indian Ocean, on which the theory focuses, was the real "Ocean of the Atlanteans". It seems that Avienus placed the Hesperides and the island of Geryon, Erytheia, in this ocean. On the other hand, Avienus and other sources claimed that Erytheia was found in the Orient, thus the connection between the Indian and the "original" Atlantic Ocean.

Troy, Thera, and the capital of the Incas were imitations, re-creations of the original capital of Atlantis. Since Atlantis was a group of islands, its location in the Indian Ocean is possible. The area is part of Pacific Ocean's Ring of Fire (a chain of volcanoes), that is still active nowadays. The area is also prone to calamities such as volcanic eruptions, earthquakes and tsunamis. In conclusion, Plato's diluvian world could have taken place here.

Another point of interest is the Holy Mountain. Each culture seemed to have one – starting with Golgotha or Mount Calvary from the Bible, or Mount Qaf in Islamism, Mount Olympus in Greece, *etc.* The sacred mountain idea, just like the capital of Atlantis, points to Atlantis as the source.

On his list, Professor Santos also checked the similarities in the climate of Atlantis and the East Indies. Plato states that Atlanteans had two crops a year and a tropical climate, which matches again the Indonesian climate. It is also known that agriculture was started in the Far East over a ten thousand years ago, which proves the abundance of food needed to sustain a civilization large enough to create an army matched only by Plato's Atlantean army.

About the Pillars of Heracles – the pillars of Europe (Strait of Gibraltar) were originally called Calpe and Habila, and that the original Pillars were actually the Sunda Strait. The Phoenicians created the confusion between the two different pillars in order to stop the Greeks from reaching the true Paradise.

Atlantis was supposed to lie in the middle of the sea, making the connection between this world and the true continent. Java, Sumatera and the Malay Peninsula are between the Pacific and the Indian Oceans, breaking them in two. It can also be a resting spot for travelers from the continent to the Americas.

Professor Santos' theory refers to the innavigable seas or the mud barrier. The Strait of Gibraltar always had deep waters, while the Indian Ocean around the islands and peninsulas have murky waters.

STEPHEN OPPENHEIMER

Stephen Oppenheimer was trained in medicine at Oxford and London universities, qualifying in 1971. From 1972 he worked as a clinical pediatrician, mainly in Malaysia, Nepal and Papua New Guinea. He carried out and published clinical research in the areas of nutrition, infectious disease (including malaria), and genetics, focusing on the interactions between nutrition, genetics and infection, in particular iron nutrition, thalassemia and malaria. From 1979 he moved into medical research and teaching, with positions at the Liverpool School of Tropical Medicine, Oxford University, a research center in Kilifi, Kenya, and the Universiti Sains Malaysia in Penang.

He spent three years undertaking fieldwork in Papua New Guinea, studying the effects of iron supplementation on susceptibility to infection. His fieldwork, published in the late 1980s, identified the role of genetic mutation in malarious areas as a result of natural selection due to its protective effect against malaria, and those different genotypes for alpha-thalassemia traced different migrations out to the Pacific. Following that work, he concentrated on researching the use of unique genetic mutations as markers of ancient migrations.

From 1990 to 1994 Oppenheimer served as chairman and chief of clinical service in the Department of Pediatrics in the Chinese University of Hong Kong. He worked as senior specialist pediatrician in Brunei from 1994 to 1996.

He returned to England in 1997, writing the book *Eden in the East: The Drowned Continent of Southeast Asia*, published in 1998. The book synthesized work across a range of disciplines, including oceanography, archaeology, linguistics, social anthropology and human genetics. The book challenged the orthodox view of the origins of Polynesians as rice farmers from Taiwan and was widely acclaimed. Oppenheimer's paradigm change, using a synthesis of genetics, archaeology, geology and linguistics, has since been endorsed by reviewers in *Science*. *Out of Eden* has been the subject of a Channel 4 program of the same name and a Discovery Channel film *The Real Eve*.

In his book *Eden in the East: The Drowned Continent of Southeast Asia*, Oppenheimer makes a case that the rise in ocean levels that accompanied the waning of the ice age – as much as 150 m – during the period 14,000 – 7,000 years ago, must be taken into account when trying to understand the flow of genes and culture in Eurasia. Citing evidence from geology, archaeology, genetics, linguistics, and folklore, he hypothesizes that the Southeast Asian subcontinent of Sundaland was home to a rich and original culture that was dispersed when Sundaland was mostly submerged and its population moved westward. According to Oppenheimer, Sundaland's culture may have reached India and Mesopotamia, becoming the root for the innovative cultures that developed in those areas. He also suggests that the Austronesian languages originate from Sundaland and that a Neolithic Revolution may have started there.

THE BOOK

The biblical flood really did occur at the end of the last Ice Age. The flood drowned for ever the huge continental shelf of Southeast Asia, and caused a population dispersal which fertilized the Neolithic cultures of China, India, Mesopotamia, Egypt and the eastern Mediterranean, thus creating the first civilizations. The Polynesians did not come from China but from the islands of Southeast Asia. The domestication of rice was not in China but in the Malay Peninsula, 9,000 years ago. In this ground breaking book Stephen Oppenheimer reveals how evidence from oceanography, archaeology, linguistics, genetics and folklore overwhelmingly suggests that the lost "Eden" – the cradle of civilization – was not in the Middle East, as is usually supposed, but in the drowned continent of Southeast Asia.

Eden in the East overturns conventional ideas of the origins of western civilization in Mesopotamia. In this book Professor Oppenheimer place Southeast Asia for the first time as the key to the first roots of civilization. At the same time he provide scientific explanations for numerous, and previously unexplained, cultural links between early Eastern and Western cultures. Notable among these links are the hundreds of myths of a great flood which forced people into boats and left only a few survivors. He can now identify this flood as the dramatic rise in sea level at the end of the Ice Age that suddenly inundated vast areas of Eurasia. In other words the Biblical Flood really did occur. It had its most disastrous effects, however, in the continent of Southeast Asia – now a lost and half-sunken Eden.

As the Ice Age ended, there were three catastrophic and rapid rises in sea level. The last of these, which finished shortly before the start of civilization in Mesopotamia, may have been the one that was remembered. These three floods drowned the coastal cultures and all the flat continental shelves of Southeast Asia. As the sea rolled in, there was a mass emigration from the sinking continent. These flood-driven refugees carried their domestic animals with them in large ocean-going canoes in all directions. The networks of sea trade, created by their settlements around the Indian Ocean, fertilized the Neolithic cultures of China, India, Mesopotamia and Egypt.

The Southeast Asian contributions to the building of the first cities in Mesopotamia may not have been solely technological. While they may have brought the new ideas and skills of megalithic construction cereal domestication, sea-faring, astronomy, navigation, trade and commerce, they may also have introduced the tools to harness and control the labor of the farmers and artisans. These included magic, religion, and concepts of state, kingship and social hierarchy.

While most alternative prehistories are based more on speculation than fact, Professor Oppenheimer has found some very solid evidence; and have built on the work of specialists in many fields in addition to his own research, to support a comprehensive new picture.

The most solid facts come from oceanographic research of the last decade. It now appears that the great rise in sea level after the last Ice Age, known about for many years, was not gradual; three sudden ice-melts, the last of which was only 8,000 years ago, had catastrophic effects on tropical coasts with flat continental shelves. Rapid land loss was compounded by super waves, set off by cracks in the earth's crust as the weight of ice shifted to the seas.

Archaeology holds the most accurately dated clues to the past. Professor Oppenheimer has devoted two chapters to archaeological evidence found on coasts and in caves throughout the Indo-Pacific region. All of the technological 'firsts' which signaled man's emergence from the long Paleolithic era towards the end of the Ice Age come from the Pacific Rim islands. These include evidence of deliberate long-distance sailing and grinding of cereal flour in the Solomon Islands from 30,000 years ago. The world's first pots, 12,500 years old, come from Japan. The first evidence that swamps were drained for agriculture comes from the New Guinea Highlands 9,000 years ago.

These snapshots hint at a much older history to the discovery of Neolithic skills in the East. The better archaeological preservation of the later stages of human development in Mesopotamia and Egypt, however, has given rise to the view that civilization started in the West.

Professor Oppenheimer reviews the evidence of the spoken word in the two linguistic chapters. Experts in the history of language now recognize that Southeast Asia not Europe or West Asia was the center of language dispersal at the end of the Ice Age. The ancestral language of the Micronesians and Polynesians did not come out of China, as has been recently assumed, but further south over 8,000 years ago out of the drowning islands of Indonesia. As the flood engulfed Indo-China and separated Sumatera from Malaysia the ancestral languages of the Khmers, whose descendants built Angkor Wat, moved west into India.

The most dramatic new findings in this book come out of his own research field. He has published more than 25 scientific papers on the genetic prehistory of the Indo-Pacific region over the past 15 years. Building on his initial work, in *Eden in the East* he has shown that genetic disorders can be used as people-markers revealing a new view of prehistoric migrations in the Indo-Pacific region. His latest finding, made in collaboration with the Oxford Institute of Molecular Medicine, was published in the *American Journal of Human Genetics* in October 1998. This paper arose directly out of his research for *Eden in the East*. It provides compelling evidence that Polynesians and other Argonauts of the Indian and Pacific Oceans originated in eastern Indonesia back in the Ice Age rather than in China, as previously thought. This finding alone forces the realization that the Polynesians' skills of sailing, navigation, astronomy and agriculture had their origins, back in Indonesia, during the Ice Age.

Another objective tool that he uses to explore ancient East-West cultural influence in the last part of the book is comparative mythology. Uniquely shared folklore shows that counterparts and originals for nearly every Middle Eastern and European mythological archetype, including the flood, can be found in the islands of eastern Indonesia and the southwest Pacific. Southeast Asia is revealed as the original "Garden of Eden" and the "Flood" as the force which drove people from "Paradise".

His multidisciplinary approach to prehistoric enquiry has been recognized in the academic fields of linguistics and comparative folklore. He has been invited to present papers on his work on prehistory at international linguistic meetings.

INTERACTIVE GENETIC MAP

The Bradshaw Foundation, in association with Stephen Oppenheimer, presents a virtual global journey of modern man over the last 160,000 years, an interactive genetic map created collaboratively with Professor Stephen Oppenheimer, based on his book *Out of Eden/The Real Eve*, titled *Journey of Mankind: The Peopling of The World* in their website. The map shows for the first time the interaction of migration and climate over the period. The modern mankind is the descendants of a few small groups of tropical Africans who united in the face of adversity, not only to the point of survival but to the development of a sophisticated social interaction and culture expressed through many forms. Based on a synthesis of the *mtDNA** and Y†† chromosome evidence with archaeology, climatology and fossil study, Stephen Oppenheimer has tracked the routes and timing of migration, placing it in context with ancient rock art around the world.

The following figures were captured from the interactive map.

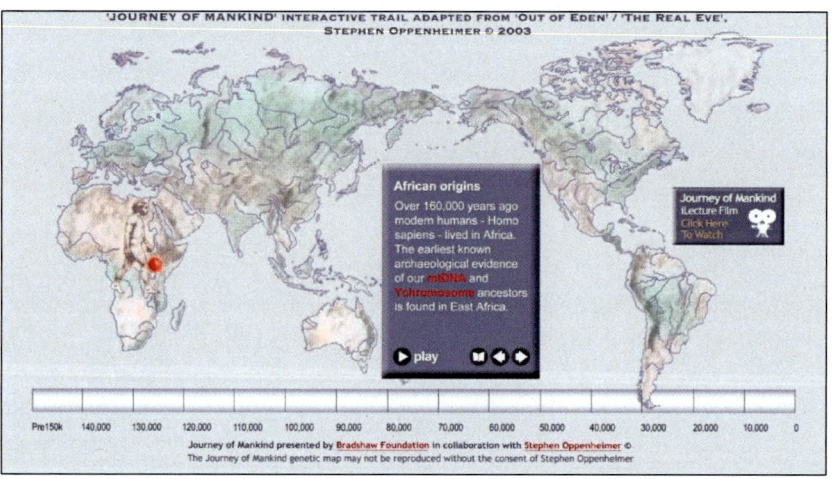

Figure 1 – Screen capture of interactive map *Journey of Mankind: The Peopling of The World* by Bradshaw Foundation collaboratively with Professor Stephen Oppenheimer

---

* Mitochondrial DNA (mtDNA or mDNA) is the DNA located in mitochondria; cellular organelles within eukaryotic cells that convert chemical energy from food into a form that cells can use, adenosine triphosphate (ATP).
† The Y chromosome is one of two sex chromosomes (allosomes) in mammals, including humans, and many other animals.

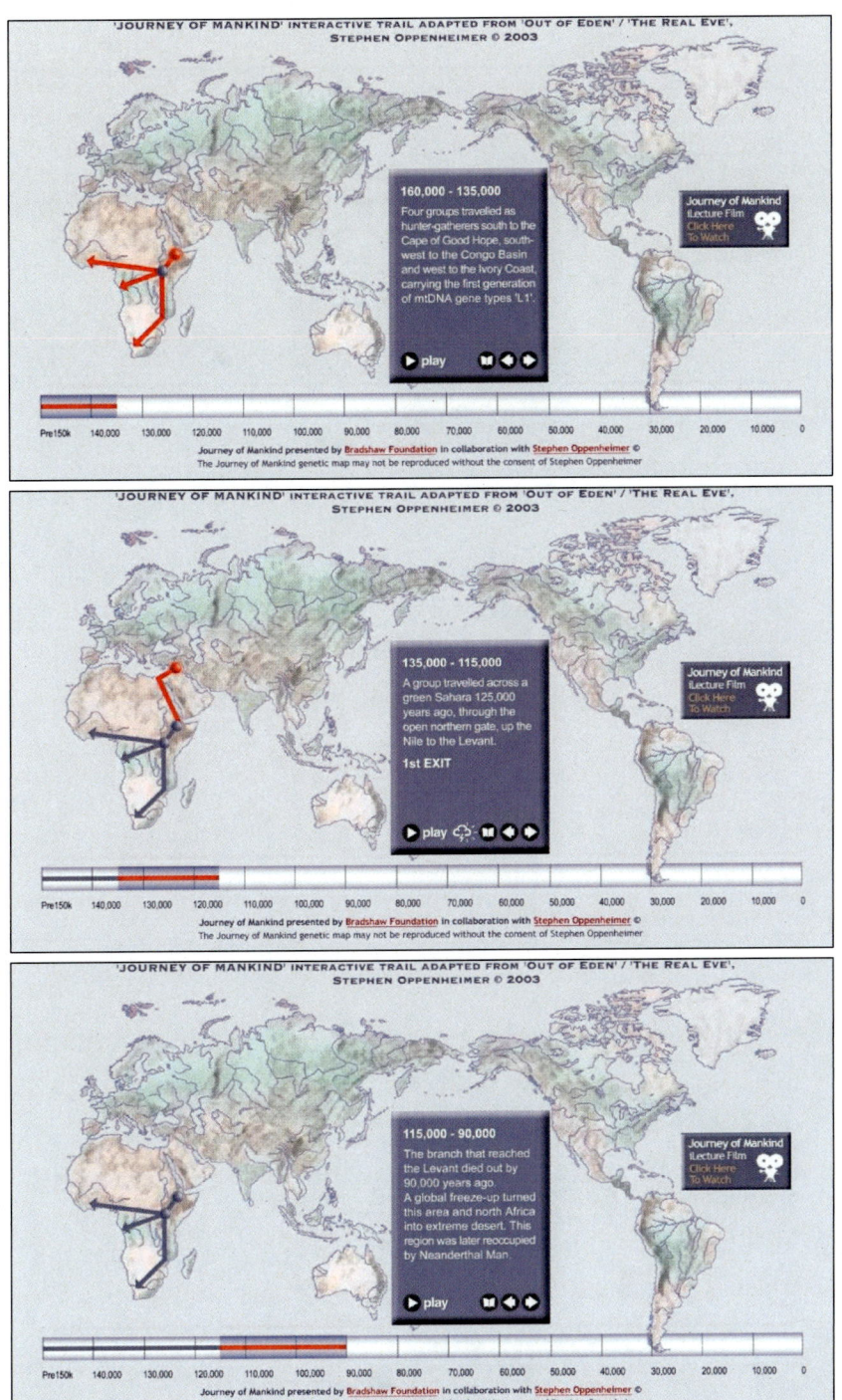

Figure 1 – Screen capture of interactive map *Journey of Mankind: The Peopling of The World* by Bradshaw Foundation collaboratively with Professor Stephen Oppenheimer (continued)

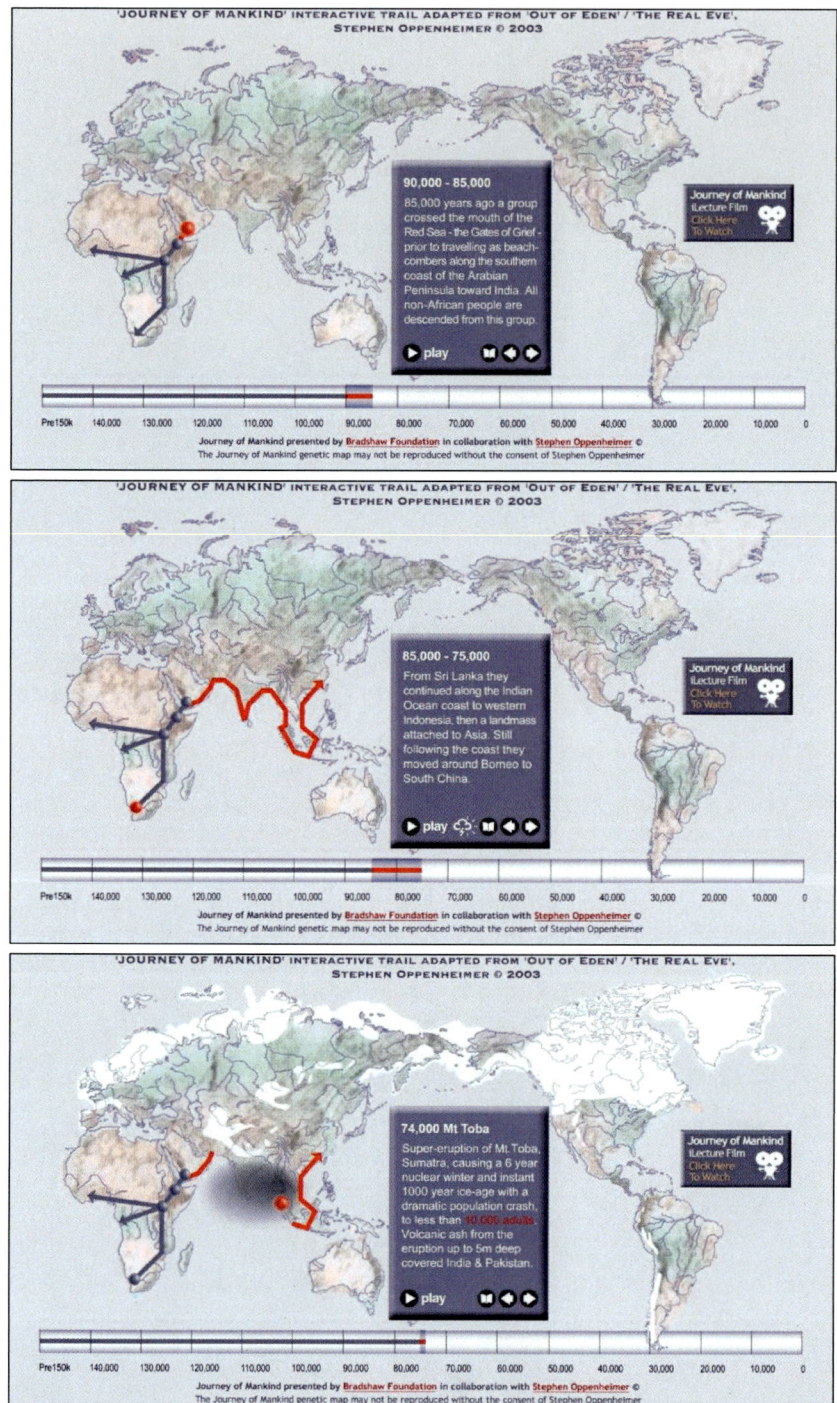

Figure 1 – Screen capture of interactive map *Journey of Mankind: The Peopling of The World* by Bradshaw Foundation collaboratively with Professor Stephen Oppenheimer (continued)

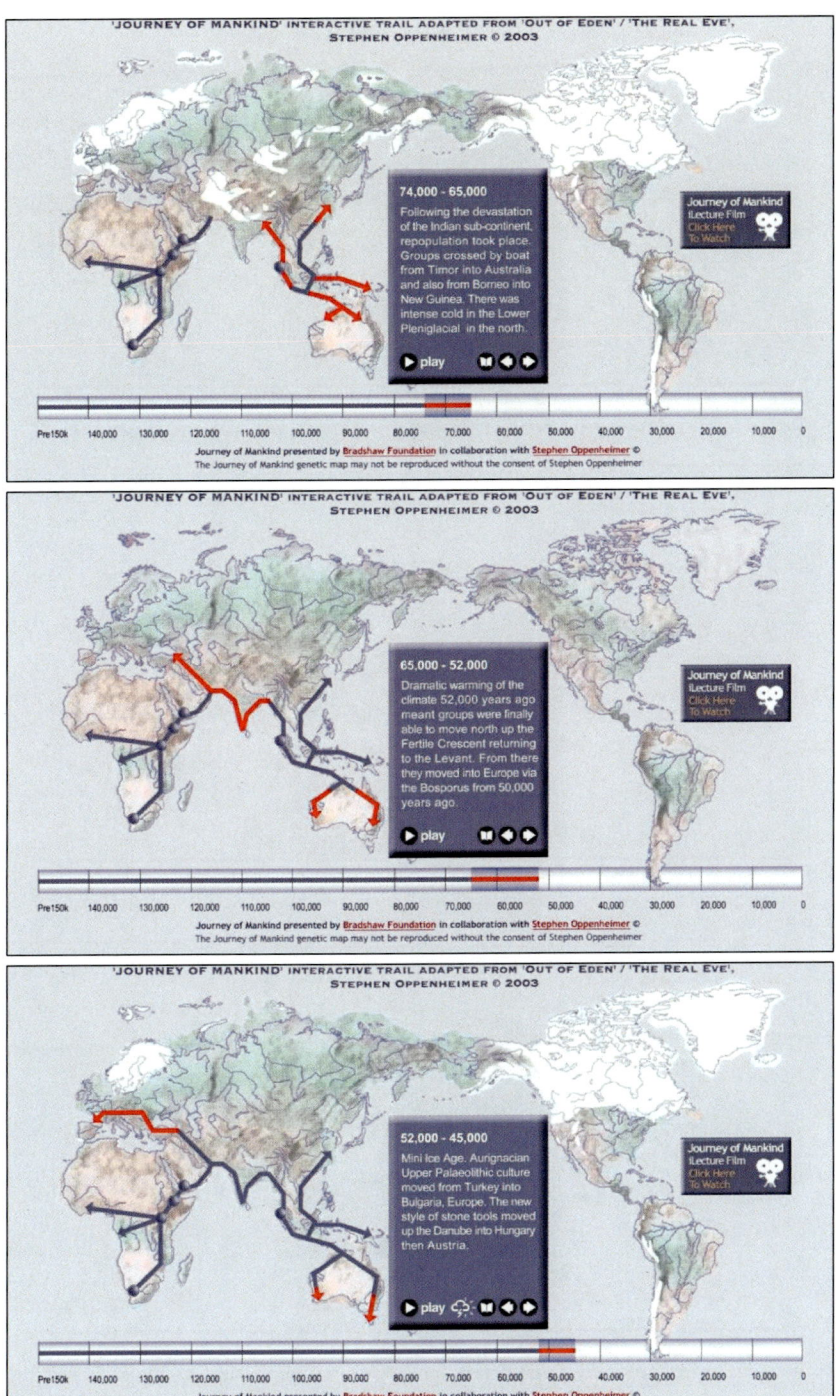

Figure 1 – Screen capture of interactive map *Journey of Mankind: The Peopling of The World* by Bradshaw Foundation collaboratively with Professor Stephen Oppenheimer (continued)

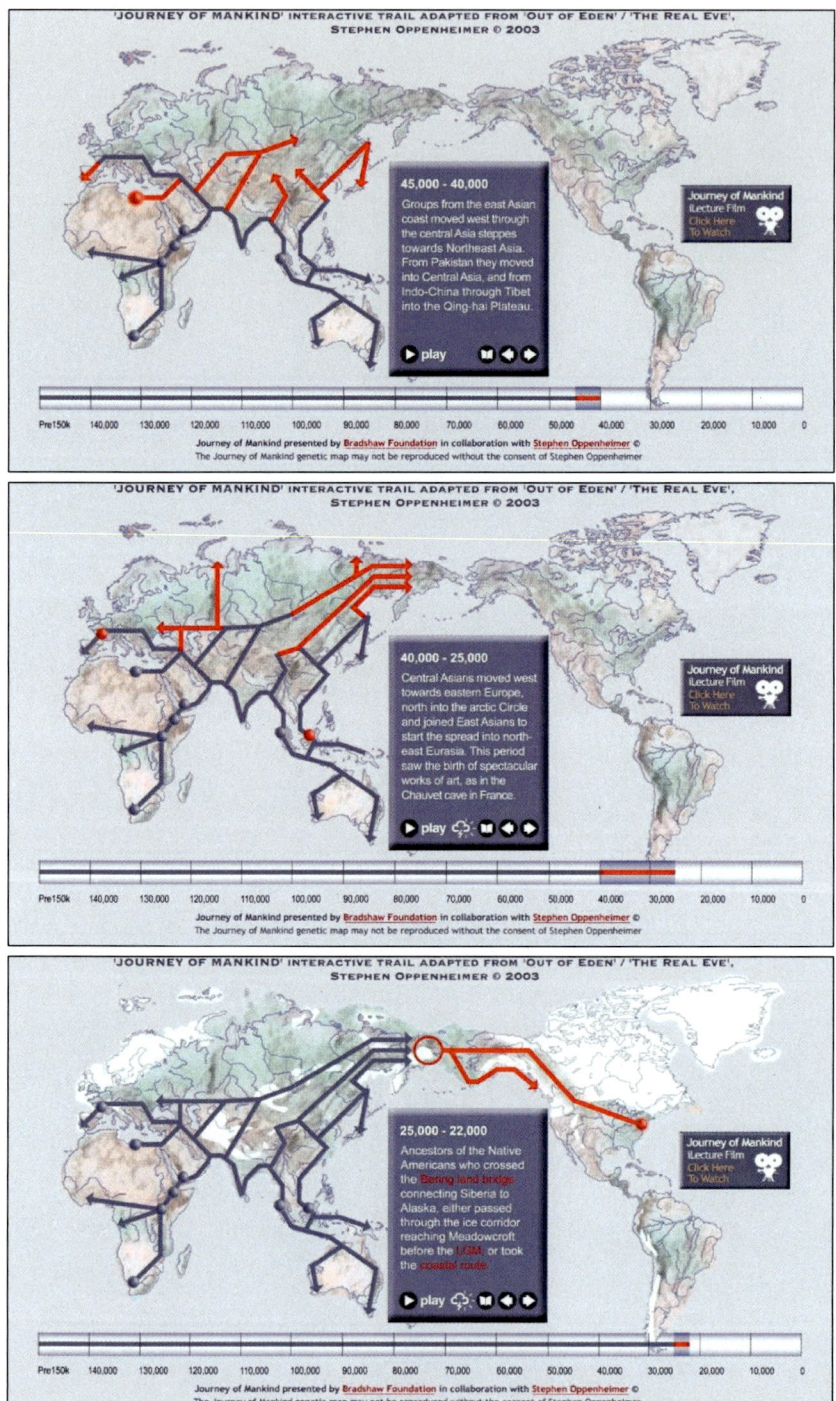

Figure 1 – Screen capture of interactive map *Journey of Mankind: The Peopling of The World* by Bradshaw Foundation collaboratively with Professor Stephen Oppenheimer (continued)

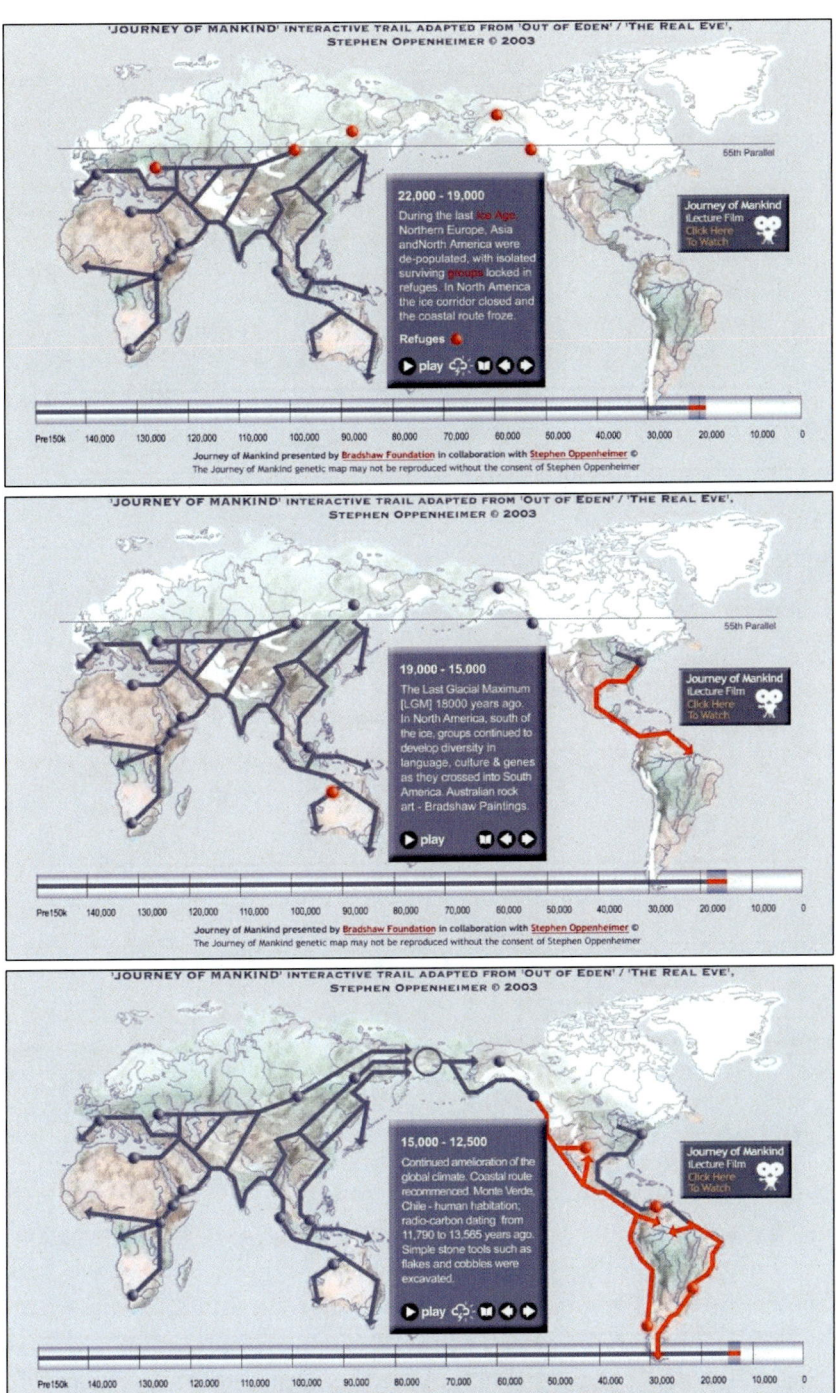

Figure 1 – Screen capture of interactive map *Journey of Mankind: The Peopling of The World* by Bradshaw Foundation collaboratively with Professor Stephen Oppenheimer (continued)

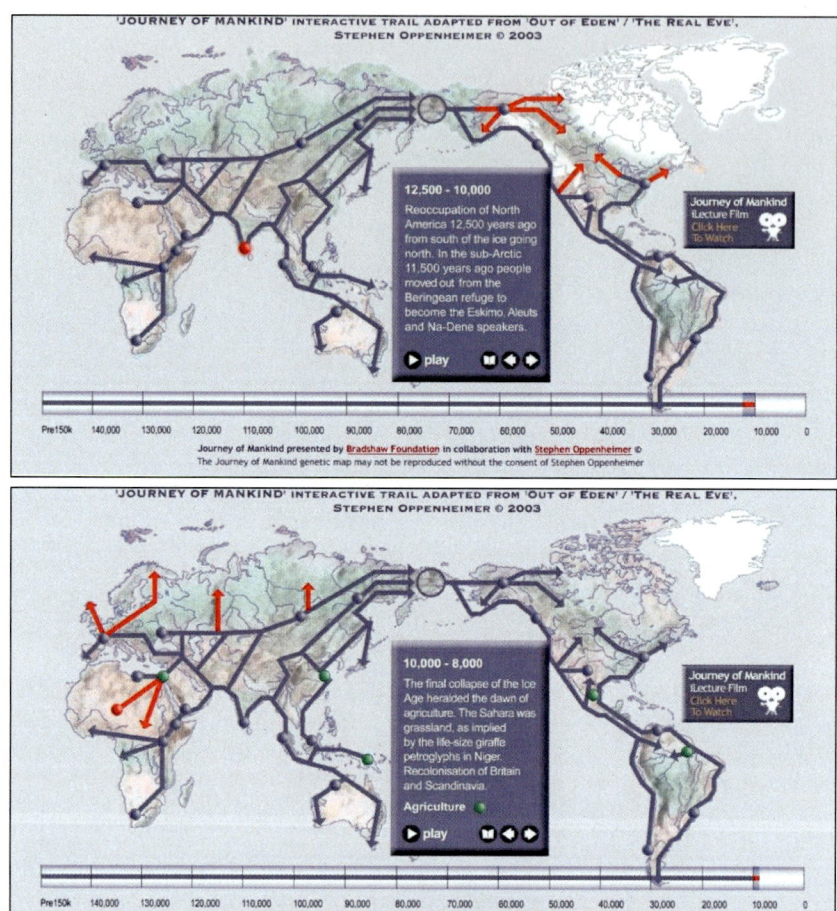

Figure 1 – Screen capture of interactive map *Journey of Mankind: The Peopling of The World* by Bradshaw Foundation collaboratively with Professor Stephen Oppenheimer (continued)

WILHELM SOLHEIM

Wilhelm G Solheim II was an American anthropologist recognized as most senior practitioner of archaeology in Southeast Asia, and as a pioneer in the study of Philippine and Southeast Asian prehistoric archaeology. He is perhaps best known, however, for hypothesizing the existence of the *Nusantao Maritime Trading and Communication Network* (NMTCN), one of two dominant hypotheses regarding the peopling of the Asia-Pacific region during the Neolithic age.

Solheim began his archaeological training at the University of California, Berkeley, and then spent several semesters at the University of the Philippines under Professor H Otley Beyer. He completed his PhD at the University of Arizona in 1959. He has been Professor Emeritus Department of Anthropology, University of Hawaii at Mānoa since he retired in December 1991. In 1997, he joined the staff of the Archaeological Studies Program at the University of the Philippines, Diliman.

Solheim died on July 25, 2014 at the age of 89.

In a hypothesis developed by Professor Wilhelm Solheim, the *Nusantao Maritime Trading and Communication Network* (NMTCN) is a trade and communication network that first appeared in the Asia-Pacific region during its Neolithic age, or beginning roughly around 5,000 BC. "Nusantao" is an artificial term coined by Solheim, derived from the Austronesian root words *nusa* "islands" and *tao* "man, people". Solheim's suggestions are in contrast to the more widely accepted *Out-of-Taiwan* hypothesis (OOT) by Peter Bellwood.

Solheim first suggested the concept in 1964. The NMTCN attempts to explain the diffusion of cultural traits throughout the Asia-Pacific region, a pattern that does not seem to match the projections of cultural spread by simple migration theories. Today, it is one of the dominant theories for the early peopling of the Southeast Asian region.

Solheim suggests that "[if] elements of culture were spread by migrations, then the spread would have been primarily in one direction." He suggests that since the pattern of cultural diffusion in the Asia-Pacific region is spread in all directions, it is likely that the spread of cultural traits happened via some kind of trading network, rather than a series of migrations.

In Solheim's hypothesis, the people who constituted this trading network are referred to as "the Nusantao".

In essence, the Nusantao would thus refer to groups of people in Southeast Asia who have or at least had a maritime-oriented culture in their beginnings.

At this point it is perhaps necessary to point out that Solheim does not view the word "people" in a biological sense but in a cultural sense – "as bearers of a living, evolving, variable culture". Thus, the Nusantao would also encompass groups in Southeast Asia that may not be biologically (genetically) related to one another, but share similarities in some aspects of their respective cultures. In effect, by conceptualizing the Nusantao and subsequently, the *Nusantao Maritime Trading and Communication Network* (NMTCN), Solheim was finding the agency responsible for the shared aspects of culture found widespread not only in Southeast Asia, but Asia in general out into the Pacific.

The term *Nusantao Maritime Trading and Communication Network* (NMTCN) is actually one which Solheim has only coined quite recently. The concept, however, has been in his mind almost the same time he formulated that of the Nusantao. The NMTCN, as the term connotes, is a trade and communication network that has been in place in the Asia-Pacific region for the past 10,000 years or so. It is this concept that Solheim puts forward as an alternative to simple migration theory in explaining why shared aspects of culture are found widespread in the Asia-Pacific region. He points out that if "elements of culture were spread by migrations, then the spread would have been primarily in one direction"; but since the observed shared elements of culture in the Asia-Pacific region were spread in all directions, the logical explanation is that they have been carried thus through some sort of trading network.

Solheim divides the NMTCN into four lobes: central, northern, eastern and western lobes.

Central lobe. The Central Lobe of the NMTCN is further divided into 2 smaller lobes – the Early Central Lobe and the Late Central Lobe. The Early Central Lobe is considered the homeland of the early NMTCN; it is located in eastern coastal Vietnam and is also dated earlier than the development of the Austronesian language. The Late Central Lobe, on the other hand, constitutes "the area where Austronesian became the original language family and Malayo-Polynesian developed". It includes southeastern Taiwan and South China from south Fujian, and may extend westwards including the Cambodian coast, both sides of the Gulf of Thailand, the eastern coast of Peninsular Malaysia, as well as some islands of western Indonesia.

Northern lobe. The Northern Lobe extends from Taiwan and Fujian to include coastal China, an unknown distance up the Chinese rivers that drain into the China Sea, coastal Korea and eastern Japan, possibly including the west coast and northern end of Honshu and extending further on to the Americas.

Eastern lobe. The Eastern Lobe is also further divided into 2 smaller lobes – an Early Eastern Lobe and a Late Eastern Lobe. The former includes Maluku in eastern Indonesia and the Bismarck archipelago in northwest Melanesia. The latter, on the other hand, extends from the Maluku eastward to Wallacea, and from there outwards throughout the Pacific (except the interior and much of the coast of New Guinea) as far as Easter Island.

Western lobe. Last but not the least is the Western Lobe. This extends from Malaysia and western Indonesia, along coastal India and Sri Lanka up to the western coast of Africa and Madagascar.

All of the three latter lobes overlap with the Late Central Lobe. As the names for the subdivisions of the Central and Eastern Lobes imply, all these four lobes of the NMTCN did not appear simultaneously, but developed as the Nusantao extended their trading network out from their original homeland in Vietnam. The possible order of expansion is thus also somewhat concentric and may be summarized as follows.

1. From the Early Central Lobe eastwards to start the local development of the Early Eastern Lobe. This is dated approximately between 5,000 BC, when the Early Central Lobe (in place since *ca* 9,000 BC) expanded eastwards to form the Late Central Lobe, and 3,000 – 4,000 BC, when the latter expanded from Northern Luzon in the Philippines into western Micronesia to form the Early Eastern Lobe.

2. From the beginning of the Late Central Lobe northwards including northern and western Taiwan, coastal China from Fujian north to Korea and Japan. This dates to approximately 5,000 BC based on a sample of rice excavated from Guah Sireh in Sarawak (AMS date of 3,850 ± 260 BP). Probably an early variety of *Oryza sativa javanica*, a similar variety is also found to have been introduced in Japan before the Yayoi period (*ca* 300 BC – *ca* 250 AD), suggesting a south-to-north movement of peoples.

3. From the Central Lobe to the west. This expansion of the Central Lobe into the Western Lobe probably dates earlier than 2,000 BC, as attested by the presence of decorated pottery belonging to the Sahuynh-Kalanay pottery tradition in sites like Gua Cha in northern Malaysia, Kok Phanom Di in southeastern Thailand (both from the second millennium BC) and Laang Spaan in western Cambodia (dated *ca* 1,990 – *ca* 1,550 BC).

4. The Late Eastern Lobe from the Central Lobe to the east.

Figure 2 – Map showing the extent of Solheim's *Nusantao Maritime Trading and Communication Network* (reproduced after Flessen, 2006)

SUNIL PRASANNAN

Dr Sunil Prasannan is a molecular biologist who has worked among others at Imperial College of London. Pasannan in 2004 has contributed to a number of internet forums relating to Atlantis, including the Graham Hancock site. On balance he believes that Plato's description best fits the Sundaland Hypothesis. He gives a lengthy outline of his opinions on the sites.

As mentioned in Graham's latest book, *Underworld*, the land area thought to have been lost during the meltdown at the end of the Ice Age would have been something like 25,000,000 square kilometers, assuming a ball park figure of 100 meters of sea-level rise. Much of this would have been relatively narrow strips of land parallel to modern coastlines, such as those off much of Africa, but in other places, such as the Persian Gulf and off the coast of NW India, significant areas were inundated. But would there have been anywhere in the world where a continent-sized, or near-continent-sized, landmass would have been lost forever? The Sunda Shelf off modern Indonesia, Malaysia and Indo-China, which at LGM (last glacial maximum, about 16,000 years ago) would have been a gigantic plain, "Sundaland", linking together the three countries above into a single peninsula-shaped landmass twice the size of India (itself 3,000,000 square kilometers in area today). Mention also has to be made of the considerable land

52

bridge joining nearby New Guinea with modern Australia, forming "Sahul", or "Greater Australia", which would also have incorporated Tasmania.

As for mountains and rivers, Sundaland would have had them in abundance, the mountains of course still with us today due to their loftiness, in Sumatera, Java and Kalimantan in particular. Underwater mapping of the Sunda Shelf reveals that modern rivers in Indonesia, Malaysia and Indo-China would have been extended and would often combine to form much bigger rivers in the area inundated. And of course, being smack-bang on the equator, this region must surely have enjoyed a warm climate for thousand of years either side of LGM. So this must have seemed like a veritable Garden of Eden to the multitude of people who would surely have taken advantage of this Ice Age refugium to settle long term and develop any civilized culture, and consequent technology.

We know that the Greek philosopher, Plato, wrote the only known account referring directly to Atlantis. In his dialogues, *Timaeus* and *Critias* dating from about 360 BC, he tells the story of how the much earlier Greek philosopher, Solon, visited Egypt in about 600 BC, and learnt of Atlantis from a priest. One of the key features in the priest's description of Atlantis was its size, being some sort of landmass (whether "island" or "continent") "bigger than Libya and Asia combined", that was lost "in a single day and night of misfortune". Of course, in Classical times, Asia was simply Asia Minor (modern Turkey), and Libya was the northern Mediterranean coast of Africa. And, of course, size has been alluded to above as a prerequisite for a landmass supporting a lost civilization. The best way to go about this is to simply pick out passages in *Timaeus* or *Critias*, not in any particular order, and rationalize them in terms of Sundaland and/or modern Indonesia and its neighbors. The size given for Plato's Atlantis, the observation that the inundated areas of Sundaland formed, perhaps the largest continuous stretch of territory inundated at the end of Ice Age. The "way to the other islands" could be a reference to Oceania, including, of course, the enlarged "Sahul", greater Australia, which would have combined Oz, Tasmania and New Guinea. Also, Plato (or rather, Solon's priestly guide) could have had the myriad Polynesian islands in mind too. Finally, "the opposite continent" must be a reference to the Americas, which if you stop to think about it, is "opposite" whether you sail west from Europe or Africa, or eastwards from Asia. Clearly, irrespective of any controversy regarding the location of Atlantis, this demonstrates pre-Columbian knowledge of there being an American continent.

The statement "*nine thousand was the sum of years that had elapsed*" does tie in well with the latest scientific research into the meltdown at the end of the Ice Age. The bulk of the submerged Sunda Shelf was inundated relatively rapidly between 14,000 and 11,000 years ago. Whilst much of the territory would have been lost in the first of three "global super floods", 14,000 years ago, almost all the antediluvian continental shelf would have been inundated during the second flood roughly 11,000 years ago. The only significant event of the third super flood of approximately 7,500 years ago would have been the opening of the Strait of Malacca between Malaya and Sumatera. If we forgive him for omitting the first flood, either Plato's observation of events 11,600 years ago is just a fluke, or we could justifiably speculate that the Egyptians did keep records, or at least traditions, that dated back to the epoch of 9,600 BC.

Both in *Timaeus*: "…*the sea in those parts is impassable and impenetrable, because there is a shoal of mud in the way; and this was caused by the subsidence of the island*" and again in *Critias*: "[the sea] *became an impassable barrier of mud to voyagers sailing from hence to any part of the ocean*". Plato clearly alludes to unfavorable maritime conditions caused by underwater debris and obstacles in the region of the sunken Atlantis landmass after its demise. The present day South China Sea in the vicinity of the sunken Sunda Shelf is very shallow for such a large expanse of water, being never much deeper than 50 to 60 meters. This is in sharp contrast to the precipitous depths of the Atlantic or the Pacific. We could speculate that along with catastrophic flooding, seismic activity could have occurred, which would have introduced significant amounts of volcanic ash and debris into the newly formed South China Sea. Krakatau, of 1883 explosion fame, could well have been involved, this volcano having once stood proudly between Sumatera and Java.

In *Critias*, there is much to suggest the climate was lush and tropical, for instance: "… *that sacred island that then beheld the light of the sun.*" This could be an archaic version of the modern English "seeing the light of day", *ie* to exist (before the flood, Sundaland saw the light of day, afterwards it no longer did, because it was underwater), but suppose it could refer to the altitude of the sun above of the horizon. An alternative translation of the same phrase is given: "… *that sacred island, then still beneath the sun.*" If tropical latitude was implied by Plato, this could explain his choice of words, because the sun would be very much higher in the sky at midday than in the temperate region of the Mediterranean. Indeed, at the equator, which neatly bisects the Indonesian region, the sun appears directly overhead.

"... *the island itself provided most of what was required by them for the uses of life ... also whatever fragrant things there are now in the earth, whether roots, or herbage, or woods, or essences which distil from fruit and flowers grew and thrived in that land.*" Quite a paradise it seems, doesn't it?! Exotic fruits and vegetables, herbs and spices too.

Another, perhaps bigger clue to a tropical, and not temperate, climate is given: "*Twice in the year they gathered the fruits of the earth — in winter having the benefit of the rains of the heavens, and in the summer the water which the land supplied by introducing streams from the canals.*" Surely this suggests a climate driven by a seasonal monsoon, as is the case in much of southern and Southeastern Asia today. By "winter", Plato refers to the wet season, and "summer" would refer to the dry season. Of course, there must have been some difference from the pattern today, due to slight cooling during the Ice Age, and the extra landmass that Sundaland presented to any weather system coming in off the ocean. Also, it is clear from the above passage that the Atlanteans devised effective irrigation schemes.

Apparently, the land that was Atlantis was extensively forested, because Plato makes a number of references to the number of trees, as well as the resultant amount of timber available to the Atlanteans: "*there was an abundance of wood for carpenters*" and slightly later: "*and much wood was available of various sorts, abundant for each and every kind of work*" and even in a "grove" in the capital city: "[there were] *all manner of trees of wonderful height and beauty owing to the excellence of the soil.*" The latter passage surely conveys the picture of a region dominated by tropical rainforest. We know the Indonesian islands today have Asia's largest total rainforest area, some 113 million hectares (279 million acres) in 1990. And Malaysia's rainforests cover some 63% of its total area of 330,000 square kilometers (128,000 square miles). Of course, the figures today would be significantly smaller, due to extensive logging, but who knows just how extensive the forests would have been on the plain now forming the Sunda Shelf, that was flooded at the end of the Ice Age?

He also makes a curious, but rather specific, reference to "elephants" roaming the lost Atlantis: "*there were a great number of elephants in the island; for there was ample provision for food for all sorts of animals, both for those which live in lakes and marshes and rivers, and also those which live in mountains and on plains, so there was for the animal that is the largest and most voracious of all.*" The very mention of elephants immediately brings Southern and Southeastern Asia, and Africa too, to mind. Although, Africa would include the Atlantic seaboard of Morocco, and Mastodons were around in Florida at the end of the Ice Age, though the latter didn't outlive it.

However, bearing in mind what Plato wrote about the climate and vegetation (see above), it is clear conditions were lush enough to support a large population of pachyderms. And although no exact species are specified, many other kinds of animals are mentioned, and those *"that live in lakes and marshes and rivers"* could have included crocodiles and the like.

Also intriguing is the physical description of the landscape, which does paint a reasonably accurate picture of the Sundaland region as it would have been during the Ice Age: *"The whole country was said by* [Solon] *to be very lofty and precipitous on the side of the sea, but the country immediately about and surrounding the city was a level plain...smooth and even, and of an oblong shape."* Sundaland, as it was, would have had high mountains along the south coast, in the present day islands of Sumatera and Java, and also in the east, in Kalimantan, and all three regions would have been immediately bounded by the main ocean, but the central portion, now forming the submerged Sunda Shelf, would indeed have been a flat plain. A further geographical feature is described, namely: *"near the plain again, in the center of the island....there was a mountain not very high on any side."* Could this be a reference to the present day island of Natuna Besar, part of Indonesia, but halfway between Malay Peninsula (west Malaysia) and northern Kalimantan (east Malaysia)? The highest point on the island is 959 meters above sea level, and adding a maximum 100 m for the lower sea level during the Ice Age would not make it much higher than 1,060 meters, comparable to Mount Snowdon in Wales, UK. This would make it "not very high" if compared to the much loftier peaks in Malaya, Sumatera, Java and Kalimantan, regularly soaring to well over 2,000 or even 3,000 meters in height above the modern sea level. While there are other much smaller (and flatter) islands in the vicinity, Natuna Besar surely must be the best candidate for the mountain described in *Critias*.

It seems there a number of activities described in *Critias*, and that we could reconcile with a Southeast Asian location for the civilization described. The first of these is the construction of an effective and extensive irrigation system, as described in passages such as that: *"The depth, and width, and length of this ditch were incredible, and gave the impression that a work of such extent, in addition to so many others, could never have been artificial... Further inland, likewise, straight canals of a hundred feet in width were cut from it through the plain, and again let off into the ditch leading to the sea."* Dr Stephen Oppenheimer, in his *Eden in the East*, suggests that there are visible signs of settled agriculture in the Southeast Asian region at least as early as those in the Middle East. For instance, the cultivation of rice, which needs a fair amount of irrigation, seems to have been undertaken in the Malay Peninsula as early as 9,000 years ago, about 2,000 years before the first signs in India or China. A similar date is given for the extensive drainage of swamps by the New Guinea Highlanders to grow crops such as taro. Although the latter site is not in Sundaland, it is not terribly far away, and we could speculate that it was descendants of refugees from the flooded Sunda Shelf who could have been responsible for these very early signs of irrigation in the Asia-Pacific region. Of course, the Malay and New Guinea sites are both above water; no underwater archaeology has been undertaken on the Sunda Shelf.

Another aspect of human endeavor is an allusion to a vast trade network in the region: "*For because of the greatness of their empire, many things were brought to them from foreign countries….meanwhile they went on constructing* [their] *harbors and docks.*" Is there any evidence of Southeast Asia being a hub of oceanic commerce in deepest antiquity? According to Stephen Oppenheimer, the evidence available, sadly, doesn't go as far back as the epoch of 11,500 years ago, but what is known is that there are definite signs of a cultural and genetic diffusion from Southeast Asia dating from at least 7,000 years ago, the epoch of the third global super flood. For instance, there are 6,000 year-old statuettes found as far apart as Mesopotamia and New Guinea depicting rather Oriental looking ladies with slanting eyes, and a type of skin scarification (performed ritually) found today only in Oceania. So there must have been available the kind of ships capable of sailing right across the Indian Ocean. After all, the Malagasy people of Madagascar speak an Austronesian language related to modern Indonesian. Populations as far apart as Polynesia, Korea, Australia, India and the Middle East show both nuclear and mitochondrial DNA links with the population of Southeast Asia. An example is Thalassemia, an anemia associated with resistance to Malaria, which is endemic in a vast arc of territory stretching from the Western Mediterranean and Southern Africa right across to northern Australia and farthest Polynesia. This suggests some degree of settlement by peoples from Sundaland in the areas mentioned above.

Also consideration has to be made of the "Sundadont" teeth mentioned by Graham Hancock in *Underworld*, found in the deepest habitation layer in Mehrgarh, in Pakistan, the oldest known settlement in the Indian subcontinent (*ca* 7,000 BC). However this type of shovel-like incisor, associated with Southeast Asian populations, died out by the time of the next habitation layer. Graham suggests that the "Sundadont" people who founded Mehrgarh could have moved inland to western Pakistan from the flooding of the wide continental shelf off northwestern India between 14,000 and 7,000 years ago.

Interestingly, the inundation maps for the second global super flood of approximately 11,000 years ago show little change from the situation following the first of approximately 14,000 years ago. Of course that would mean that there were Southeast Asians living on India's northwest coast before the epoch of 9,500 BC, but because the Mehrgarh teeth were in actual fact not true Sundadont, but "Sundadont"-like, a degree of intermarriage could perhaps have occurred with the native Indian tribes, who have the "European" dental complex, by the time of their final migration inland.

Another tantalizing piece of evidence is the Cantino Map of *ca* 1502 AD. This early Portuguese map of the world shows what can only be a fair representation of Southeast Asia (and India) as it would have appeared during the Ice Age – namely a massive peninsula approximating to the Sunda Shelf. As the Portuguese only reached Malacca on the Malay Peninsula in *ca* 1509 AD, obviously someone must have had the need, and ability, to map the Indonesian region upwards of 7,000 years ago. And, of course, knowing that there are underwater structures off the coast of India (such as Poompuhur), as well as off Taiwan (such as Yonaguni), that were likely to have been above water 11,000 years ago, demonstrates there would indeed have been plenty of scope for a trading network centered on Southeast Asia in such a distant epoch.

The third major application of technology seems to be that of both mining of metal ores, and the manufacture of metal alloys. In *Critias*, Plato informs us: *"they dug out of the earth whatever was to be found there, solid as well as fusil"* and, also, that the citadel in the capital city was coated in various kinds of metals: *"The entire circuit of the wall, which went round the outermost zone, they covered with a coating of bronze, and the circuit of the next wall they coated with tin, and the third, which encompassed the citadel, flashed with the red light of orichalcum."* "Orichalcum" was some sort of brass (an alloy of copper and zinc). But the mention of bronze (an alloy of copper and tin), and tin itself, suggests that the Atlanteans had a considerable amount of both copper and tin available, considering the observation they were covering whole walls with them. And are not modern Indonesia and Malaysia two of the world's largest producers of tin, as well as having significant copper reserves, along with several other metals? As far as tin goes, only Brazil and China produce more. Much of Indonesia's tin is extracted from offshore "placer" deposits, and in fact, it is thought that about 40% of Indonesia's potential reserves are actually offshore, on the Sunda Shelf! The neighboring countries of Malaysia and Thailand also have significant tin deposits, including "placers". In fact, the three Southeast Asian countries produce approximately one third of all the tin metal in the world.

Following on from the description of the citadel above is the curious passage describing the layout of the capital: *"Now the largest of the zones into which a passage was cut from the sea was three stadia in breadth, and the zone of land which came next of equal breadth; but the next two zones, the one of water, the other of land, were two stadia, and the one which surrounded the central island was a stadium only in width... All this including the zones and bridge, which was the sixth part a stadium in width, they surrounded by a stone wall on every side, placing towers and gates on the bridges where the sea passed in."* How can this not be interpreted as a mandalic construction, similar to (for example) Angkor Wat in Cambodia, a massive temple which consists of internesting rectangles surrounded by a moat and connected to the surrounding country by causeways? Could the "sea" and "bridges" Plato described have really been a moat and causeways similar to those of Angkor and its surrounding temples? The mandala motif seems to be a hallmark of Indian and Southeast Asian temples built to Hindu or Buddhist specifications. But what really got the hairs raised on the back of the neck, even a chill down the spine, is the location of Angkor – because 11,600 years ago, Cambodia would have been an integral part of the antediluvian Sundaland landmass! So what, you might ask, given that Angkor was built sometime between the 9th and 13th centuries AD, some 10,000 years after the demise of Atlantis as rendered by Plato? We know that the "modern" sites of Angkor and its neighbors were actually built on "primeval mounds" dating back to the deepest antiquity, probably dated by the so-called "Draco correlation" highlighted by Graham in his *Heaven's Mirror* to 10,500 BC. Let's assume this correlation is both correct with respect to the constellations and in the correct time-frame – could it have been survivors of the flooding of the lower-lying regions of Sundaland to the south of Cambodia who first began venerating the "primeval mounds"?

There is one other thing, and that is to point out a weird inconsistency in Plato's account that needs to be put in context with respect to Atlantis' location. We are led to believe that there was a war between Atlantis (which had conquered Egypt) and the Hellenic city-state of Athens, which would of course mean that Athens would have to be as old as Atlantis before inundation in 9,600 BC. An example from *Timaeus* is given: *"and then, Solon, your country shone forth, in the excellence of her virtue and strength, among all mankind. She was pre-eminent in courage and military skill, and was the leader of the Hellenes."* And yet, somewhat earlier in *Timaeus*, the Egyptian priest pointedly ridicules Solon (and by implication all

Greeks) by telling him this: "*O, Solon, Solon, you Hellenes are never anything but children, and there is not an old man among you.*" What on earth could be going on here? Why this complete and utter contradiction regarding the venerability of the Hellenes? But, we needn't speculate too much, because in *Critias*, Plato seems to partially explain what could be going on: "*you must not be surprised if you should perhaps hear Hellenic names given to foreigners. I will tell you the reason of this: Solon, who was intending to use the tale for his poem, enquired into the meaning of the names, and found that the early Egyptians in writing them down had translated them into their own language, and he recovered the meaning of several names and when copying them out again translated them into our language.*"

Could it have been the case that what actually happened was that Solon had "Hellenized" a tale originating in Egypt, transposing "foreign" places for those of a more Mediterranean setting? Moreover, we have to consider Plato's own role, given that the era of 360 BC was one of increasing Greek confidence. The story of a "war" in the Mediterranean region itself could be apocryphal, giving a jingoistic edge to the whole saga. The following line in *Timaeus* suggests this to a high degree: "*Athens was first in war and in every way the best governed of all cities.*" After all, orthodox history tells us the only civilizations on the northern side of the Mediterranean dated from about 2,000 BC at the earliest, these being Mycenae on the Greek mainland and the earlier Minoan civilization on Crete. Neither could possibly have been around 11,600 years ago. The only likely candidate would have been the mysterious civilization on Malta, though this island, which at the end of the Ice Age would have formed a lengthy land bridge stretching all the way to Italy via Sicily, would surely have been too far west to have been considered a "primeval Athens" which brings neatly back to the four words so eloquently avoided in the explanation earlier in this essay for the location of Atlantis: the Pillars of Heracles! Plato writes in *Timaeus* that Atlantis was: "*situated in front of the straits which are by you called the Pillars of Heracles.*"

This would obviously be the present day Strait of Gibraltar, if put in a Greek, Mediterranean context. But if there was a degree of borrowing undertaken by either Solon or Plato, as alluded to in the passages quoted immediately above, where else could "Pillars of Heracles" have been situated? There are two other straits situated in the Middle East, both to the east of Egypt and Greece, both joining smaller seas with the main Ocean (Indian Ocean in this case). These are the Strait of Hormuz at the eastern end of the Persian Gulf, and the Bab-el-Mandeb, at the southern end of the Red Sea. Since the latter is situated so much closer to Egypt, suspect that the Bab-el-Mandeb could have been the "Pillars" in the original, assuming the Egyptians referred to them as such – they certainly wouldn't have named them after the Greek hero Heracles! However, it is possible it wouldn't have been completely navigable 11,600 years ago, because it is relatively shallow in parts, which then points at Hormuz, which according to the data of Kurt Lambeck would have been a small inlet, not a strait, 16,400 years ago, but would have opened up completely by 10,600 years ago, only a millennium after the date in question. So we could assume it was navigable 11,600 years ago.

But what about Atlantis being "in front" of the straits? Indonesia and its neighbors are not in front of either Hormuz or the Bab-el-Mandeb, are they? Actually, it pertinent to consider the original Greek rendering of the phrase, which reliably informed is: *"huper Hêrakleias stêlas."* "Huper" in time came to be rendered as "hyper", and is a prefix we recognize in modern English as meaning "very much of", "excessive", *etc*, as in hypertension, hypermarket, and so forth. The original Greek meaning of "hyper" in the above context as an adverb is something on the lines of "beyond", or "further out". So the real meaning is probably nearer "beyond the Pillars of Heracles" – *ie* some considerable distance away from the Strait, and not right next door to it. So, this does not in any way contradict a Southeast Asian location for Atlantis.

Even Plato's insistence that: *"this power came forth from the Atlantic"* isn't fatal to this theory, because we have no evidence that the Greeks thought that there was more than one "Ocean Sea". The Phoenicians rounded the Horn of Africa as early as *ca* 595 BC, some 250 years before Plato's Dialogues, so the Greeks would have been aware of this. They had their "oikumene", or known world, encircled by what they thought was an all-encompassing ocean. After all, wasn't "the Ocean" exactly what Alexander the Great (who came to power in Greece not too long after Plato's time) sought in his arduous adventures as far eastward as India? "Beyond the Pillars of Heracles" would therefore have meant anywhere in this "Ocean Sea".

Also, another big clue is given in the source of the Atlantis story – ancient Egypt itself. Now, what could possibly link ancient Egypt with Southeast Asia? Well, is it not the case that the Egyptians considered their "paradise", or "primeval homeland", where their civilizing heroes such as Thoth and Osiris originated, as being far away to the East, "in the sea of the Rising Sun"? And this brings back to the subject of Angkor Wat in modern Cambodia, which as has been speculated earlier in this essay could have been originally "ear-marked" by refugees escaping the flooded plains to the south. Graham Hancock suggests in *Heaven's Mirror* that if a meridian (line of longitude) is drawn through Giza in Egypt (the site of the Pyramids), Angkor is almost exactly 72° east of it. But suppose that the Giza site had been chosen by the "civilizers" of the Egyptians because it was 72° west of a meridian running through Angkor.

Consider the following description of the Egyptians' "Abode of the Blessed": *"situated away beyond a large expanse of water."* Sir EA Wallis Budge, the eminent Egyptologist, noted this regarding how to reach the said "abode": *"the Egyptians believed that this land could only be reached by means of a boat, or by the personal help of the gods."* And intriguingly, in an almost Plato-esque fashion, that it consisted of: *"rectangular in shape, and that it was intersected by canals supplied from the stream by which the whole region was enclosed."*

So what could Plato's account of a "war" be based on? Wallis Budge reasoned that the Egyptian legend of the god Horus avenging his father Osiris, by defeating his "evil" uncle Set could have been based on historical events, given that Horus was aided by followers rendered as "blacksmiths": *"It is, of course, impossible to say who were the blacksmiths that swept over Egypt from south to north, or where they come from, but the writer believes that they represent invaders in pre dynastic times, who made their way into Egypt from a country in the East, by way of the Red Sea.....They brought with them the knowledge of working in metals and of brickmaking, and having conquered the indigenous peoples in the south* [ie the city of Edfu] *then proceeded to conquer and occupy other sites."* So could this have been the "war" which engulfed Egypt that Plato based his account in *Timaeus* on?

And what of *Critias*, which the philosopher never finished, but left incomplete with this intriguing passage regarding the Greek god Zeus' response to the Atlanteans' increasingly decadent lifestyle? *"Zeus, the god of gods, who rules according to law, and is able to see into such things, perceiving that an honorable race was in a woeful plight, and wanting to inflict punishment on them, that they might be chastened and improve, collected all the gods into their most holy habitation, which, being placed in the center of the world, beholds all created things. And when he had called them together, he spoke as follows..."*

Can we speculate that Plato had in mind the following utterance by the god Thoth in the *Egyptian Book of the Dead* when he wrote the above? *"They have fought fights, they have upheld strives, they have done evil, they have created hostilities, they have made slaughter, they have caused trouble and oppression ...* [therefore] *I am going to blot out everything which I have made. This earth shall enter into the watery abyss by means of a raging flood, and will become even as it was in primeval time."*

Then we have the mentions in Plato's dialogues of a large land mass, disappearing for ever under the flood; a shallow sea left in its place; lush, fertile soil; tropical climate; herds of elephants; an abundance of metals; early engagement in agriculture and irrigation; construction of mandalic edifices; an extensive trading network...

DANNY HILMAN NATAWIDJAJA

Danny Hilman Natawidjaja was trained in geology at Bandung Institute of Technology and The Auckland University. He completed his doctoral degree at The California Institute of Technology. He is currently a senior geologist at The Center for Geotechnology Research, The Indonesian Institute of Sciences. Natawidjaja is also a member of The Integrated and Independent Research Team of Gunung Padang Megalithic Site. Natawidjaja published his Atlantis theory in a Kindle eBook, *Plato Never Lied: Atlantis Is in Indonesia* in 2013.

Natawidjaja makes a case that destruction of Atlantis by an earthquake and a great flood was mentioned at a definite time: 11,600 years ago, the time in the history of Quaternary geology known as the end of the Younger Dryas (YD), or Late Pleistocene and Early Holocene period. At this YD, global catastrophes that destroyed life on earth were allegedly occurred and interestingly the history of civilization as we know was began in the aftermath of the YD.

Natawidjaja discusses the Plato manuscripts critically and sharply from logical and scientific point of views. In accordance with Natawidjaja's background, the contents of the Plato's manuscripts are analyzed from viewpoints of a geologist. Natawidjaja also describes more about the concept of natural disaster cycle and its relation to human being from the modern geological knowledge, accompanied by descriptions of a case study of major natural disasters that occurred in parts of Indonesia, including the drowning of ancient land of Sundaland that occurred at the end of the Ice Age.

In the last section, he briefly discusses the results of geological studies at the Gunung Padang megalithic site and whether there is any connection with Atlantis.

***

SUNDALAND

Sundaland (also called the Sundaic region) is a biogeographical region of Southeastern Asia which encompasses the Sunda Shelf, the part of the Asian continental shelf that was exposed during the last Ice Age. The last glacial period, popularly known as the Ice Age, was the most recent glacial period within the current Ice Age occurring during the last years of the Pleistocene, from approximately 110,000 to 12,000 years BP (before present). It included the Malay Peninsula on the Asian mainland, as well as the large islands of Kalimantan, Java, and Sumatera and their surrounding islands. The eastern boundary of Sundaland is the Wallace Line*, as the eastern boundary of the range of Asia's land mammal fauna, and thus the boundary of the Indomalaya and Australasia ecozones.

The South China Sea and adjoining landmasses had been investigated by scientists such as Molengraaff and Umbgrove, who had postulated ancient, now submerged drainage systems. These were mapped by Tjia in 1980 and described in greater detail by Emmel and Curray in 1982 complete with river deltas, floodplains and back swamps. The ecology of the exposed Sunda Shelf has been investigated by analyzing cores drilled into the ocean bed. The pollens found in the cores have revealed a complex ecosystem that changed over time. The flooding of Sundaland separated species that had once shared the same environment such as the river *threadfin* (*Polydactylus macrophthalmus*, Bleeker 1858) that had once thrived in a river system now called "North Sunda River" or "Molengraaff River". The fish is now found in the Kapuas River on the island of Kalimantan, and in the Musi and Batanghari rivers in Sumatera.

The last glacial period, popularly known as the Ice Age, was the most recent glacial period within the current ice age occurring during the last years of the Pleistocene, from approximately 110,000 to 12,000 years BP. Scientists consider this Ice Age to be merely the latest glaciation event in a much larger ice age, one that dates back over two million years and has seen multiple glaciations.

---

* The Wallace Line is a faunal boundary line drawn in 1859 by the British naturalist Alfred Russel Wallace that separates the ecozones of Asia and Wallacea, a transitional zone between Asia and Australia. West of the line are found organisms related to Asiatic species; to the east, a mixture of species of Asian and Australian origin is present. The line is named after Alfred Russel Wallace, who noticed this clear division during his travels through the East Indies in the 19th century. The line runs through Indonesia, between Kalimantan and Sulawesi, and through the Lombok Strait between Bali and Lombok.

During this period, there were several changes between glacier advance and retreat. The maximum extent of glaciation within this last glacial period was approximately 22,000 years BP. While the general pattern of global cooling and glacier advance was similar, local differences in the development of glacier advance and retreat makes it difficult to compare the details from continent to continent.

From the point of view of human archaeology, it falls in the Paleolithic and Mesolithic periods. When the glaciation event started, *Homo sapiens* were confined to Africa and used tools comparable to those used by Neanderthals in Europe and the Levant and by *Homo erectus* in Asia. Near the end of the event, *Homo sapiens* spread into Europe, Asia, and Australia. The retreat of the glaciers allowed groups of Asians to migrate to the Americas and populate them.

The Younger Dryas stadial, also referred to as the Big Freeze, was a geologically brief (1,300 ± 70 years) period of cold climatic conditions and drought which occurred between approximately 12,800 and 11,500 years BP. The Younger Dryas stadial is thought to have been caused by the collapse of the North American ice sheets, although rival theories have been proposed. It followed the Bølling-Allerød interstadial (warm period) at the end of the Pleistocene and preceded the preboreal of the early Holocene. It is named after an indicator genus, the alpine-tundra wildflower Dryas Octopetala.

The Dryas stadials were cold periods which interrupted the warming trend since the Last Glacial Maximum 20,000 years BP. The Older Dryas occurred approximately 1,000 years before the Younger Dryas and lasted about 3000 years. The Oldest Dryas is dated between approximately 18,000 and 15,000 BP.

POST-GLACIAL FLORA AND FAUNA

In warmer regions of the world, climates at the Last Glacial Maximum were cooler and almost everywhere drier. In extreme cases, such as South Australia and the Sahul, rainfall could be diminished by up to ninety percent from present, with floras diminished to almost the same degree as in glaciated areas of Europe and North America. Even in less affected regions, rainforest cover was greatly diminished, especially in West Africa where a few refugia were surrounded by tropical grassland. The Amazon rainforest was split into two large blocks by extensive savanna, and it is probable that the tropical rainforests of Southeast Asia were similarly affected, with deciduous forests expanding in their place except on the east and west extremities of the Sundaland shelf. Only in Central America and the Chocó region of Colombia did tropical rainforests remain substantially intact – probably due to the extraordinarily heavy rainfall of these regions.

Most of the world's deserts expanded. Exceptions were in what is now the western United States, where changes in the jet stream* brought heavy rain to areas that are now desert and large pluvial lakes formed, the best known being Lake Bonneville in Utah. This also occurred in Afghanistan and Iran where a major lake formed in the Dasht-e Kavir. In Australia, shifting sand dunes covered half the continent, whilst the Chaco and Pampas in South America became similarly dry. Present-day subtropical regions also lost most of their forest cover, notably in eastern Australia, the Atlantic Forest of Brazil, and southern China, where open woodland became dominant due to drier conditions. In northern China – unglaciated despite its cold climate – a mixture of grassland and tundra prevailed, and even here, the northern limit of tree growth was at least twenty degrees farther south than today.

In the period immediately before the Last Glacial Maximum, many areas that became completely barren desert were wetter than they are today, notably in southern Australia, where Aboriginal occupation is believed to coincide with a wet period between 40,000 and 60,000 years BP.

During the Last Glacial Maximum, shifts in climate altered the world's vegetation patterns from what they had been prior to the formation of the ice sheets. However, the types of vegetation present during the glaciation are similar to those found today. Many such trees, mosses, flowering plants, insects, birds, shelled mollusks, and mammals are examples.

Some mammals also went extinct around the world during this time but it is clear that they did live during the last glacial period. Mammoths, mastodons, long-horned bisons, saber-toothed cats, and giant ground sloths are among these.

Human history also began in the Pleistocene and we were heavily impacted by the last glaciation. Most importantly, the drop in sea level aided in our movement from Asia into North America as the landmass connecting the two

---

* Jet streams are fast flowing, narrow air currents found in the atmospheres of some planets, including Earth. The main jet streams are located near the altitude of the tropopause, the transition between the troposphere and the stratosphere (where temperature increases with altitude).

areas in the Alaska's Bering Straight (Beringia) surfaced to act as a bridge between the areas.

The Sundaland vegetation during the Last Glacial Maximum (20,000 years BP) consist of mainly tropical rainforest, tropical grasslands, monsoon or dry forest and a few tropical semi deserts.

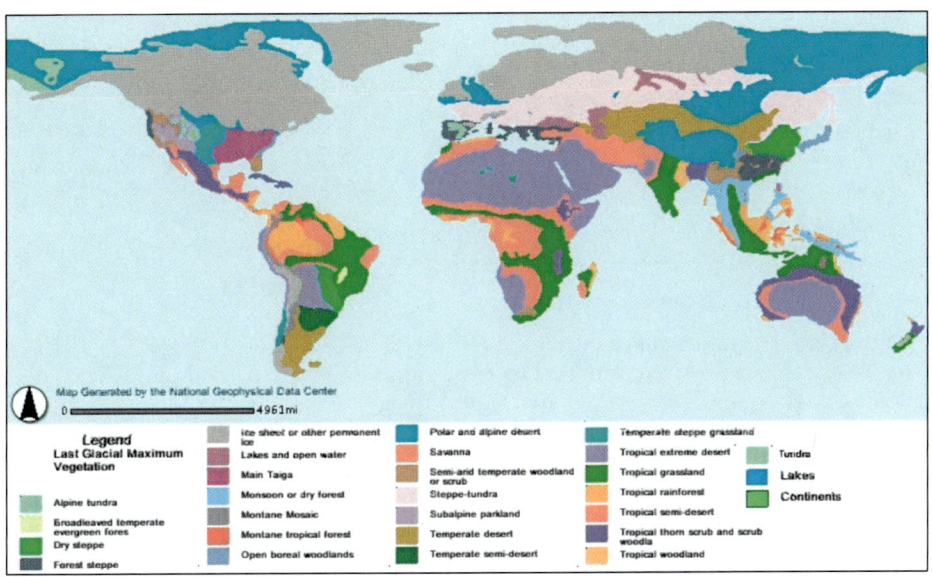

Figure 3 – Reconstructed vegetation cover at the Last Glacial Maximum period about 18,000 years ago, describing the type of vegetation cover present, based on fossil pollen samples recovered from lake and bog sediments. Derived from reconstructions by Jonathan Adams in the QEN Atlas, and Ray and Adams (2001). Original source has moved. Image seems to be from data used for N Ray and JM Adams, 2001, a GIS-based Vegetation Map of the World at the Last Glacial Maximum (25,000-15,000 BP). (*Source: Wikipedia®*)

POST-GLACIAL SEA SURFACE TEMPERATURE CHANGE

Gagan *et al* in 2004 reconstructed the post-glacial temperature history, relative to late 20th century values, in the Indo-Pacific region during the last 20,000 years using foraminiferal Mg/Ca, alkenone, and coral Sr/Ca thermometry. Foraminiferal Mg/Ca suggests that the near equatorial portion of the warm pool cooled by 2 – 4 °C during the Last Glacial Maximum. Interestingly, it shows a rapid rise to early Holocene sea surface temperatures which were as warm as modern values. Comparisons of Mg/Ca and $\delta^{18}O$ measured in the same foraminifers clearly indicate that the rise in sea surface temperature led deglaciation by 3,000 years (Lea *et al*, 2000; Stott *et al*, 2002).

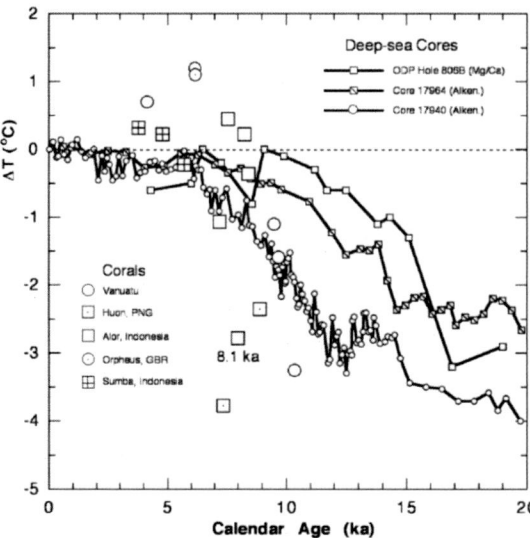

In general, the results of alkenone unsaturation paleotemperature estimates for the Indo-Pacific region are consistent with the 3 °C cooling during the Last Glacial Maximum indicated by foraminiferal Mg/Ca. Like the foraminiferal Mg/Ca, the alkenone records show sea surface temperatures within 1 °C of modern values by the early Holocene.

Figure 4 – Comparison of reconstructed sea surface temperatures, relative to late 20th century values, in the Indo-Pacific region during the last 20,000 years using foraminiferal Mg/Ca, alkenone, andcoral Sr/Ca thermometry
(Gagan *et al*, 2004)

Revised coral Sr/Ca estimates of post glacial sea surface temperatures using a single Sr/Ca shows a clearer picture emerges for the Southern Hemisphere portion of the Indo-Pacific region. The Vanuatu Coral sea surface temperature estimates for the early Holocene indicates cooling of 1 – 3 °C. New coral Sr/Ca records from Alor, southeast Indonesia, show that sea surface temperatures reached modern values by 8,500 years, in good agreement with the Mg/Ca and alkenones. This generally warm period is interrupted by a brief cold-spike centered on 8,100 years (Gagan, unpublished data). Mid-Holocene sea surface temperatures in Indonesia (Sumba) fall within 0.5 °C of modern values, whereas corals from the inshore Great Barrier Reef, Australia, indicate sea surface temperatures ~1 °C warmer than the present.

The sea surface temperature in Sundaland region during the Younger Dryas period (12,800 – 11,500 years BP) was approximately 1 °C below the present-day temperature.

POST-GLACIAL SEA LEVEL CHANGE

Fleming *et al* (1998), Fleming (2000) and Milne *et al* (2005) collected data from various reports and adjusted them for subsequent vertical geologic motions, primarily those associated with post-glacial continental and hydroisostatic rebound. The first refers to deformations caused by the weight of continental ice sheets pressing down on the land, the latter refers to uplift in coastal areas resulting from the increased weight of water associated with rising sea levels. It should be noted that because of the latter effect and associated uplift, many islands, especially in the Pacific, exhibited higher local sea levels in the mid Holocene than they do today. Uncertainty about the magnitude of these corrections is the dominant uncertainty in many measurements of sea level change.

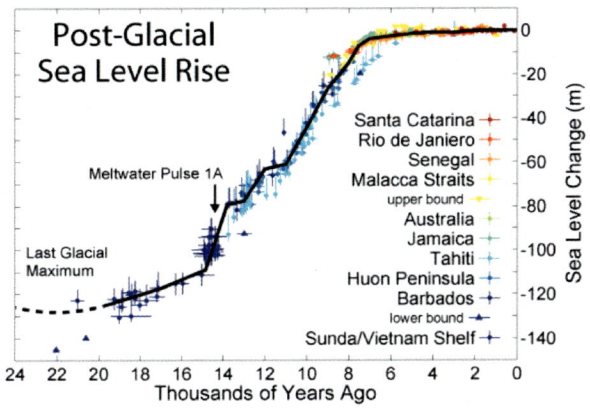

Figure 5 – Post-Glacial sea level (*source: Wikipedia*[8])

The black curve is based on minimizing the sum of squares error weighted distance between this curve and the plotted data. It was constructed by adjusting a number of specified tie points, typically placed every 1,000 years but at times adjusted for sparse or rapidly varying data. A small number of extreme outliers were dropped. It should be noted that some authors propose the existence of significant short-term fluctuations in sea level such that the sea level curve might oscillate up and down about this ~1000 years mean state. Others dispute this and argue that sea level change has largely been a smooth and gradual process. However, at least one episode of rapid deglaciation, known as Meltwater Pulse 1A*, is agreed upon and indicated on the plot. A variety of other accelerated periods of deglaciation have been proposed (*ie* MWP-1B, 2, 3, 4), but it is unclear if these actually occurred or merely reflect misinterpretation of difficult measurements. No other events are evident in the data presented above.

---

* Meltwater Pulse 1A was a considerable post-glacial sea level rise of about 20 m in less than 500 years, perhaps just 200 years. The sea level is estimated to have risen at a rate of 37 to 65 mm/yr – the pulse was much larger than current sea level rise, which has been judged to be in the region of 2 to 3 mm/yr. The meltwater event occurred in a period of rapid climate change when the Holocene glacial retreat was going on during the end of the last ice age. Several researchers have narrowed the period of the pulse to between 13,000 and 14,600 years ago. The pulse is framed historically between the Bølling-Allerød (B-A) interstadial and the Antarctic Cold Reversal/Older Dryas events.

The lowest point of sea level during the last glaciation is not well constrained by observations (shown here as a dashed curve), but is generally argued to be approximately 130 ± 10 meters below present sea level and to have occurred at approximately 22 ± 3 thousand years ago. The time of lowest sea level is more or less equivalent to the last glacial maximum. Prior to this time, ice sheets were still increasing in size so that sea level was decreasing almost continuously over a period of approximately 100,000 years.

Observations made by Kurt Lambeck *et al* in 2014 shows the major cause of sea-level change during ice ages is the exchange of water between ice and ocean and the planet's dynamic response to the changing surface load. Inversion of around 1,000 observations for the past 35,000 years from localities far from former ice margins has provided new constraints on the fluctuation of ice volume in this interval. The key results are:

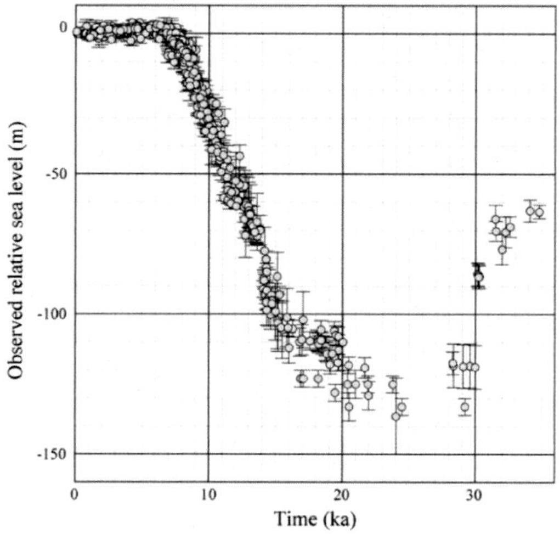

1. a rapid final fall in global sea level of about 40 m in less than 2,000 years at the onset of the glacial maximum about 30,000 year before present;

2. a slow fall to -134 m from 29,000 to 21,000 years BP with a maximum grounded ice volume of about 52 million km^3 greater than today;

Figure 6 – Depth-age relationship of all data with 2σ error estimates (Lambeck *et al*, 2014)

3. after an initial short duration rapid rise and a short interval of near-constant sea level, the main phase of deglaciation occurred from around 16,500 years BP to about 8,200 years BP at an average rate of rise of 12 m per 1,000 years punctuated by periods of greater, particularly at 14,500 – 14,000 years BP at more than 40 mm per year, and lesser, from 12,500 to 11,500 years BP (Younger Dryas), rates;

4. no evidence for a global rapid rise event at around 11,300 years BP; and

5. a progressive decrease in the rate of rise from around 8,200 years to around 2,500 years BP, after which ocean volumes remained nearly constant until the renewed sea-level rise at 100 – 150 years ago, with no

evidence of oscillations exceeding 15 – 20 cm in time intervals more than 200 years from 6,000 to 150 years BP.

The sea level in the Younger Dryas period (12,800 – 11,500 years BP) was approximately 60 meters below the present-day sea level.

TOPOGRAPHY AND BATHYMETRY

Present-day topographic and bathymetric data covering the Sunda Shelf in geographic projection (latitude and longitude) are extracted from the GTOPO30 elevation grids published by USGS*. GTOPO30 refers to 30-arc second (approximately 0.9 km near equator) horizontal latitude and longitude spatial resolution of digital elevation model (DEM) file format. Other similar grids like GEBCO_8 published by IHO† and IOC/UNESCO‡, and ETOPO1 published by NOAA§ are also used as references. A color scheme is applied to the DEM in which areas below -120 m are represented by blue colors so that the Last Glacial Maximum coastlines can be easily identified.

Several assumptions are made in the analytical procedures (Sathiamurthy *et al*, 2006). First, it is assumed that the current topography and bathymetry of the region approximate the physiography that existed during the span of time from 21,000 years BP to present. However, because sedimentation and scouring processes have affected the bathymetry of the Sunda Shelf over the last 21,000 years (Schimanski and Stattegger, 2005), we know that this is only an approximation. Thus, it should be emphasized that the depth and geometry of the Sunda Shelf and the existing present-day submerged depressions do not reflect past conditions precisely.

Second, it is assumed that the present-day sea bed are likely to have existed during the Last Glacial Maximum and have not resulted from seabed scouring

---

* The United States Geological Survey (USGS) is a scientific agency of the United States government. The scientists of the USGS study the landscape of the United States, its natural resources, and the natural hazards that threaten it.
† The International Hydrographic Organization (IHO) is an inter-governmental organization representing the hydrographic community.
‡ The Intergovernmental Oceanographic Commission of UNESCO (IOC/UNESCO) was established by resolution 2.31 adopted by the General Conference of UNESCO. The IOC assists governments to address their individual and collective ocean and coastal management needs.
§ The National Oceanic and Atmospheric Administration (NOAA) is a scientific agency within the United States Department of Commerce focused on the conditions of the oceans and the atmosphere.

by currents, limestone solution, or tectonic movement-possibilities that were pointed out by Umbgrove (1949) as perhaps taking place during early post-Pleistocene transgression. In the case of tectonic movement, Geyh *et al* (1979) mentioned that the Sumatera Strait was tectonically stable at least during the Holocene. Furthermore, Tjia *et al* (1983), state that the Sunda Shelf has been largely tectonically stable since the beginning of the Tertiary. Nevertheless, Tjia *et al* (1983) indicated that sea level rise in this region may be attributed to a combination of actual sea level rise and vertical crust movement. Hill (1968) in reference to earlier work done by Umbgrove (1949), suggested the possibility of limestone solution as a mode of depression formation (as in the case of the Lumut pit off the coast of Perak, Malaysia), and gave an alternative explanation, which was of tectonic origin.

Sea bed sedimentation data are rarely available but approximation of sedimentation process is made in generating the topographic and bathymetric regional map of Sundaland. In similar conditions, other processes like littoral drift, delta formation, meandering, river regime change and river bed movement are also approximated and incorporated on the maps. Ancient lakes are reconstructed from the DEM and any geological history that exist. Small and insignificant islands are removed.

Along with the topographic and bathymetric map, shorelines at certain sea water levels, ground surface slope, river watersheds and flow pattern of rivers are also generated and place them in different layers.

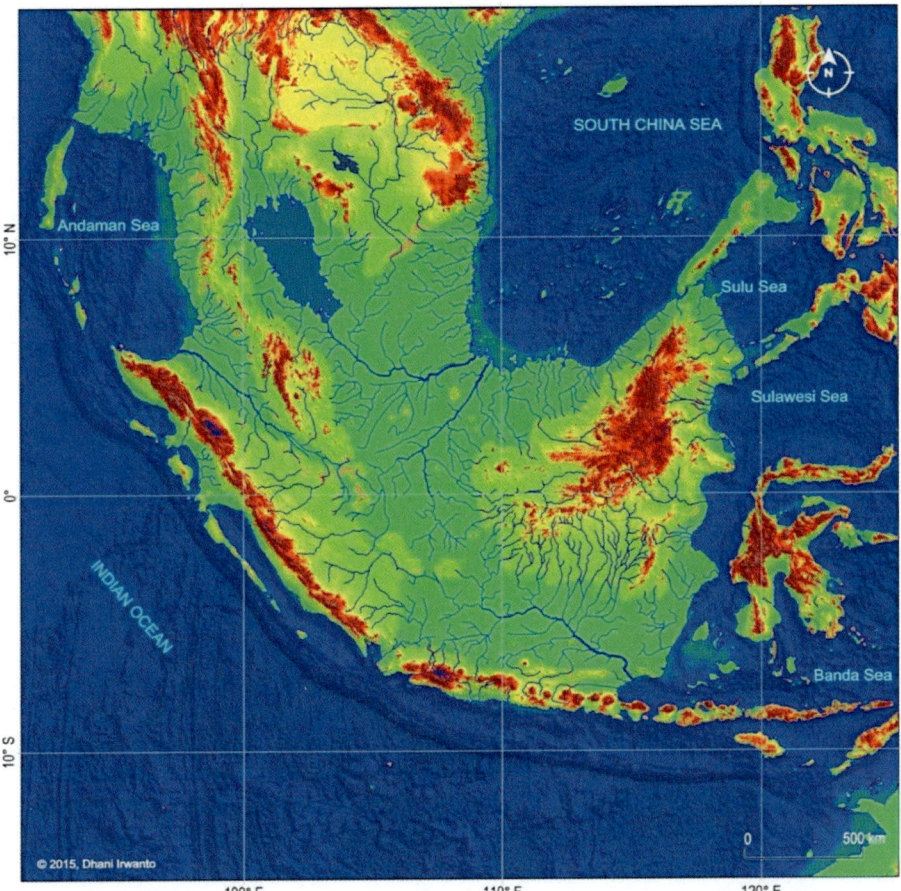

Figure 7 – A map showing the Sundaland around the Last Glacial period (21,000 years BP) generated by the author from the GTOPO30 elevation grids published by USGS. The sea water level was around 120 meter below the present-day sea water level. The flow pattern of the rivers below the present-day sea water level is generated using the same grids and approximations of sea sedimentation, littoral drift, delta formation, meandering, river regime change and river bed movement. The present-day inland rivers are combined. The colors other than blue represent the ground levels. The thin red lines are the present-day shorelines.

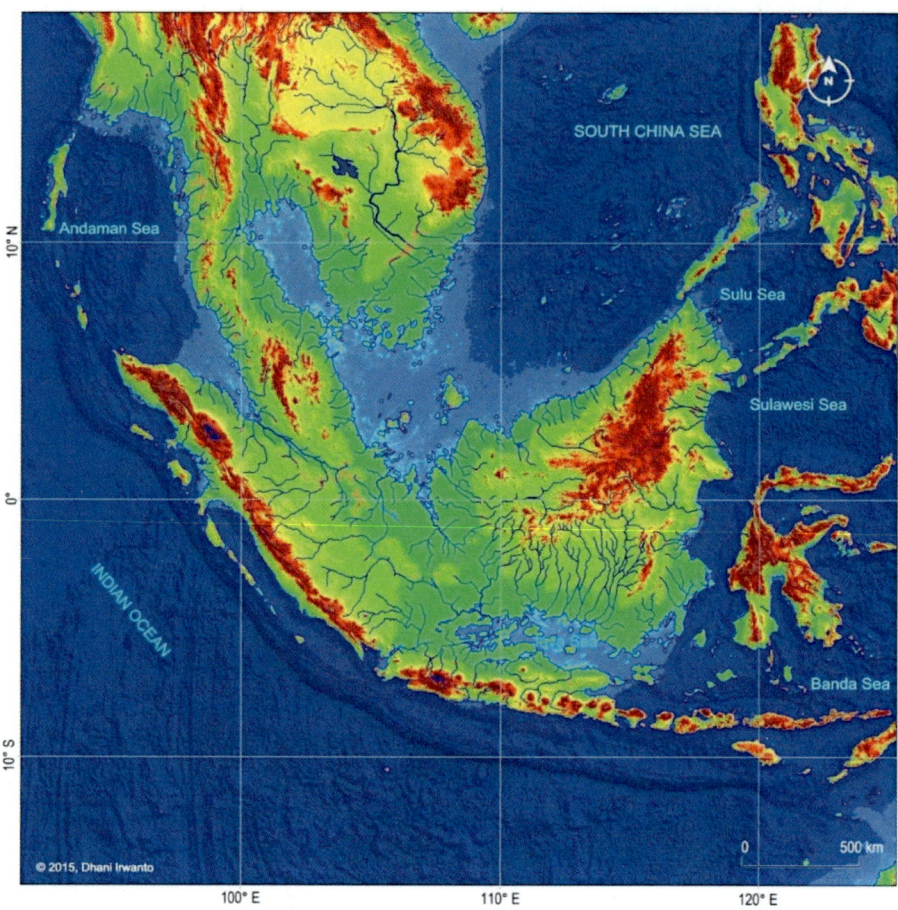

Figure 8 – A map showing the Sundaland around the Younger Dryas period (12,800-11,500 years BP) generated by the author using the same method as in the previous figure. The sea water level was around 60 meter below the present-day sea water level.

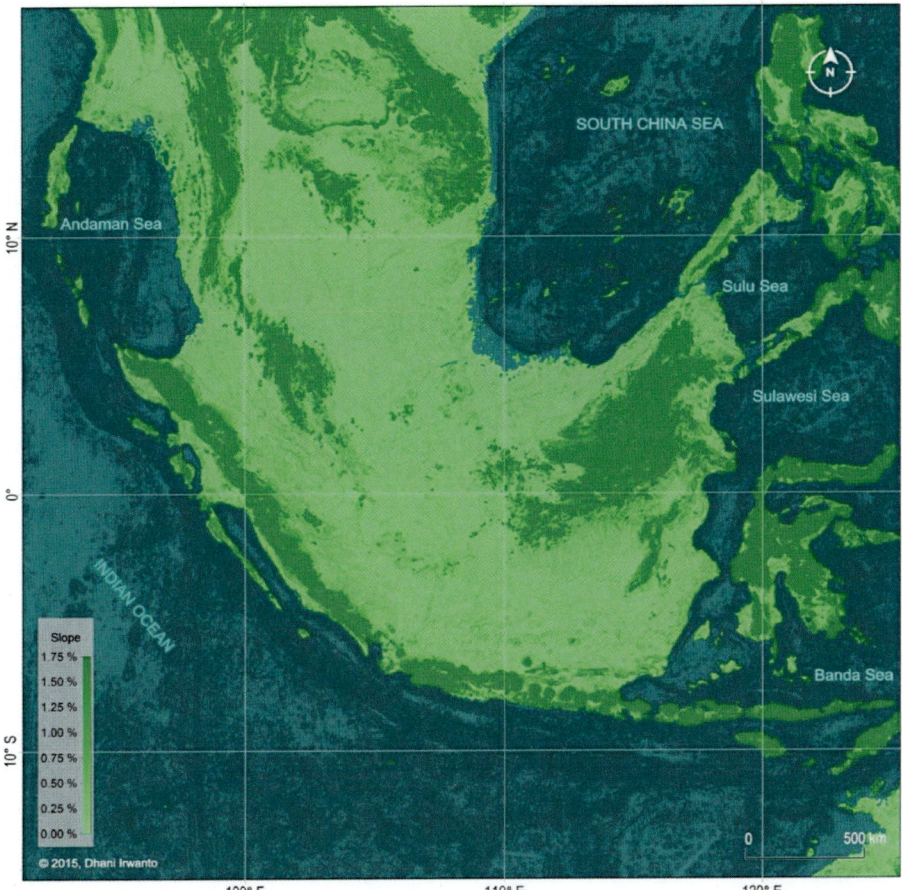

Figure 9 – A map showing the Sundaland ground slope around the Last Glacial Maximum period (21,000 years BP) generated by the author using the same method as in the previous figures. 1% slope and flatter (light green color) are highlighted to show the widely spread plains in the Sundaland. Dark green color represents slopes steeper than 1%.

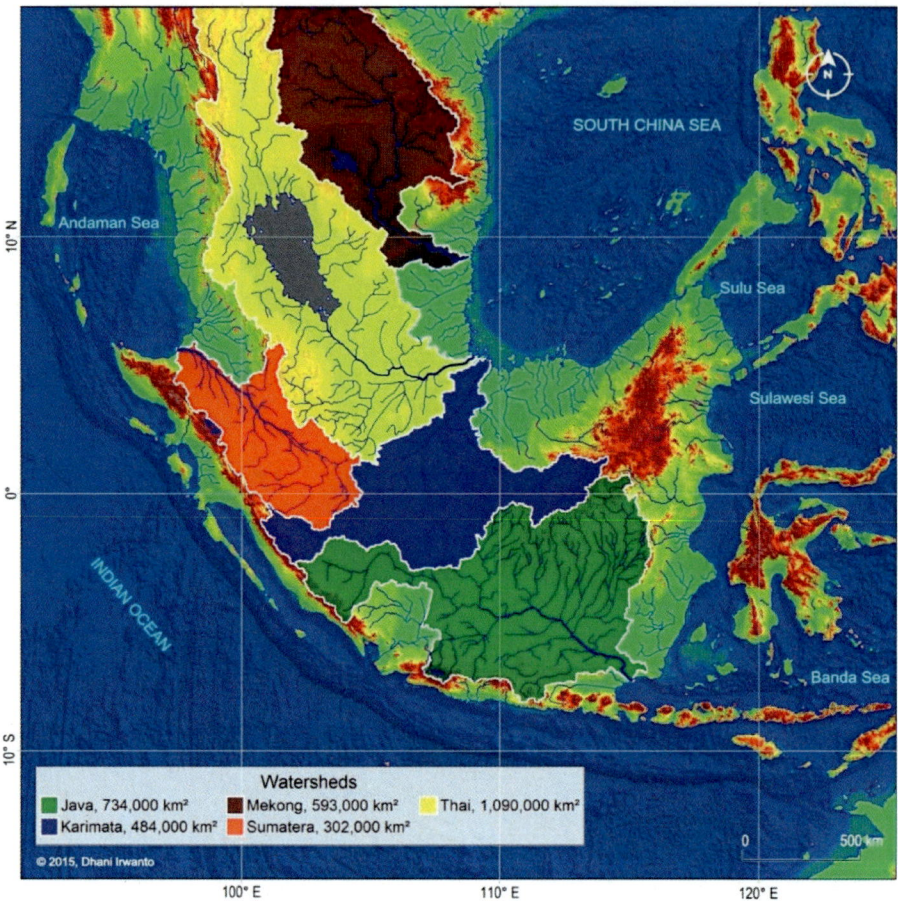

Figure 10 – A map showing the Sundaland major watersheds around the Last Glacial Maximum period (21,000 years BP) generated by the author using the same method as in the previous figures. River names are given referring to the sea, strait, gulf, island or present day river names occupied by the watersheds.

PRESENT-DAY FEATURES

TECTONIC FRAMEWORK

Sundaland comprises a complex assembly of continental blocks, arc terranes, suture zones and accreted continental crust. The principal continental blocks that form the core of Sundaland and their volcanic arc terranes have been identified and established over the last two decades.

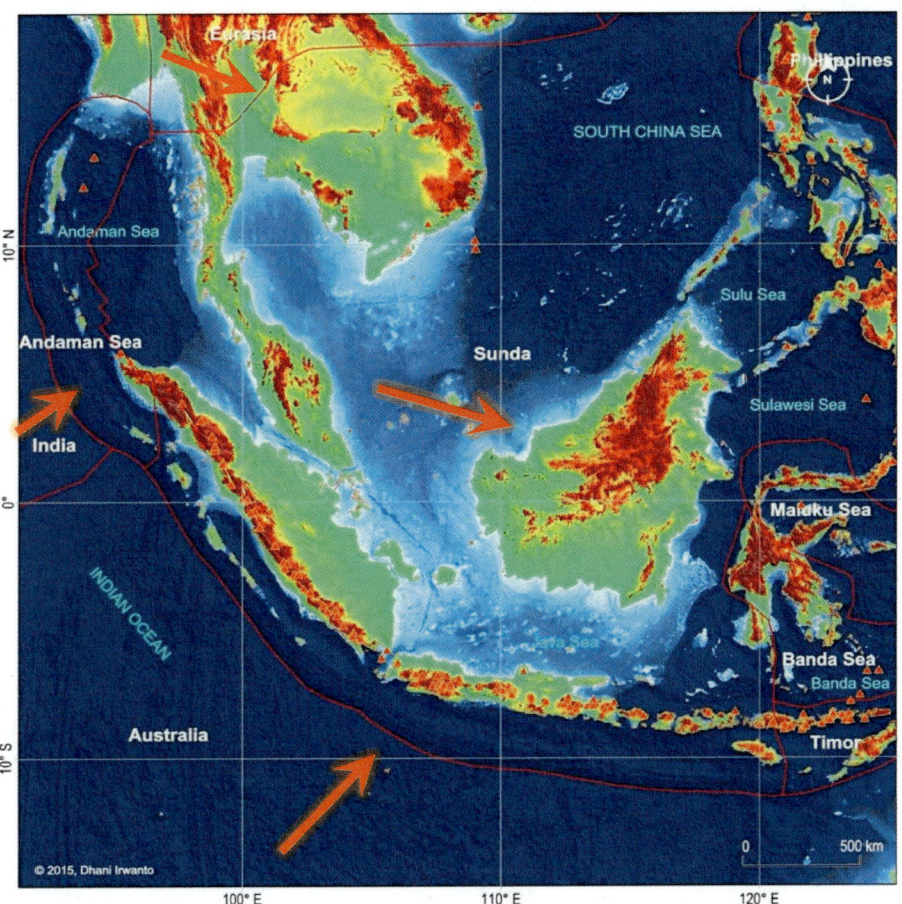

Figure 11 – Main active faults in Sundaland at the zone of convergence of the plates of Sunda, Eurasia, Philippines, India and Australia. Smaller plates of Timor and Banda Sea (part of Sunda), Maluku (part of Philippines) and Andaman (part of Eurasia) are also shown. Large arrows represent absolute motions of plates. Red triangles are the volcanoes.

EARTHQUAKES

The subduction of the Indo-Australian Plate beneath a block of the Eurasian Plate is associated with numerous earthquakes. Several of these earthquakes are notable for their size.

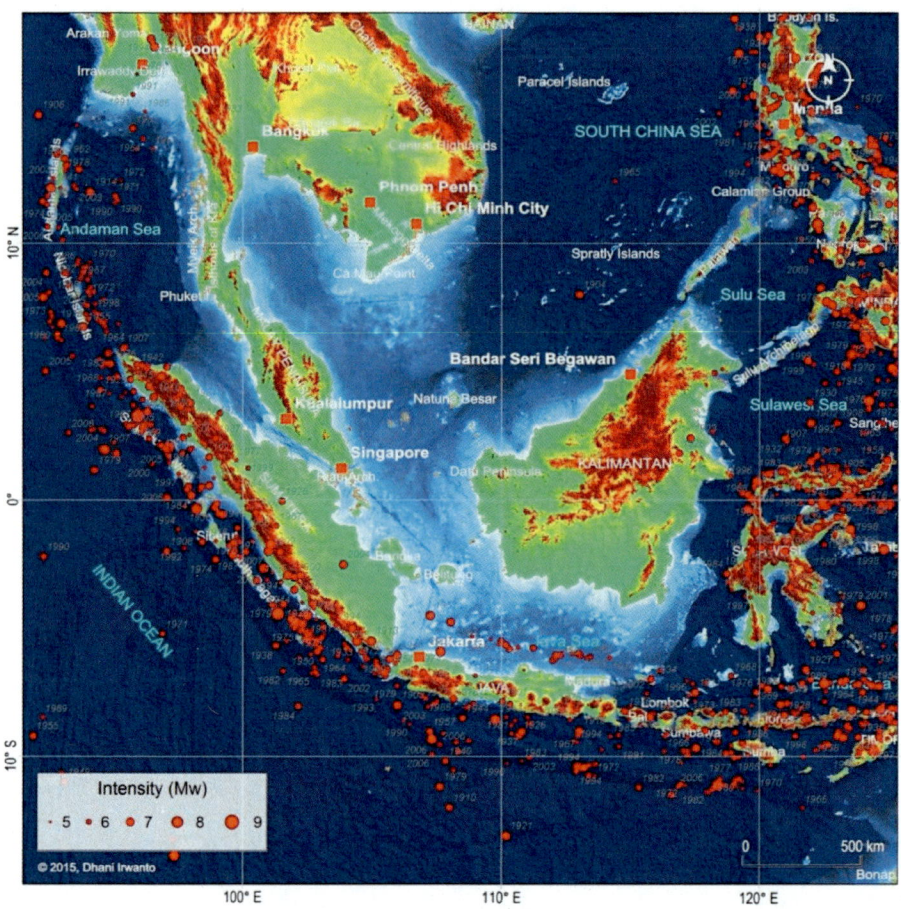

Figure 12 – Plots of major earthquake occurrences ever recorded and their intensities in M_w scales*. Note that Sundaland is encircled by earthquake prone lines. (*Source: USGS*)

---

* Moment Magnitude (M_w) is a scale of earthquake in terms of the energy released, which is equal to the rigidity of the Earth multiplied by the average amount of slip on the fault and the size of the area that slipped.

TSUNAMIS

A tsunami is a series of waves generated by an impulsive disturbance in the ocean or in a small, connected body of water. As the tsunami approaches the coastline, the wave energy is compressed into a much shorter distance, creating potentially large destructive waves.

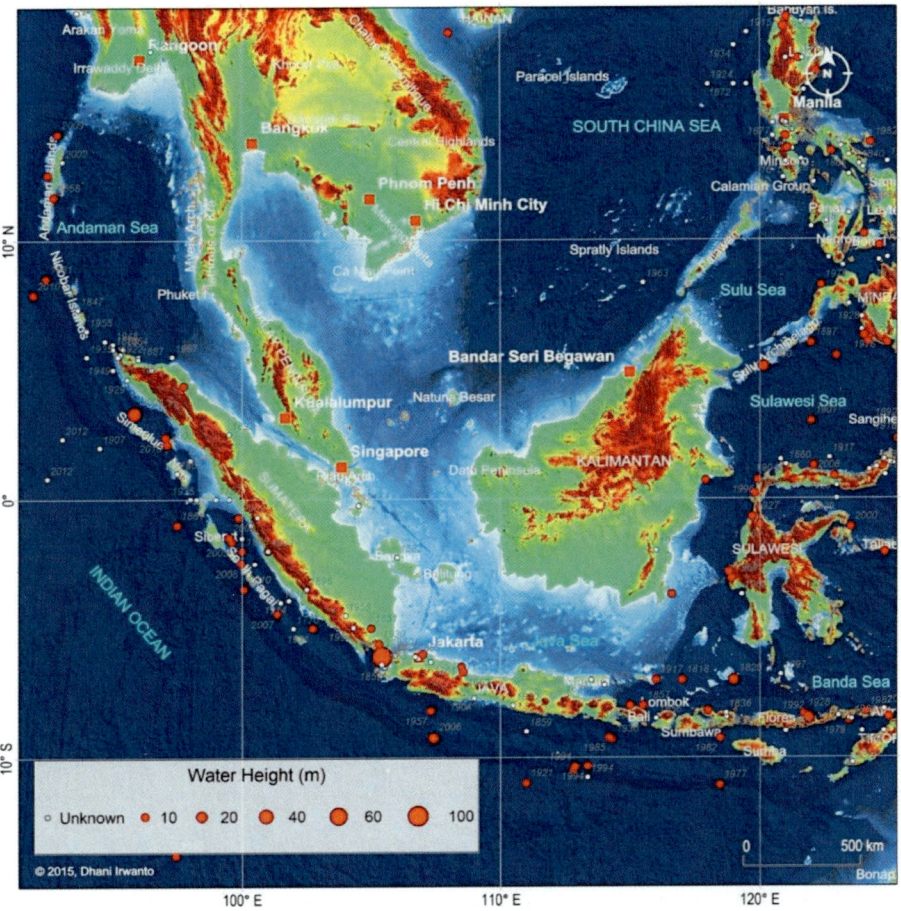

Figure 13 – Plots of tsunami sources ever recorded and their created water heights. Note that tsunamis occurred frequently in Banda Sea and Sulawesi Sea that could affect the inner islands. (*Source: NOAA*)

VOLCANO ERUPTIONS

A volcano is a rupture on the crust of a planetary mass object, such as the Earth, which allows hot lava, volcanic ash, and gases to escape from a magma chamber below the surface. Volcanoes are generally found where tectonic plates are diverging or converging.

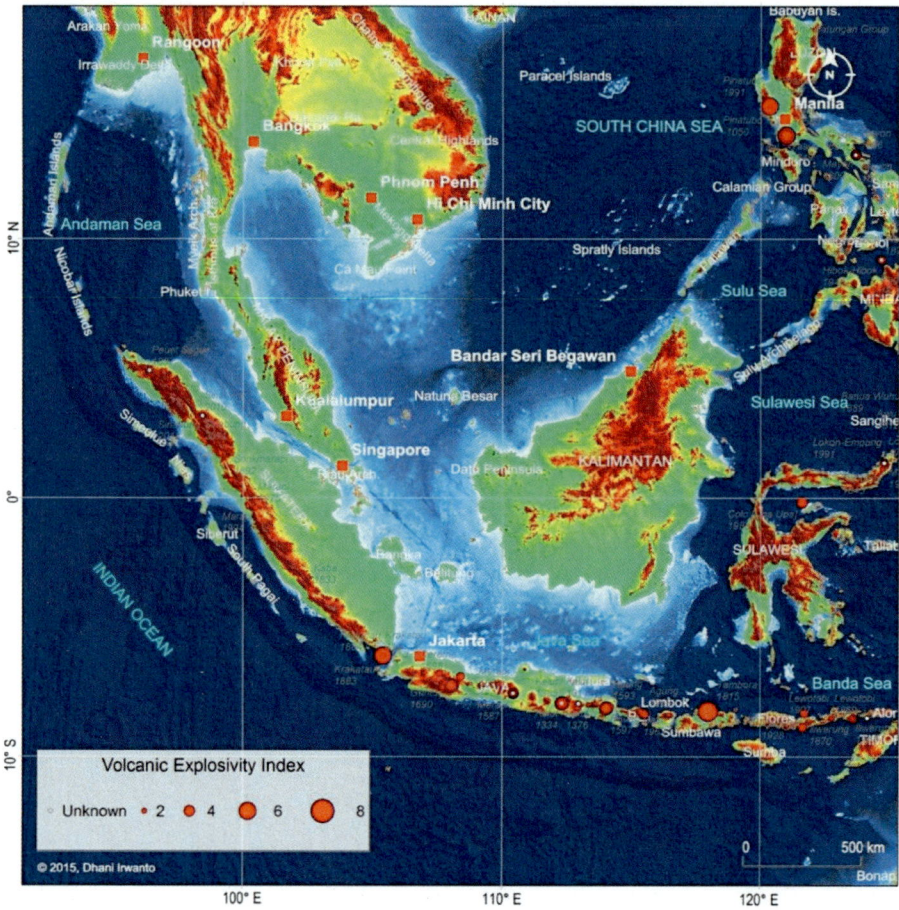

Figure 14 – Plots of volcano eruptions ever known and their Volcanic Explosivity Indices (VEI)*. Note for large scale Tambora eruption in 1815 and frequent Krakatau eruptions being the largest in 1883. (*Source: NOAA*)

---

* Volcano eruption is scaled in Volcanic Explosivity Index (VEI) determined by its volume of products, eruption cloud height and qualitative observations values.

PRECIPITATION

In meteorology, precipitation is any product of the condensation of atmospheric water vapor that falls under gravity. The main forms of precipitation include drizzle, rain, sleet, snow, graupel and hail.

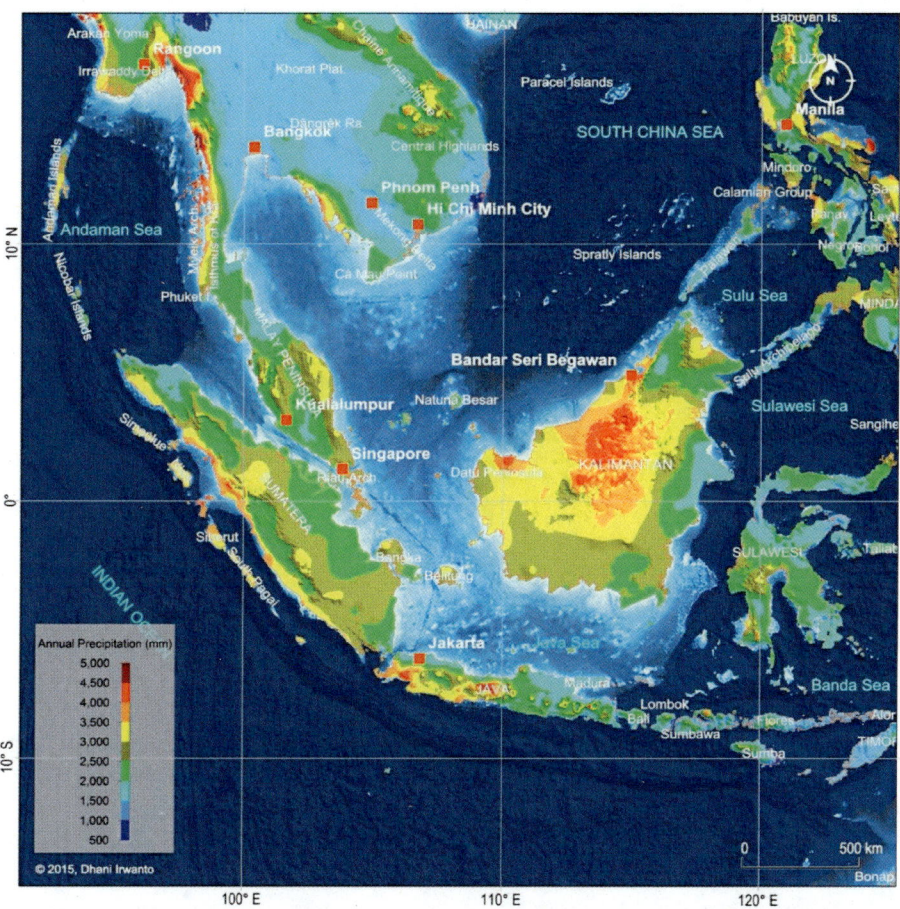

Figure 15 – A map showing the average annual precipitation in millimeters. Note that Kalimantan Island is mostly precipitous. (*Source: WorldClim**)

---

* WorldClim is a set of global climate layers (climate grids) with a spatial resolution of about 1 square kilometer developed by RJ Hijmans, SE Cameron, JL Parra, PG Jones and A Jarvis (2005).

TEMPERATURE

Although air temperature changes little from season to season or from one region to the next, cooler temperatures prevail at higher elevations. In general, temperatures drop approximately 1 °C per 90-meter increase in elevation from sea level.

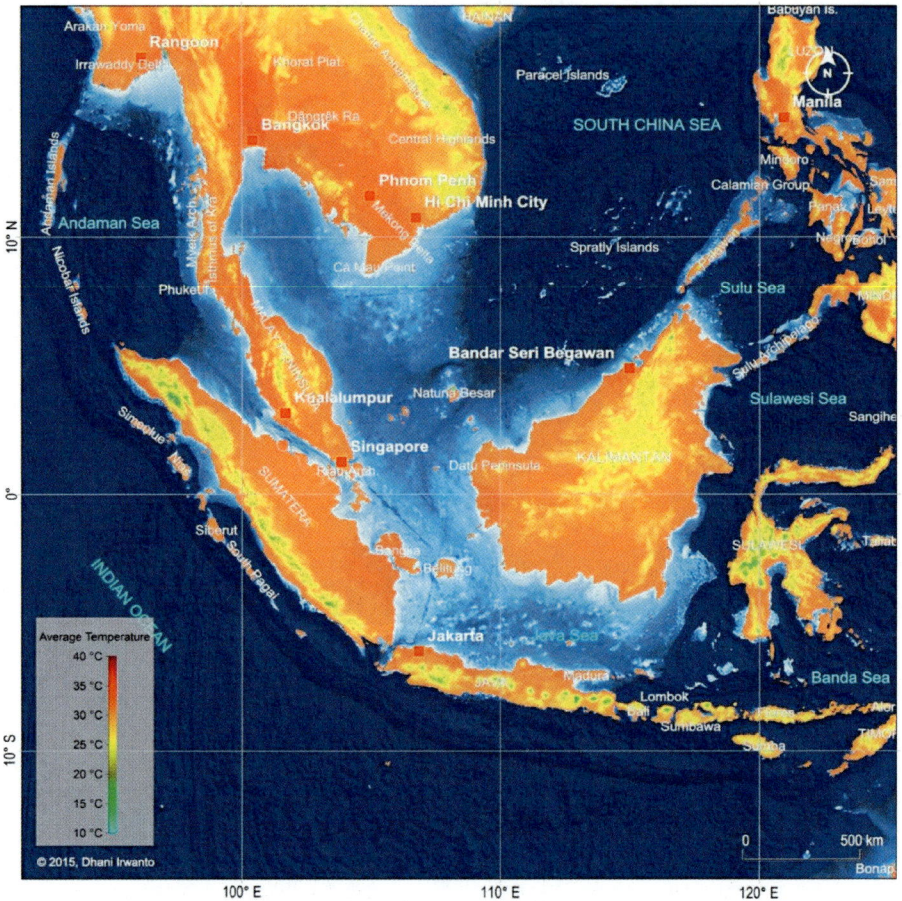

Figure 16 – A map showing the average temperature in °C. Note that the plains in Sundaland have relatively warm temperature around 30 °C. (*Source: WorldClim*)

LAND COVER

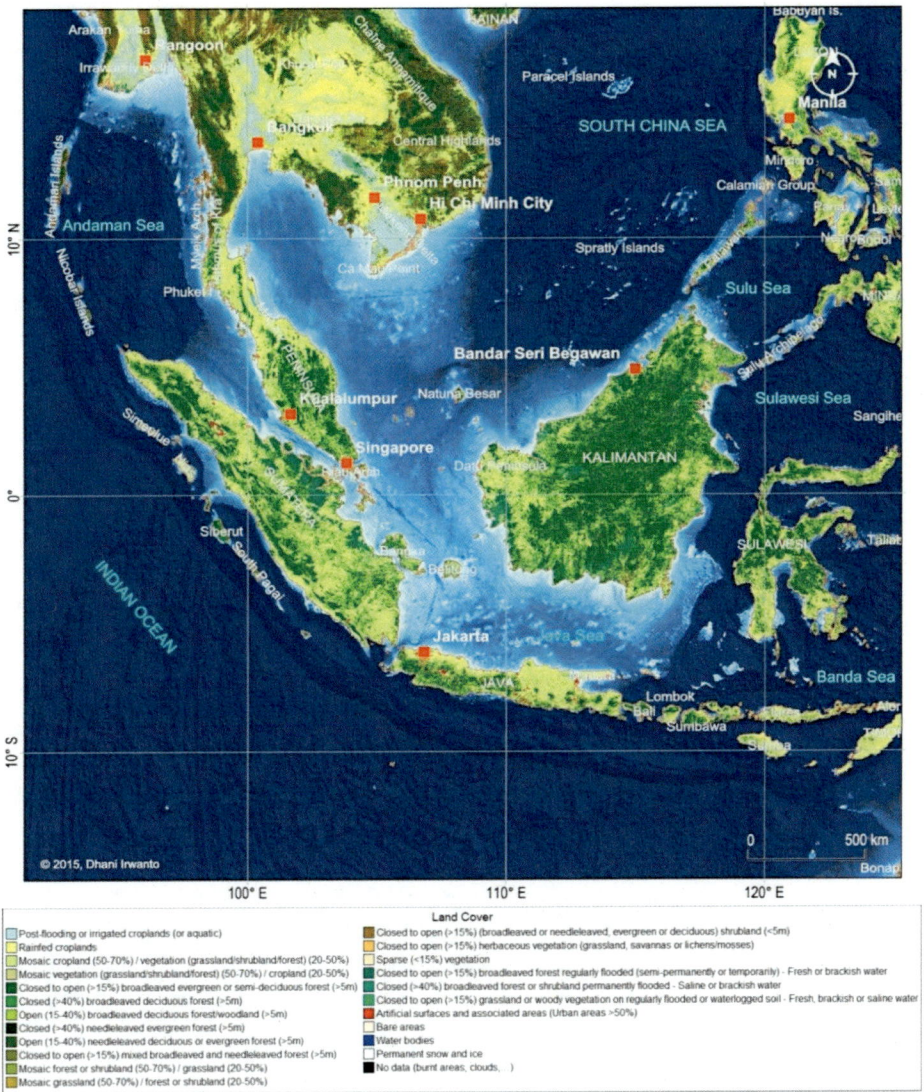

Figure 17 – A map showing the land cover in 2009. Note that Kalimantan Island is covered mostly by broadleaf forest, grassland and cropland. (*Source and copyright of the land cover: ESA and UC Louvain*)

83

FLORA

Sundaland holds about 25,000 different species of plants. 15,000 of them are endemic to this region and cannot be found anywhere else. *Scyphostegiaceae* is a plant family represented by a single species, *Scyphostegia borneensis*, which is endemic to Kalimantan. Another 155 species of *Dipterocarpus* are also endemic to this island. Kalimantan also has more than 2,000 species of orchids. The forests in Sumatera include more than 100 species of *Dipterocarpus*; nearly a dozen of them are endemic to this island. Java has about 270 endemic orchid species.

At least 117 plant genera are endemic in this biodiversity hotspot. 59 of them are found in Kalimantan and 17 in Sumatera. Unique plants from this region are similar to ones from the Asian continent, mentioning *Rafflesia arnoldii*, the pitcher plants and Javanese Edelweiss (*Anaphalis javanica*) as examples.

Melati (Jasminum sambac), a small white flower with a sweet fragrance, is the national flower of Indonesia, together with *Anggrek Bulan (Phalaenopsis amabilis)* and *Padma Raksasa Rafflesia (Rafflesia arnoldii)*. All three were chosen on World Environment Day on 5 June 1990 by President Soeharto. On the other occasion *Bunga Bangkai (Titan arum)* was also added as *Puspa Langka* (rare flowers) together with Rafflesia.

FAUNA

Sundaland fauna share similar characteristics with the mainland Asian fauna. During the ice age, lower sea levels connected the Asian continent with the western Indonesian archipelago. This enabled animals from the Asian mainland to migrate over dry land to Sundaland. As a result, large species such as tiger, rhinoceros, orangutan, elephant, and leopard exist in this region. Many of these species are now categorized as endangered. The Makassar Strait, between Kalimantan and Sulawesi, and the Lombok Strait, between Bali and Lombok, are the deep-water Wallace Line separators, marking the limit of the Sundaland region.

Sundaland has a total of 381 mammal species, of which 173 are endemic to this region. Most of these species are currently endangered. Two species of orangutans, *Pongo pygmaeus* (Kalimantan orangutans) and *Pongo abelii* (Sumatran orangutans) are listed in the International Union for Conservation of Nature (IUCN) red list. Other mammals, such as the Kalimantan proboscis monkey (*Nasalis larvatus*), the Sumateran rhinoceros (*Dicerorhinus sumatrensis*) and the Javan rhinoceros (*Rhinoceros sondaicus*), are also seriously threatened.

According to the Conservation International*, a 771 bird species are found in Sundaland. 146 of them are endemic to the region. Java and Bali have at least 20 endemic species, including the Bali starling (*Leucopsar rothschildi*) and the Javan plover (*Charadrius javanicus*). 449 species in 125 genera of reptiles are estimated to live in Sundaland. 249 species and 24 genera are endemic. Three reptile families are endemic to this region: *Anomochilidae*, *Xenophidiidae* and *Lanthanotidae*, the last represented by the Kalimantan earless monitor (*Lanthanotus borneensis*), a rare and little-known lizard. Around 242 species of amphibians in 41 genera live in this region. 172 species of them, including caecilians, and six genera are endemic.

Around 1000 fish species are known to live in the rivers, lakes, and swamps of Sundaland. Kalimantan has about 430 species, with 164 of them considered endemic. Sumatera has 270 species, 42 of which are endemic. The golden *arowana* (*Scleropages formosus*) originates from this region. Around 200 new species of fish have been identified in the last ten years.

---

* Conservation International (CI) is an American nonprofit environmental organization headquartered in Arlington, Virginia. The organization's intent is to protect nature.

MINERAL RESOURCES

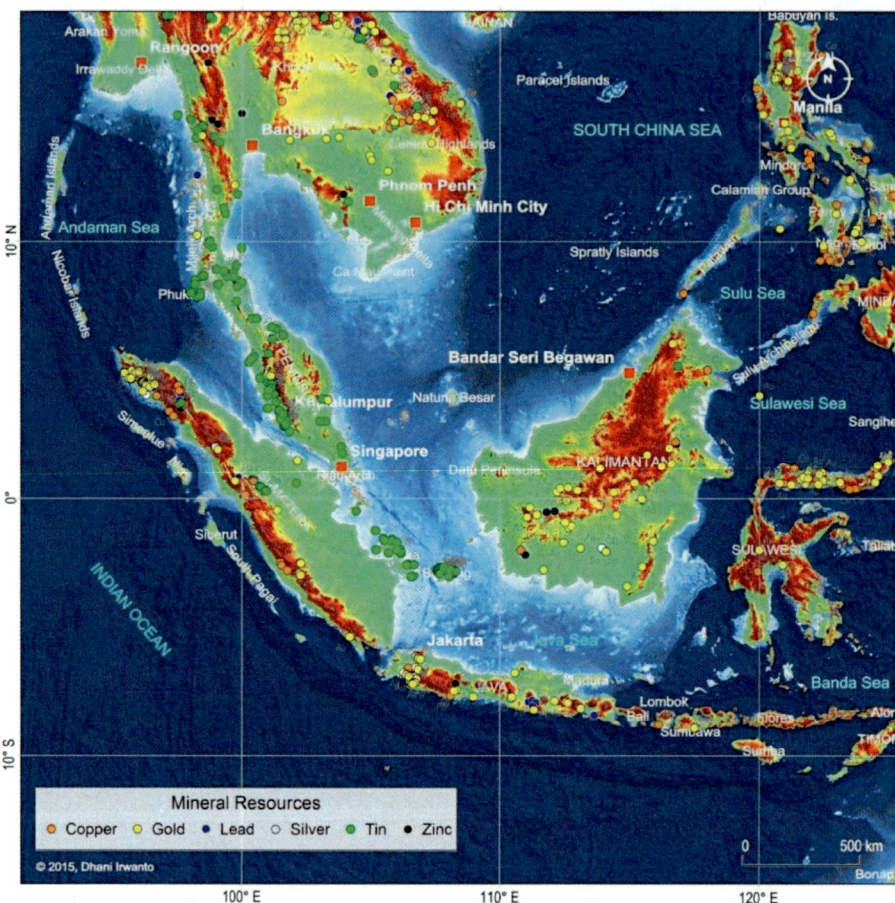

Figure 18 – A map showing identified locations of mineral resources, especially copper (Cu), gold (Au), lead (Pb), silver (Ag), tin (Sn) and zinc (Zn). Some minerals are in the same locations as the others so they are overlaid and not shown on the figure. Note that Kalimantan Island is rich for gold while Malay Peninsula, Bangka Island and Belitung Island are rich for tin. Copper, lead and zinc are spotted and scattered. (*Sources: USGS and various*)

PRE-HISTORIC REMAINS

Pre-history refers to the period of human existence before the availability of those written records with which recorded history begins. Pre-historic remains presented here may consist of human skeleton, potteries, metal works, cave painting, burial sites, stone tools, megalithic stones and step pyramids.

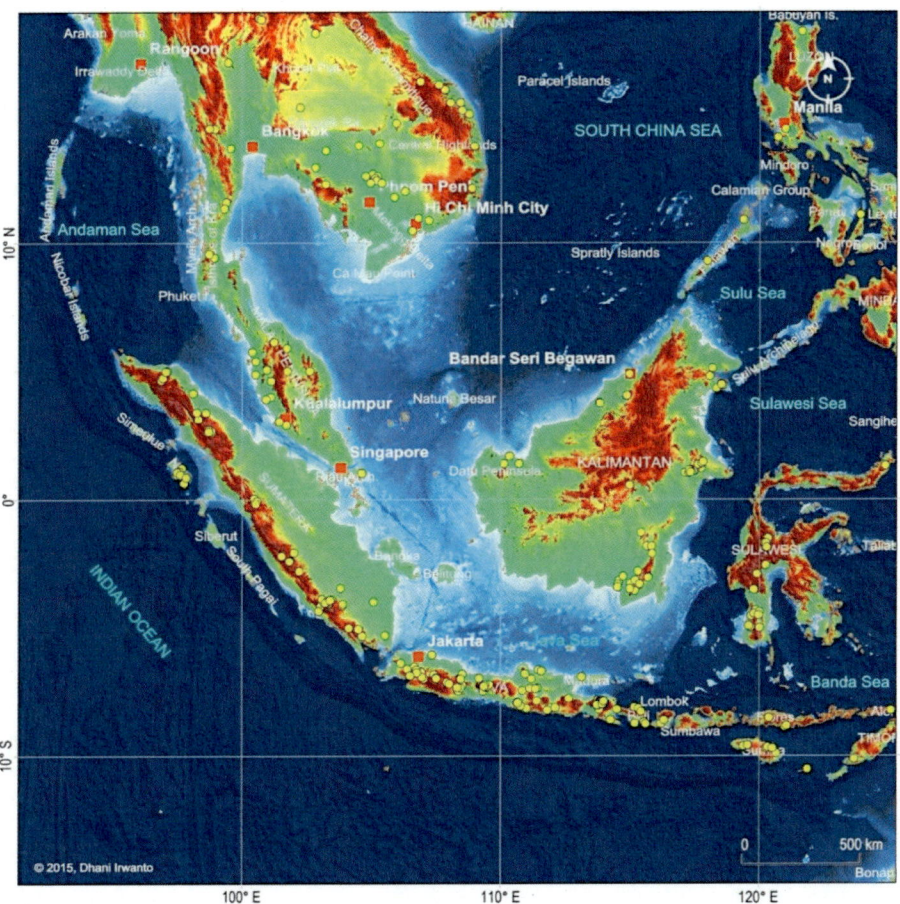

Figure 19 – A map showing the locations of pre-historic remains. Note that the remains are densely found in Java, Bali, southern Sumatera, southern Sulawesi and southern Kalimantan. No undersea remain has been investigated.
(*Sources: various, collected by the author*)

***

PLATO'S ATLANTIS IS IN SUNDALAND

From Plato's *Critias* Section 108e: "*... nine thousand was the sum of years which had elapsed since the war which was said to have taken place between those who dwelt outside the Pillars of Heracles and all who dwelt within them ...*"

From Plato's *Timaeus* Section 24e: "*... the island was larger than Libya and Asia* [Minor] *put together, and was the way to other islands, and from these you might pass to the whole of the opposite continent which encompasses the true ocean ...*"

From Plato's *Critias* Section 108e: "*... the combatants on the other side were commanded by the kings of Atlantis, which, as was saying, was an island greater in extent than Libya and Asia* [Minor] *...*"

9,000 years before Solon's day (*ca* 600 BC) means approximately 11,600 years BP. The sea level at this time was around 60 meters below the present-day sea level. The map showing the lands at 11,600 BP is extracted by the author from the GTOPO30 elevation grids published by USGS.

See the map on Figure 20. Traveling further from Sundaland, one may reach some islands like Nusatenggara Islands, Sulawesi, Maluku Islands, Mindanau and Luzon. Passing through these islands, one may reach the opposite continent, *ie* the large "Sahul Continent" combining the Australian Continent, Papua and the land connecting them. This continent encompassed Pacific and Indian Oceans. So that Plato's statement: "*... was the way to other islands, and from these you might pass to the whole of the opposite continent which encompasses the true ocean ...*" is true to point that Atlantis is hypothesized located in Sundaland.

Looking at the map, we will see that Sundaland is larger than Libya and Asia Minor*, precisely what Plato affirms in his discourse on Atlantis.

PLATO'S ATLANTIS WAS IN A TROPICAL CLIMATE

Other supporting arguments to conclude that Plato's Atlantis is Sundaland are as follows.

From Plato's *Critias* Section 111c: "*...the land reaped the benefit of the annual rainfall ...*"

From Plato's *Critias* Section 111e: "*...abundance of water, and in the heaven above an excellently attempered climate.*"

---

* Asia Minor, a peninsula also called Anatolia, comprises most of the Asian part of modern Turkey and the Armenian highland. Most people there today speak Turkish. The seas surrounding Asia Minor are the Black Sea, the Aegean Sea and the Mediterranean Sea.

From Plato's *Critias* Section 112d: "*... the fountain gave an abundant supply of water for all and of suitable temperature in summer and in winter.*"

From Plato's *Critias* Section 118e: "*Twice in the year they gathered the fruits of the earth – in winter having the benefit of the rains of heaven, and in summer the water which the land supplied by introducing streams from the canals.*"

Although some of the above phrases describe the nature of the land of the Atlantis' opponent, the author assumes that they were in the same region and in the same climate so that both have the same nature.

Figure 20 – A map showing continents and lands during the Plato's Atlantis era (about 11,600 BP)

The modern Sundaland is characterized that it is located in a tropical climate in which all twelve months have mean temperatures of at least 18 °C, remains relatively constant throughout the year and seasonal variations are dominated by precipitation: wet and dry seasons (Indonesian "musim hujan" and "musim kemarau"). All twelve months have average precipitation of at least 60 mm. The climate usually occurs within 5 – 10° latitude of the equator. Based on Köppen climate classification*, the climate is within the "tropical rainforest climate (Af)".

Most areas within the tropics are hot year-round, with diurnal variations in temperature exceeding seasonal variations. Seasonal variations in tropical climate are dominated by changes in precipitation, which are in turn largely influenced by the tropical rain belt or Intertropical Convergence Zone (ITCZ), a zone of low pressure near the equator – a portion of the Hadley cell[†] – where the trade winds converge and create heavy convectional precipitation. The northeast trade winds and southeast trade winds converge in a low pressure zone. Solar heating in the region forces air to rise through convection which results in a plethora of precipitation. Sundaland is located in the ITCZ (red color on Figure 21).

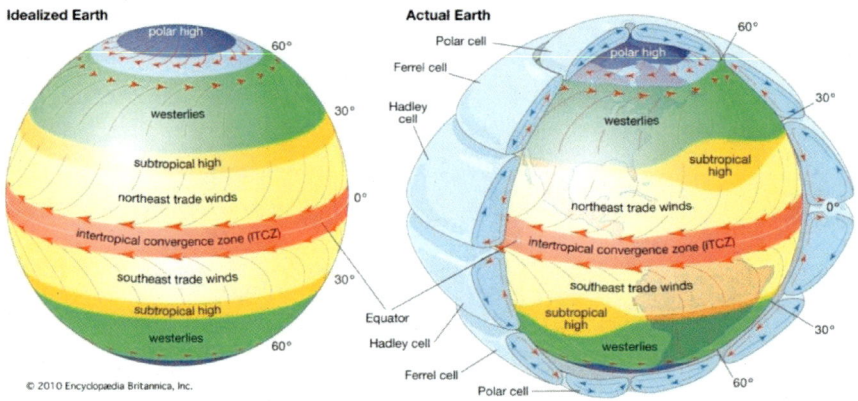

Figure 21 – General patterns of atmospheric circulation over an idealized Earth with a uniform surface (left) and the actual Earth (right). Both horizontal and vertical patterns of atmospheric circulation are depicted in the diagram of the actual Earth. (*Source: Encyclopedia Britanica, Inc*)

---

* The Köppen climate classification was first published by Russian German climatologist Wladimir Köppen in 1884, with several later modifications by Köppen himself, notably in 1918 and 1936. Later, German climatologist Rudolf Geiger collaborated with Köppen on changes to the classification system, which is thus sometimes referred to as the Köppen-Geiger climate classification system. The system is based on the concept that native vegetation is the best expression of climate. Thus, climate zone boundaries have been selected with vegetation distribution in mind. It combines average annual and monthly temperatures and precipitation, and the seasonality of precipitation.
† The Hadley cell, named after George Hadley, is a tropical atmospheric circulation that is defined by the average over longitude, which features rising motion near the equator, poleward flow 10 – 15 kilometers above the surface, descending motion in the subtropics, and equatorward flow near the surface. This circulation is intimately related to the trade winds, tropical rainbelts and hurricanes, subtropical deserts and the jet streams.

Plato's words of *"benefit of the annual rainfall"*, *"abundance of water"*, *"excellently attempered climate"*, *"summer and winter"*, *"very lofty and precipitous"* and *"twice in the year ... in winter ... and in summer"* are strongly interpreted as characteristics of a tropical climate. Plato uses the words "summer" and "winter" to describe the "dry season" and "wet season" as there are no such seasons and there were no such words in Greece.

PLATO'S ATLANTIS WAS AN AGRICULTURAL COUNTRY

Further supporting arguments to conclude that Plato's Atlantis is Sundaland are as follows.

> From Plato's *Critias* Section 111c: *"... full of rich earth, and there was abundance of wood in the mountains."*
>
> From Plato's *Critias* Section 111e: *"... the natural state of the country, which was cultivated, as we may well believe, by true husbandmen, who made husbandry their business, and were lovers of honor, and of a noble nature, and had a soil the best in the world, and abundance of water, and in the heaven above an excellently attempered climate."*
>
> From Plato's *Critias* Sections 114e, 115a and 115b: *"There was an abundance of wood for carpenter's work, and sufficient maintenance for tame and wild animals. Moreover, there were a great number of elephants in the island; for as there was provision for all other sorts of animals, both for those which live in lakes and marshes and rivers, and also for those which live in mountains and on plains, so there was for the animal which is the largest and most voracious of all. Also whatever fragrant things there now are in the earth, whether roots, or herbage, or woods, or essences which distil from fruit and flower, grew and thrived in that land; also the fruit which admits of cultivation, both the dry sort, which is given us for nourishment and any other which we use for food-we call them all by the common name pulse, and the fruits having a hard rind, affording drinks and meats and ointments, and good store of chestnuts and the like, which furnish pleasure and amusement, and are fruits which spoil with keeping, with which we console ourselves after dinner ..."*
>
> From Plato's *Critias* Section 118e: *"Twice in the year they gathered the fruits of the earth - in winter having the benefit of the rains of heaven, and in summer the water which the land supplied by introducing streams from the canals."*

Agriculture is defined as the cultivation of animals, plants, fungi, and other life forms for food, fiber, biofuel, medicinal and other products used to sustain and enhance human life. Agriculture was the key development in the rise of sedentary human civilization, whereby farming of domesticated species created food surpluses that nurtured the development of civilization. For plants, this usually requires some form of irrigation, although there are methods of dry land farming. Livestock are raised in a combination of grassland-based and landless systems. Pre-industrial agriculture was typically subsistence agriculture/self-

91

sufficiency in which farmers raised most of their crops for their own consumption instead of cash crops for trade.

The major agricultural products can be broadly grouped into foods, fibers, fuels, and raw materials. Specific foods include cereals (grains), vegetables, fruits, oils, meats and spices. Fibers include cotton, wool, hemp, silk and flax. Raw materials include lumber and *bambu*. Other useful materials are produced by plants, such as resins, dyes, drugs, perfumes, biofuels and ornamental products such as cut flowers and nursery plants.

With its vast and abundant fertile soils, Indonesia is a major global key producer of a wide variety of agricultural tropical products. Agriculture shares the country's gross domestic product (GDP) (15% in 2013) and still provides income for the majority of Indonesian households today. The World Bank sources indicate that in 2012 this sector employed around 49 million Indonesian individuals, which represents 41% of the total Indonesian labor force. Between the mid-1960s and mid-1980s the percentage of Indonesian land area that was used for agriculture stayed constant at around 21% of Indonesia's total land area. However, in the mid-1980s this number rose to almost 25% until the late 1990s. Starting from 1998 another upsurge (due to the establishment of large scale plantations – in particular palm oil) made this number reach the current level of 30%.

The agricultural sector of Indonesia comprises large plantations (both state-owned and private) and smallholder production modes. The large plantations tend to focus on commodities which are important export products (palm oil and rubber), while the small hold farmers focus on rice, soybeans, corn, fruits and vegetables.

Agriculture remains an important sector of Malaysia's economy, contributing 12% to the national GDP and providing employment for 16% of the population. The British established large-scale plantations and introduced new commercial crops (rubber in 1876, palm oil in 1917, and cocoa in the 1950s). The 3 main crops – rubber, palm oil, and cocoa – have dominated agricultural exports ever since, although the Malaysian share of the world's production of these crops declined steadily during the last 2 decades. In addition to these products, Malaysian farmers produce a number of fruits and vegetables for the domestic market, including bananas, coconuts, durian, pineapples, rice, and others. The Malaysian tropical climate is very favorable for the production of various exotic fruits and vegetables, especially since Peninsular Malaysia seldom experiences hurricanes or droughts.

Indonesia's size, tropical climate, and archipelagic geography, support the world's second highest level of biodiversity (after Brazil), and its flora and fauna is a mixture of Asian and Australasian species. The flora of Indonesia consists of many unique varieties of tropical plants, 55,000 species are endemic. Among about 10,000 species of vascular plants found solely in Indonesia are the world's largest compound flowers.

The flora of Malaysia comprises a vast assemblage of plant species estimated to over 15,500 vascular plants. Malaysia boasts 8,019 species of seed plants: 19 species of *Gymnosperms* and 8,000 *Angiosperms*.

The fauna of Indonesia is characterized by high levels of biodiversity and endemicity due to its distribution over a vast tropical archipelago. Indonesia is second only to Australia in terms of total endemic species, with 36% of its 1,531 species of bird and 39% of its 515 species of mammal being endemic. The Indonesian archipelago is home to roughly 12% of the world's mammals, 16% of the world's reptiles and amphibians, 17% of the world's birds and 25% of global fish populations.

The fauna of Malaysia are some of the most diverse on earth. There are approximately 210 mammal species, 620 bird species, 250 reptile species, and 150 frog species found in Malaysia. Its large marine territory also holds a great diversity of life, with the country's coastal waters comprising part of the Coral Triangle.

The Plato's Atlantis, as in *Critias*, was characterized as being an agricultural country. The country was full of rich earth, abundance of wood, cultivated by true husbandment, had a noble nature, had a best soil in the world, abundance of water, had an excellently attempered climate, abundance of animals including elephants; roots, herbage, woods or essences which distil from fruit and flower; and two harvests each year, in the winter fed by the rains and in the summer fed by irrigation from the canals. It had similar characteristic as the present-day Indonesia and Malaysia.

Abundance of animals and plants were found in the country, as in *Critias* as follows.

1. *"... there were a great number of elephants in the island; for as there was provision for all other sorts of animals, both for those which live in lakes and marshes and rivers, and also for those which live in mountains and on plains, so there was for the animal which is the largest and most voracious of all ..."* may mean elephants, bears, tigers, rhinos, pigs, apes (orangutans), monkeys, buffalos, cows, goats, horses, deer, chickens, crocodiles and so on.

2. *"... roots, or herbage, or woods, or essences which distil from fruit and flower ..."* may mean Indonesian and Malaysian "jamu", herbal medicine made from natural materials, or "bumbu", mixtures of spices or seasoning.

3. *"... fruit which admits of cultivation, both the dry sort, which is given us for nourishment and any other which we use for food — we call them all by the common name pulse ..."* may mean rice (Indonesian and Malaysian "beras").

4. *"... fruits having a hard rind, affording drinks and meats and ointments ..."* may mean coconut.

5. *"... chestnuts and the like, which furnish pleasure and amusement ..."* may mean coffee.

6. *"... fruits which spoil with keeping, with which we console ourselves after dinner ..."* may mean fermented cassava or rice (Indonesian "tape" or "tapai", Malaysian and Bruneian "tapai", Sundanese "peuyeum", Thai "khao-mak", Cambodian "chao" or "tapai", and The Philippines "tapay" or "binuburang").

Others also translate "fruits" as "crops", "groceries" or "produces". The above products are abundant and become the local characteristics of the present-day Sundaland and its surroundings especially Indonesia and Malaysia. Indonesia and Malaysia are famous for their specific herbal medicines called "jamu" and flavorings or spices called "bumbu". Indonesia bears a famous predicate of "Pulau Kelapa" means the islands of coconut.

Moreover, *"Twice in the year they gathered the fruits of the earth — in winter having the benefit of the rains of heaven, and in summer the water which the land supplied by introducing streams from the canals"* is exactly the rice cultivation practices alive until today. Dr Stephen Oppenheimer, in his *Eden in the East,* suggests that there are visible signs of settled agriculture in the Southeast Asian region at least as early as those in the Middle East. For instance, the cultivation of rice, which needs a fair amount of irrigation, seems to have been undertaken in the Malay Peninsula as early as 9,000 years ago, about 2,000 years before the first signs in India or China. A similar date is given for the extensive drainage of swamps by the New Guinea Highlanders to grow crops such as taro. Although the latter site is not in

Sundaland, it is not terribly far away, and we could speculate that it was descendants of refugees from the flooded Sunda Shelf who could have been responsible for these very early signs of irrigation in the Asia-Pacific region (Pasannan, 2004). The Malay and New Guinea sites are both above water; no underwater archaeology has been undertaken on the Sunda Shelf.

PLATO'S ATLANTIS WAS RICH OF MINERALS

From Plato's *Critias* Section 114e: "*… they dug out of the earth whatever was to be found there, solid as well as fusile, and that which is now only a name and was then something more than a name, orichalcum, was dug out of the earth in many parts of the island, being more precious in those days than anything except gold.*"

From Plato's *Critias* Sections 116b and 116c: "*The entire circuit of the wall, which went round the outermost zone, they covered with a coating of brass, and the circuit of the next wall they coated with tin, and the third, which encompassed the citadel, flashed with the red light of orichalcum.*"

From Plato's *Critias* Section 116c: "*… in the center was a holy temple dedicated to Cleito and Poseidon, which remained inaccessible, and was surrounded by an enclosure of gold …*"

From Plato's *Critias* Sections 116d and 116e: "*All the outside of the temple, with the exception of the pinnacles, they covered with silver, and the pinnacles with gold. In the interior of the temple the roof was of ivory, curiously wrought everywhere with gold and silver and orichalcum; and all the other parts, the walls and pillars and floor, they coated with orichalcum. In the temple they placed statues of gold: there was the god himself standing in a chariot – the charioteer of six winged horses - and of such a size that he touched the roof of the building with his head; around him there were a hundred Nereids riding on dolphins, for such was thought to be the number of them by the men of those days. There were also in the interior of the temple other images which had been dedicated by private persons. And around the temple on the outside were placed statues of gold of all the descendants of the ten kings and of their wives …*"

From Plato's *Critias* Section 120a: "*… they drew from the bowl in golden cups and pouring a libation on the fire …*"

From Plato's *Critias* Section 120c: "*… at daybreak they wrote down their sentences on a golden tablet …*"

A mineral is a naturally occurring substance that is solid and inorganic representable by a chemical formula, usually abiogenic, and has an ordered atomic structure. It is different from a rock, which can be an aggregate of minerals or non-minerals and does not have a specific chemical composition.

Metals are substantial minerals found in almost all rocks and soils. Most metals form compounds, called minerals, which are naturally occurring, inorganic solids with regular chemical compositions and crystal structures. Although most metal-bearing mineral compositions comprise several elements, there are a few exceptions such as gold, which is found in its elemental form as a mineral called native gold.

Metals can form, or be part of, many different minerals. The number of metals (over 70 in the periodic table) and their compounds results in an enormous array of minerals. Iron, for instance, which is very abundant in nature, is found in over 1,100 minerals. The brilliant colors frequently associated with gems such as emerald, ruby and sapphire reflect the variety of metal-containing minerals. Chalcopyrite, an important copper-bearing mineral, is bright yellow, while the copper-phosphate mineral, turquoise, has a blue color.

Metals combine to become the rocks that make up our planet. Most rocks form considerably below the surface of the earth under the influence of pressure and heat. Geologic processes can cause them to move upward toward the surface. There, in the presence of oxygen and water, they break down, releasing elements – including metals – into solutions, and forming new minerals. This process, known as weathering, forms our soils. From soil, metals are taken up by plants and then by animals and humans in food. As soils are eroded, metal-bearing sediment is carried into streams and rivers, and eventually into the ocean. These sediments contribute to new rocks through ongoing geologic processes.

Metals are ubiquitous in nature, and their distribution in the earth depends on geologic processes that have taken place. Some processes may form minerals with high metal contents; rocks containing these minerals may be so enriched that they can be mined at a profit – becoming ore deposits. Rocks that contain lower enrichments are known simply as mineral deposits. The metal content of deposits can range from a few parts per million (ppm) to as much as 650,000 ppm (65%) in the case of some iron ores. Mining companies employ special technologies to extract metals from complex ores in the production of pure metals such as iron, aluminum, copper and gold.

While high concentrations of metals may lead to the formation of deposits, in many cases where the concentration of a metal is low, the metal may simply replace, or substitute for, another element in the crystal structure of common minerals. For example, rocks that make up the sea floor contain high concentrations of the metal magnesium, as well as smaller concentrations of nickel which substitute for some of the magnesium. Similarly, rocks that make up the continents can contain lead, which substitutes for the more abundant metallic element, potassium. This substitution phenomenon leads to the wide distribution of many metals at low concentrations throughout the rocks of the earth.

Natural geologic processes continue at a very slow pace to concentrate and disperse metals, forming large zones of elevated metal concentrations and constantly releasing metals into the environment. A full understanding of these natural processes and the resulting metal dispersion patterns is important in the discovery and recovery of metals and for determining the impact of metals in the environment.

Rocks and the minerals are the building blocks of the Earth. Modern technology, and our society as a whole, depends upon rocks and minerals as raw materials. In fact, rocks and minerals have supported the development of societies and civilizations throughout human history. Early humans carved tools out of minerals such as quartz. Pottery has been made of various clays since ancient times. Sodium chloride, also known as the mineral halite, has been used in food preservation techniques for millions of years. Mining of useful minerals out of ores became widespread hundreds of years ago, a practice still in use today. Gemstones have been prized since antiquity for adornment and as symbols of status and wealth. Early writing on mineralogy, especially on gemstones, comes from ancient Babylonia, the ancient Greco-Roman world, ancient and medieval China, and Sanskrit texts from ancient India and the ancient Islamic World.

Currently there are 86 known metallic minerals. Before the 19th century only 24 of these minerals had been discovered and, of these 24 minerals, 12 were discovered in the 18th century. Therefore, from the discovery of the first metals – gold and copper – until the end of the 17th century, some 7,700 years only 12 metals were known. Four of these metals, arsenic, antimony, zinc and bismuth, were discovered in the thirteenth and fourteenth centuries, while platinum was discovered in the 16th century. The other seven metals, known as the Metals of Antiquity, were the metals upon which civilization was based. These seven metals were: gold (*ca* 6,000 BC), copper (*ca* 4,200 BC), silver (*ca* 4,000 BC), lead (*ca* 3,500 BC), tin (*ca* 1,750 BC), iron (smelted, *ca* 1,500 BC) and mercury (*ca* 750 BC). These metals were known to the Mesopotamians, Egyptians, Greeks and the Romans. Of the seven metals, five can be found in their native states, *eg* gold, silver, copper, iron (from meteors) and mercury. However, the occurrence of these metals was not abundant and the first two metals to be used widely were gold and copper. And, of course, the history of metals is closely linked to that of coins and gemstones.

Sundaland, until today, is the producer of various minerals with relatively large quantities due to its geological and tectonic conditions that favor the formation of the mineral resources (see Figure 18).

Today, Indonesia is quite fortunate because it can be regarded as a mineral-rich country, as geologically prospective for the formation of various mineral resources. Some of these deposits particularly gold, silver, precious stones, and building stones have been utilized since the early centuries when the Dharmic and Chinese cultures entered this region. Scientific exploration in Indonesia was introduced by the European geologists, particularly the Dutch, starting in the 18th century, after the industrial revolution in Europe. Since then, numerous mineral resources such as gold, copper, tin, nickel, iron, aluminum, diamond, and various non-metallic minerals and rocks, have been uncovered. In line with this important discovery, the geological characteristic of Indonesia was also starting to be understood.

The country's mineral industry – primarily the cement, metal mining, and oil and gas industries – contributed modestly to its industrial production. The value of mineral commodity production accounted for 12.2% of the GDP of Indonesia in 2011. Production of gold in 2010 was recorded as 105 tons, silver as 272 tons, tin as 43 thousand tons, nickel as 5.4 million tons and bauxite as 104 thousand tons, were quite numerous.

Malaysia had identified mineral resources of barite, bauxite, clays, coal, copper, gold, ilmenite, iron ore, monazite, silica, silver, struverite (*tantalum*), tin, and zircon. During the 20th century, mineral production played an important role in Malaysia's national economy; after many years of exploitation, however, such minerals as barite, bauxite, copper, ilmenite, iron ore, and tin were either depleted or the capacities to produce them had decreased significantly in recent years. In terms of its contribution to the country's economy, the mining and quarrying sector accounted for 6.3% of the GDP in 2011.

Five types of minerals are mentioned in the Plato's *Critias*: gold, *orichalcum*, silver, tin and brass showing that in this country there were sources of these materials.

GOLD

According to Plato's *Critias*, the Temple to Poseidon and Cleito was surrounded by an enclosure of gold. The pinnacles outside the temple were covered with gold. The interior roof of the temple was of ivory, wrought everywhere with gold, silver and *orichalcum*. In the temple they placed a golden statue of Poseidon standing in a chariot with six winged-horses of such a size that he touched the roof of the building with his head. Around the temple on the outside were placed golden statues of all the descendants of the ten kings and of their wives.

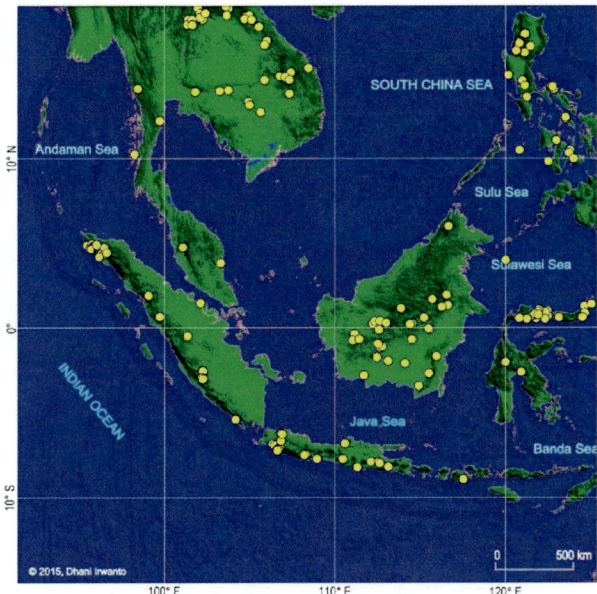

Figure 22 – Distribution of gold resources
(*Sources: USGS and various*)

Wine drawn from a bowl in golden cups was used to pour a libation on the fire in the bull sacrifice rituals every fifth and every sixth year alternately. Judgments given in the rituals were written down on golden tablets.

Gold is sometimes found free and uncombined in nature but it is usually found in conjunction with silver, quartz, calcite, tin, lead, zinc or copper. Gold can be found abundantly in Sundaland. Kalimantan, western Java and northern Sumatera have the richest gold resources, while others are spotted in the whole Sundaland. It is alleged that the gold in Atlantis was not pure gold but probably native gold which is alloyed with small content of silver or tin.

Gold articles are found extensively in antiquity mainly as jewelry *eg* bracelets, rings *etc*. Early gold artifacts are rarely pure and most contain significant silver contents. This led to the ancients naming another metal – *electrum*, which was an alloy of gold and silver, pale yellow and similar in color to amber. Therefore, early gold varied from pure through *electrum* to white gold.

Stone Age man learned to fashion gold into jewelry and ornaments, learning that it could be formed into sheets and wires easily. However, its malleability, which allows it to be formed into very thin sheet, ensures that it has no utilitarian value and early uses were only decorative. As gold is a noble metal, being virtually noncorrosive and tarnish free, it served this purpose admirably.

Gold is widely dispersed through the earth's crust and is found in two types of deposits: lode deposits, which are found in solid rock and are mined using conventional mining techniques, and placer deposits which are gravelly deposits found in stream beds and are the products of eroding lode deposits. Since gold is found uncombined in nature, early goldsmiths would collect small nuggets of gold from stream beds *etc*, and then weld them together by hammering.

ORICHALCUM

According to Plato's *Critias*, *orichalcum* was considered second only to gold in value, and was found and mined in many parts of Atlantis in ancient times. By the time of Plato, however, it was known only by name.

The third outer walls of the Temple to Poseidon and Cleito were clad, which encompassed the whole citadel, flashed with the red light of *orichalcum*. The interior walls, pillars and floors of the temple were completely covered in *orichalcum*, and the roof was variegated with gold, silver, and *orichalcum*. In the center of the temple stood a pillar of *orichalcum*, on which the laws of Poseidon and records of the first son princes of Poseidon were inscribed.

Orichalcum mentioned by Plato is composed from the Greek syllables *oros* (ὄρος, mountain) and *chalkos* (χαλκός, ore), simply means "mountain ore" that can be a compound of materials, whether metal or non metal. The Romans transliterated *orichalcum* as "aurichalcum", which was thought to literally mean "golden copper". It is known from the writings of Marcus Tullius Cicero (106 – 43 BC) that the metal they called *orichalcum*, while it resembled gold in color, had a much lower value.

By the 8th-7th century BC Assyrian cuneiform tablets mention the exploitation of the "copper of the mountains" and this may refer to "natural" brass. *Oreichalkos*, the Ancient Greek translation of this term, was later adapted to the Latin *aurichalcum* meaning "golden copper" which became the standard term for brass. In the 4th century BC Plato knew *oreichalkos* as rare and nearly as valuable as gold and Pliny the Elder (23 – 79 AD) describes how *aurichalcum* had come from Cypriot ore deposits which had been exhausted by the 1st century AD.

Orichalcum has variously been held to be a gold/copper alloy, a copper-tin or copper-zinc brass, a metal, a precious stone, or a compound no longer known. However, in *Aeneid* by Publius Vergilius Maro (70 – 19 BC) it was mentioned that the breastplate of Turnus was "stiff with gold and white orachalc" and it has been theorized that it is an alloy of gold and silver, though it is not known for certain what *orichalcum* was.

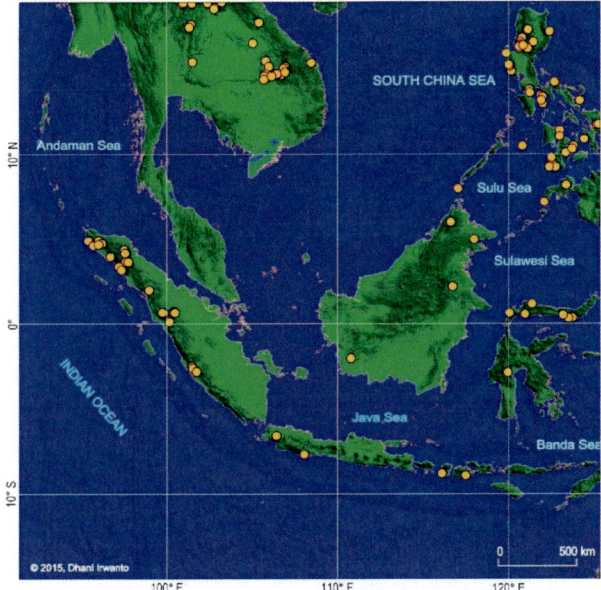

Figure 23 – Distribution of copper resources
(*Sources: USGS and various*)

In later years, *orichalcum* was used to describe the sulfide mineral chalcopyrite or brass. However, these are difficult to reconcile with the text of Plato's *Critias*, because he states that the material was "only a name" by his time, while brass and chalcopyrite continued to be very important through the time of Plato until today. Joseph Needham (1900 – 1995) notes that the 18th century Bishop Richard Watson, a professor of chemistry, wrote that there was an ancient idea that there were "two sorts of brass or orichalcum". Needham also suggests that the Greeks may not have known how *orichalcum* was made and that they might even have had an imitation of the original.

In antiquity literature, *orichalcum* is first mentioned in the 7th century BC by Hesiod in the Homeric hymn dedicated to Aphrodite, dated to the 630s, and in the *Critias* by Plato, dated *ca* 600 BC. *Orichalcum* is also mentioned in the *Antiquities of the Jews – Book VIII, section 88* by Josephus (37 – *ca* 100 AD), who stated that the vessels in the Temple of Solomon were made of *orichalcum* (or a bronze that was like gold in beauty). Pliny the Elder points out that the material has lost currency due to the mines being exhausted. Pseudo-Aristotle* in *De mirabilibus auscultationibus* (*On Marvellous Things Heard*) describes *orichalcum* as a shining material obtained during the smelting of copper with the addition of

---

* Pseudo-Aristotle is a general cognomen for authors of philosophical or medical treatises who attributed their work to the Greek philosopher Aristotle, or whose work was later attributed to him by others.

calmia (zinc oxide), a kind of earth formerly found on the shores of the Black Sea.

The author will discuss the *orichalcum* further in the next section.

SILVER

According to Plato's *Critias*, all the outside of the Temple to Poseidon and Cleito, with the exception of the pinnacles, was covered with silver. The interior roof of the temple was of ivory, wrought everywhere with gold, silver and *orichalcum*.

Silver can be obtained from pure deposits, from silver ores such as argentite (Ag_2S) and horn silver (AgCl), and in conjunction with deposits of ores containing lead, gold or copper. Silver can be found in Sundaland mainly in Java, Kalimantan and Sumatera. It is alleged that the silver in Atlantis was not pure silver.

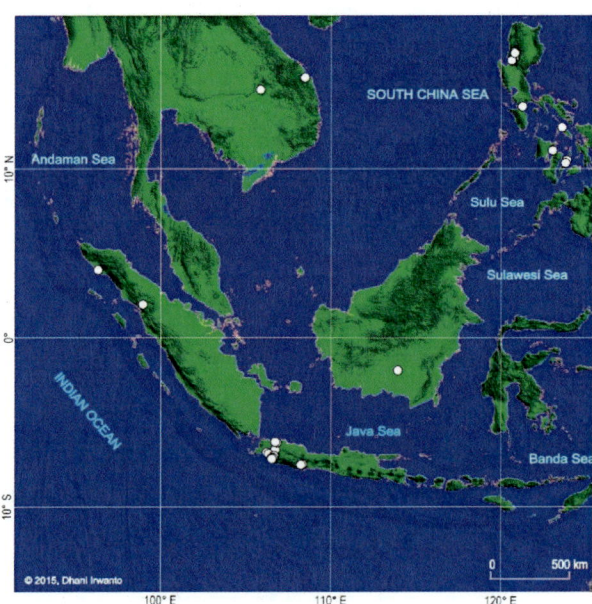

Figure 24 – Distribution of silver resources
(*Sources: USGS and various*)

Silver has been known since ancient times. Mentioned in the *Book of Genesis*, slag heaps found in Asia Minor and on the islands of the Aegean Sea indicate silver was being separated from lead as early as the 4th millennium BC using surface mining. In the Gospels, Jesus' disciple Judas Iscariot is infamous for having taken a bribe of 30 coins of silver from religious leaders in Jerusalem to turn Jesus of Nazareth over to soldiers of the High Priest Caiaphas.

After the battle of Marathon, Themistocles persuaded the Athenians to devote the anticipated revenue derived from a major silver vein strike in the mines of Laurion in *ca* 483 BC to expanding the Athenian fleet to 200 triremes, and thus laid the foundation of the Athenian naval power. The mines, which were the property of the state, were usually farmed out for a certain fixed sum and a percentage on the working; slave labor was exclusively employed. As many as 20,000 slaves were employed at the height of the mining.

The stability of the Roman currency relied to a high degree on the supply of silver bullion, which Roman miners produced on a scale unparalleled before the discovery of the New World*. Reaching a peak production of 200 tons per year, an estimated silver stock of 10,000 tons circulated in the Roman economy in the middle of the second century AD, five to ten times larger than the combined amount of silver available to medieval Europe and the Caliphate around 800 AD. Financial officials of the Roman Empire worried about the loss of silver to pay for highly demanded silk from Sinica (China).

The Chinese Empire during most of its history primarily used silver as a means of exchange. In the 19th century, the threat to the balance of payments of the United Kingdom from Chinese merchants demanding payment in silver in exchange for tea, silk and porcelain led to the Opium War because Britain had to find a way to address the imbalance in payments, and they decided to do so by selling opium produced in their colony of British India to China.

In the Americas, high temperature silver-lead cupellation technology was developed by pre-Inca civilizations as early as 60 – 120 AD.

Although silver was found freely in nature, its occurrence was rare. Silver is the most chemically active of the noble metals, harder than gold but softer than copper. It ranks second in ductility and malleability to gold. It is normally stable in pure air and water but tarnishes when exposed to ozone, hydrogen sulfide or sulfur. Due to its softness, pure silver was used for ornaments, jewelry and as a measure of wealth. In a manner similar to gold, native silver can easily be formed.

Galena always contains a small amount of silver and it was found that if the lead was oxidized into a powdery ash a droplet of silver was left behind. Another development in this process was the discovery that if bone ash was added to the

---

* The New World is one of the names used for the Western Hemisphere, specifically the Americas (including nearby islands such as those of the Caribbean and Bermuda). The term originated in the early 16th century after Europeans made landfall in what would later be called the Americas in the age of discovery, expanding the geographical horizon of classical geographers, who had thought of the world as consisting of Africa, Europe and Asia, collectively now referred to as the Old World (aka Afro-Eurasia).

lead oxide, the lead oxide would be absorbed and a large amount of material could be processed. By *ca* 2,500 BC the cupellation process was the normal mode of silver manufacture.

TIN

In the Plato's *Critias*, the second circuit of walls was coated with tin.

Tin is primarily obtained from the mineral cassiterite (SnO_2) in nature and is extracted by roasting cassiterite in a furnace with carbon. Tin is found abundantly in the western part of Sundaland and is the largest source of tin in the world nowadays.

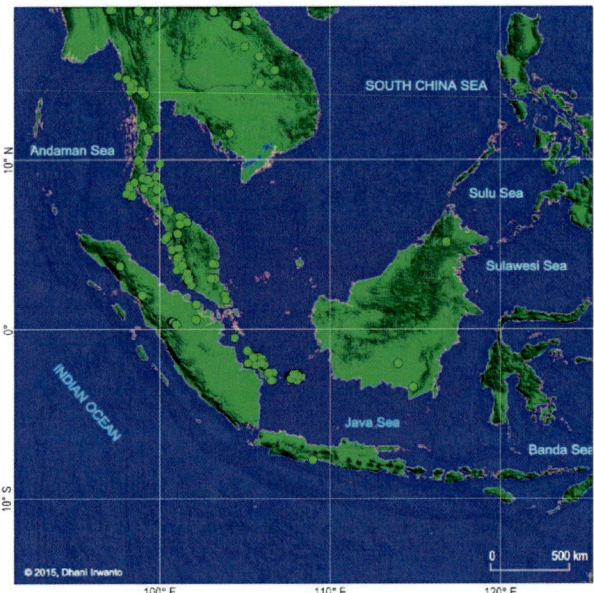

Figure 25 – Distribution of tin resources
(*Sources: USGS and various*)

The first tin artifacts date back to *ca* 2,000 BC; however, it was not until *ca* 1,800 BC that tin smelting became common in western Asia. Tin was reduced by charcoal and at first was thought to be a form of lead. The Romans referred to both tin and lead as *plumbum* where lead was *plumbum nigrum* and tin was *plumbum candidum*. Tin was rarely used on its own and was most commonly alloyed to copper to form bronze. The most common form of tin ore is the oxide casserite. By *ca* 1,400 BC bronze was the predominant metal alloy.

Tin is highly malleable and ductile and has two allotropic forms which lead to tin initially having its own disease (tin pest or blight) which was actually formation of alpha-tin below 13 °C. As alpha-tin is a highly friable cubic structure with a greater specific volume than beta-tin, during the phase change, which is kinetically limited, nodules of alpha-tin become visible on the surface of beta-tin giving rise to early belief of sickness and the first true doctors of

104

metallurgy. Tin is highly crystalline and during deformation is subject to mechanical twinning and an audible tin cry. Tin is also quite resistant to corrosion.

Tin is found as vein tin or stream tin. The tin ore is stannic oxide and is generally found with quartz, feldspar or mica. The ore is a hard, heavy and inert substance and is generally found as outcroppings as softer impurities are washed away.

BRASS

In the Plato's *Critias*, the outermost circuit of walls was coated with brass.

In modern term, brass is an alloy made of copper and zinc but Plato's brass can mean any bronze alloy, or copper, rather than the strict modern definition. It is alleged that the the Plato's brass in Atlantis is an alloy of copper, zinc, tin and lead with a dominant content of copper.

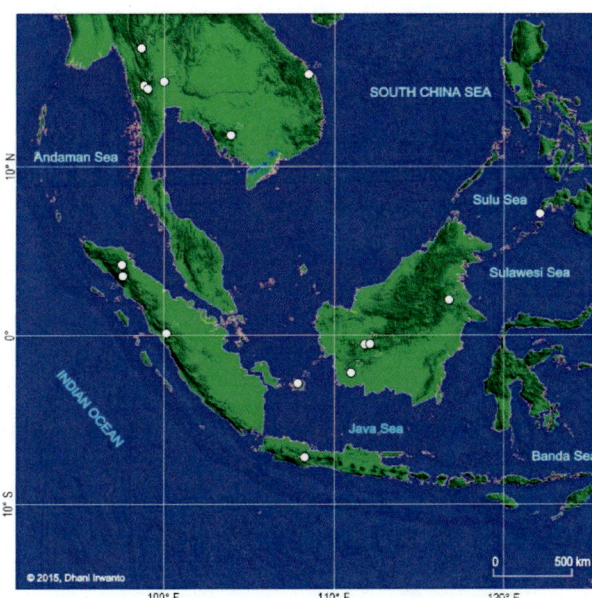

Figure 26 – Distribution of zinc resources
(*Sources: USGS and various*)

By reference, bronze is principally an alloy of copper and tin. However, a variety of alloys of copper, including alloys with arsenic, phosphorus, aluminum, manganese, and silicon, commonly termed "bronze", are applied to a variety of brasses and the distinction is largely historical. Modern practice in museums and archaeology is increasingly to avoid both terms for historical objects in favor of the all-embracing "copper alloy".

The King James Bible* makes many references to "brass". The Shakespearean English form of the word "brass" can mean any bronze alloy, or copper, rather than the strict modern definition of brass. The earliest brass may have been natural alloys made by smelting zinc-rich copper ores. By the Roman period brass was being deliberately produced from metallic copper and zinc minerals using the cementation process and variations on this method continued until the mid-19th century.

In West Asia and the Eastern Mediterranean early copper zinc alloys are now known in small numbers from a number of third Millennium BC sites in the Aegean, Iraq, the United Arab Emirates, Kalmykia, Turkmenistan and Georgia and from 2nd Millennium BC sites in West India, Uzbekistan, Iran, Syria, Iraq and Israel. However, isolated examples of copper-zinc alloys are known in China from as early as the 5th Millennium BC. The compositions of these early "brass" objects are very variable and most have zinc contents of between 5% and 15% weight which are lower than in brass produced by cementation. These may be "natural alloys" manufactured by smelting zinc rich copper ores in redox conditions. Many have similar tin contents to contemporary bronze artifacts and it is possible that some copper-zinc alloys were accidental and perhaps not even distinguished from copper. However the large number of copper-zinc alloys now known suggests that at least some were deliberately manufactured and many have zinc contents of more than 12% weight which would have resulted in a distinctive golden color.

By reference, the use of copper in antiquity is of more significance than gold as the first tools, implements and weapons were made from copper. From 4,000 to 6,000 BC was the Chalcolithic period which was when copper came into common use. Initially copper was chipped into small pieces from the main mass. The small pieces were hammered and ground in a manner similar to the techniques used for bones and stones. However, when copper was hammered it became brittle and would easily break. The solution to this problem was to anneal the copper. By *ca* 5,000 BC copper sheet was being made. By *ca* 3,600 BC the first copper smelted artifacts were found in the Nile valley and copper rings, bracelets, chisels were found. By *ca* 3,000 BC weapons, tools *etc* were widely found. Tools and weapons of utilitarian value were now within society, however,

---

* The King James Version (KJV), commonly known as the Authorized Version (AV) or King James Bible (KJB), is an English translation of the Christian Bible for the Church of England begun in 1604 and completed in 1611.

only kings and royalty had such tools; it would take another 500 years before they reached the peasants.

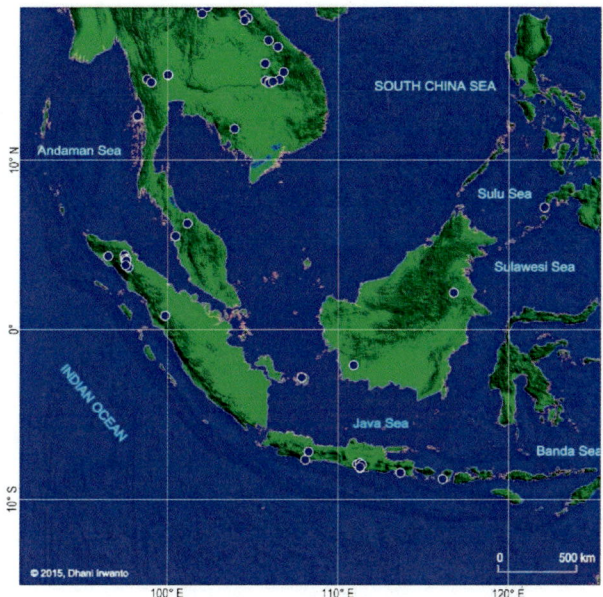

Figure 27 – Distribution of lead resources
(*Sources: USGS and various*)

Malachite, a green friable stone, was the source of copper in the early smelters. Originally it was thought that the smelting of copper was by chance dropping of malachite into campfires. However, campfire temperatures are normally in the region of 600 – 650 °C, whereas, 700 – 800 °C is necessary for reduction. It is more probable that it was discovered by ancient potters whose clay firing furnaces could reach temperatures of 1,100 – 1,200 °C. If Malachite was added to these furnaces copper nodules would easily be found. Although the first smelted copper was found in the Nile valley, it is thought that this copper was brought to Egypt by the Gerzeans and copper smelting was produced first in Western Asia between 4,000 and 4,300 BC.

Smelted copper was rarely pure, in fact, it is clear that by *ca* 2,500 BC the Sumerians had recognized that if different ores were blended together in the smelting process, a different type of copper, which flowed more easily, was stronger after forming and was easy to cast, could be made. An axe head from *ca* 2,500 BC revealed that it contained 11% tin and 89% copper. This was of course the discovery of bronze. However, by *ca* 2,000 BC copper implements contained very little tin as local reserves of tin had been exhausted. The Sumerians were forced to travel to find the necessary ores. Bronze was a much more useful alloy than copper as farm implements and weapons could be made from it; however, it needed the discovery of tin to become the alloy of choice.

***

107

PLATO'S ATLANTIS ISLAND IS IN JAVA SEA

From Plato's *Timaeus* Section 24e: "... *and there was an island situated in front of the straits which are by you called the Pillars of Heracles ; the island was larger than Libya and Asia put together ...*"

From Plato's *Timaeus* Section 25a: "... *for this sea which is within the Straits of Heracles is only a harbor, having a narrow entrance, but that other is a real sea, and the surrounding land may be most truly called a boundless continent.*"

From Plato's *Timaeus* Section 25b: "*This vast power, gathered into one, endeavored to subdue at a blow our country and yours and the whole of the region within the straits...* "

Another passage from Proclus' commentary[*] on the Plato's *Timaeus* gives a description of the geography of Atlantis: "*That an island of such nature and size once existed is evident from what is said by certain authors who investigated the things around the outer sea. For according to them, there were seven islands in that sea in their time, sacred to Persephone, and also three others of enormous size, one of which was sacred to Hades, another to Ammon, and another one between them to Poseidon, the extent of which was a thousand stadia [185 km]; and the inhabitants of it – they add – preserved the remembrance from their ancestors of the immeasurably large island of Atlantis which had really existed there and which for many ages had reigned over all islands in the Atlantic sea and which itself had like-wise been sacred to Poseidon. Now these things Marcellus[†] has written in his Aethiopica ...*"

According to Plato, the Atlantis Island where there was a harbor with a narrow entrance was in a sea surrounded by a boundless continent. The hypothesized boundless continent is the main land of Sundaland attached to the Asian Continent, and the only sea surrounded by it was in those days the ancient Java Sea. Therefore, the author hypothesizes that the Atlantis Island is located in Java Sea.

The Atlantis Island, where there was a central hill, was an island located near the main land identified from the elevation grids, where the sea water level was around 60 meter below the present-day sea water level, as shown on Figure 28. As seen on the map, the island was situated in front of a strait separating the island and the main land. There was a relatively flat plain on the north; part of it

---

[*] Proclus was a Neoplatonist of the 5th century AD. He reports on a commentary on Plato's *Timaeus* made by Crantor, a philosopher and a student of Plato's student Xenocrates. The passage in question has been represented in the modern literature either as claiming that Crantor actually visited Egypt, had conversations with priests, and saw hieroglyphs confirming the story or as claiming that he learned about them from other visitors to Egypt.

[†] Marcellus remains unidentified.

is now the southern part of Kalimantan Island. The "real sea" surrounding the island is the ancient Java Sea which is a gulf with the entrance forms a strait.

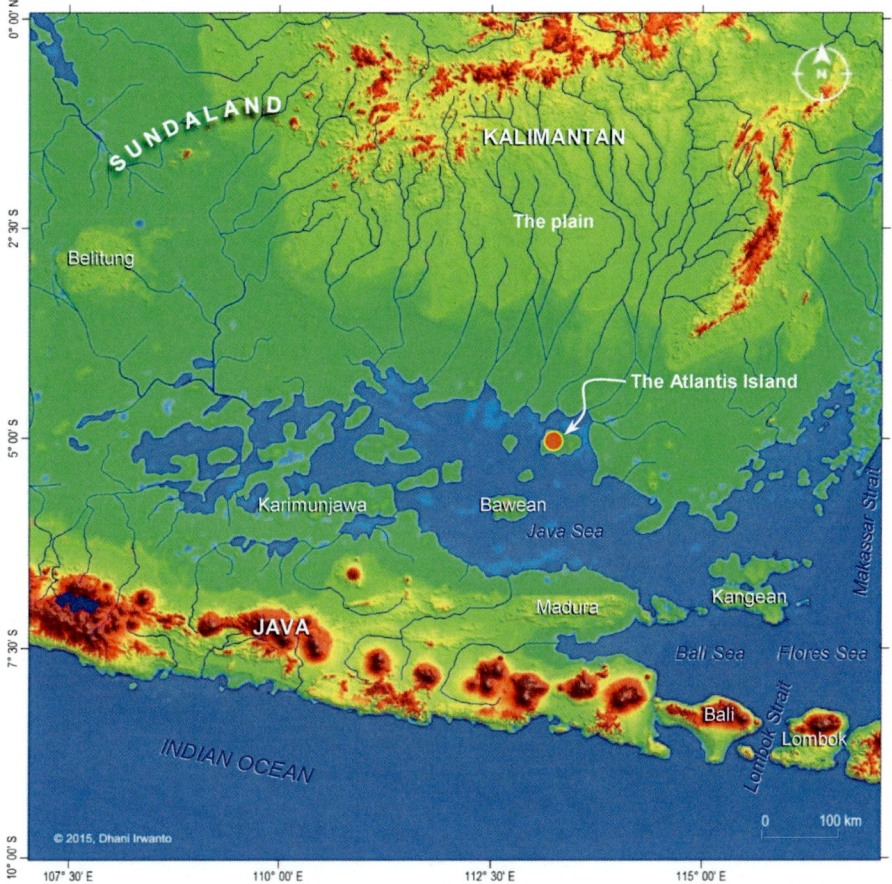

Figure 28 – A map showing the location of the Atlantis Island and the others described in the Plato's dialogues. The map was generated by the author from the GTOPO30 elevation grids published by the USGS. The sea level was around 60 meter below the present-day sea level. The colors other than blue represent the ground levels. The thin red lines are the present-day shorelines. Small islands generated from GTOPO30 were discarded.
As stated in the previous section, it should be emphasized that the topography and bathymetry do not reflect past conditions precisely, mainly due to the unknown processes of sedimentation, scouring, littoral drift, limestone solution and tectonic movement over the past 11,600 years. However, the geography can be used to describe the general conditions of the region during the Atlantis era.

Crantor's commentary as reported by Proclus is about right in describing the geography of the region in the Java Sea in those days. He describes that there were seven small islands and other three large islands, so in total there were ten islands in any sizes. Although the number as seen on the map is not exactly the same due to the unknown process of sedimentation, scouring, littoral drift, limestone solution and tectonic movement over the past 11,600 years, the elevation grids have low accuracy and the author discards the small islands, the regional geography is generally true. The statement that "the extent of which was a thousand stadia (about 185 km)" is in general also about true. One of the large islands is identified as Bawean Island.

PLATO'S ATLANTIS CITY

From Plato's *Timaeus* Section 25a: "… *for this sea which is within the Straits of Heracles is only a harbor, having a narrow entrance, but that other is a real sea, and the surrounding land may be most truly called a boundless continent.*"

From Plato's *Critias* Section 113c: "*Near the plain again, and also in the center of the island at a distance of about fifty stadia, there was a mountain not very high on any side.*"

From Plato's *Critias* Sections 113d and 113e: "… *and breaking the ground, enclosed the hill in which she dwelt all round, making alternate zones of sea and land larger and smaller, encircling one another; there were two of land and three of water, which he turned as with a lathe, each having its circumference equidistant every way from the center, so that no man could get to the island, for ships and voyages were not as yet. He himself, being a god, found no difficulty in making special arrangements for the center island, bringing up two springs of water from beneath the earth, one of warm water and the other of cold, and making every variety of food to spring up abundantly from the soil.*"

From Plato's *Critias* Sections 115c to 117e: "… *First of all they bridged over the zones of sea which surrounded the ancient metropolis, making a road to and from the royal palace. And at the very beginning they built the palace in the habitation of the god and of their ancestors, which they continued to ornament in successive generations, every king surpassing the one who went before him to the utmost of his power, until they made the building a marvel to behold for size and for beauty. And beginning from the sea they bored a canal of three hundred feet in width and one hundred feet in depth and fifty stadia in length, which they carried through to the outermost zone, making a passage from the sea up to this, which became a harbor, and leaving an opening sufficient to enable the largest vessels to find ingress. Moreover, they divided at the bridges the zones of land which parted the zones of sea, leaving room for a single trireme to pass out of one zone into another, and they covered over the channels so as to leave a way underneath for the ships; for the banks were raised considerably above the water. Now the largest of the zones into which a passage was cut from the sea was three stadia in breadth, and the zone of land which came next of equal breadth; but the next two zones, the one of water, the other of land, were two stadia, and the one which surrounded the central island was a stadium only in width. The island in which the palace was situated had a diameter of five stadia. All this including the zones and the bridge, which was the sixth part of a stadium in width, they surrounded by a stone wall on every side, placing towers and gates on the bridges where the sea passed in. The stone which was used in the work they quarried from underneath the center island, and from underneath the zones, on the outer as well as the inner side. One kind was white, another black, and a third red, and as they quarried, they at the same time hollowed*"

110

out double docks, having roofs formed out of the native rock. Some of their buildings were simple, but in others they put together different stones, varying the color to please the eye, and to be a natural source of delight. The entire circuit of the wall, which went round the outermost zone, they covered with a coating of brass, and the circuit of the next wall they coated with tin, and the third, which encompassed the citadel, flashed with the red light of orichalcum.

The palaces in the interior of the citadel were constructed on this wise:-in the center was a holy temple dedicated to Cleito and Poseidon, which remained inaccessible, and was surrounded by an enclosure of gold; this was the spot where the family of the ten princes first saw the light, and thither the people annually brought the fruits of the earth in their season from all the ten portions, to be an offering to each of the ten. Here was Poseidon's own temple which was a stadium in length, and half a stadium in width, and of a proportionate height, having a strange barbaric appearance. All the outside of the temple, with the exception of the pinnacles, they covered with silver, and the pinnacles with gold. In the interior of the temple the roof was of ivory, curiously wrought everywhere with gold and silver and orichalcum; and all the other parts, the walls and pillars and floor, they coated with orichalcum. In the temple they placed statues of gold: there was the god himself standing in a chariot-the charioteer of six winged horses-and of such a size that he touched the roof of the building with his head; around him there were a hundred Nereids riding on dolphins, for such was thought to be the number of them by the men of those days. There were also in the interior of the temple other images which had been dedicated by private persons. And around the temple on the outside were placed statues of gold of all the descendants of the ten kings and of their wives, and there were many other great offerings of kings and of private persons, coming both from the city itself and from the foreign cities over which they held sway. There was an altar too, which in size and workmanship corresponded to this magnificence, and the palaces, in like manner, answered to the greatness of the kingdom and the glory of the temple.

In the next place, they had fountains, one of cold and another of hot water, in gracious plenty flowing; and they were wonderfully adapted for use by reason of the pleasantness and excellence of their waters. They constructed buildings about them and planted suitable trees, also they made cisterns, some open to the heavens, others roofed over, to be used in winter as warm baths; there were the kings' baths, and the baths of private persons, which were kept apart; and there were separate baths for women, and for horses and cattle, and to each of them they gave as much adornment as was suitable. Of the water which ran off they carried some to the grove of Poseidon, where were growing all manner of trees of wonderful height and beauty, owing to the excellence of the soil, while the remainder was conveyed by aqueducts along the bridges to the outer circles; and there were many temples built and dedicated to many gods; also gardens and places of exercise, some for men, and others for horses in both of the two islands formed by the zones; and in the center of the larger of the two there was set apart a race-course of a stadium in width, and in length allowed to extend all round the island, for horses to race in. Also there were guardhouses at intervals for the guards, the more trusted of whom were appointed-to keep watch in the lesser zone, which was nearer the Acropolis while the most trusted of all had houses given them within the citadel, near the persons of the kings. The docks were full of triremes and naval stores, and all things were quite ready for use. Enough of the plan of the royal palace.

Leaving the palace and passing out across the three you came to a wall which began at the sea and went all round: this was everywhere distant fifty stadia from the largest

*zone or harbor, and enclosed the whole, the ends meeting at the mouth of the channel
which led to the sea. The entire area was densely crowded with habitations; and the
canal and the largest of the harbors were full of vessels and merchants coming from all
parts, who, from their numbers, kept up a multitudinous sound of human voices, and
din and clatter of all sorts night and day."*

The Plato's Atlantis city is briefly described based on Plato's dialogues as
follows.

The city of Atlantis was an island with a small mountain at its center with fertile
plains surrounding it. The central mountain had rings of water surrounding it.
Water flowed from underground – some hot, some cold. Crops flourished in
the fertile soil.

Poseidon's first child (born on Atlantis) was named Atlas and the ocean around
the island was named Atlantic. From beyond the Pillars of Heracles the city of
Atlantis controlled islands and lands as far as Egypt. They had extensive trade
with other countries. *Orichalcum* (an unknown red-colored substance) was
common on the island.

The city/island existed long enough for many rulers/kings to develop it. The
city of Atlantis had a canal from the sea to an inner lagoon. Three kinds of
stone, one red, one black and one white were quarried on the island of Atlantis.
They used brass to cover their dwellings and brass, tin and *orichalcum* to cover
the outer walls of their cities. Poseidon's temple at the center had a barbaric
appearance and the roof (interior) was made of ivory. In the temple there was a
statue of the god in a chariot. The city of Atlantis made use of private and
public baths and then saved the water for use on their fields. The later docks
had triremes and many naval supplies.

As well as the huge architectural knowledge the Atlanteans seemed to possess,
they also seem to be incredibly advanced in terms of social structure and order,
as well as having access to some superb natural resources.

The author hypothesizes the location of Atlantis Island and reconstructs the city
based on Plato's descriptions, as shown on Figure 29. The site is identified by
the sailors as Gosong Gia or Annie Florence Reef, a coral reef described as
small in extent and dries at low water.

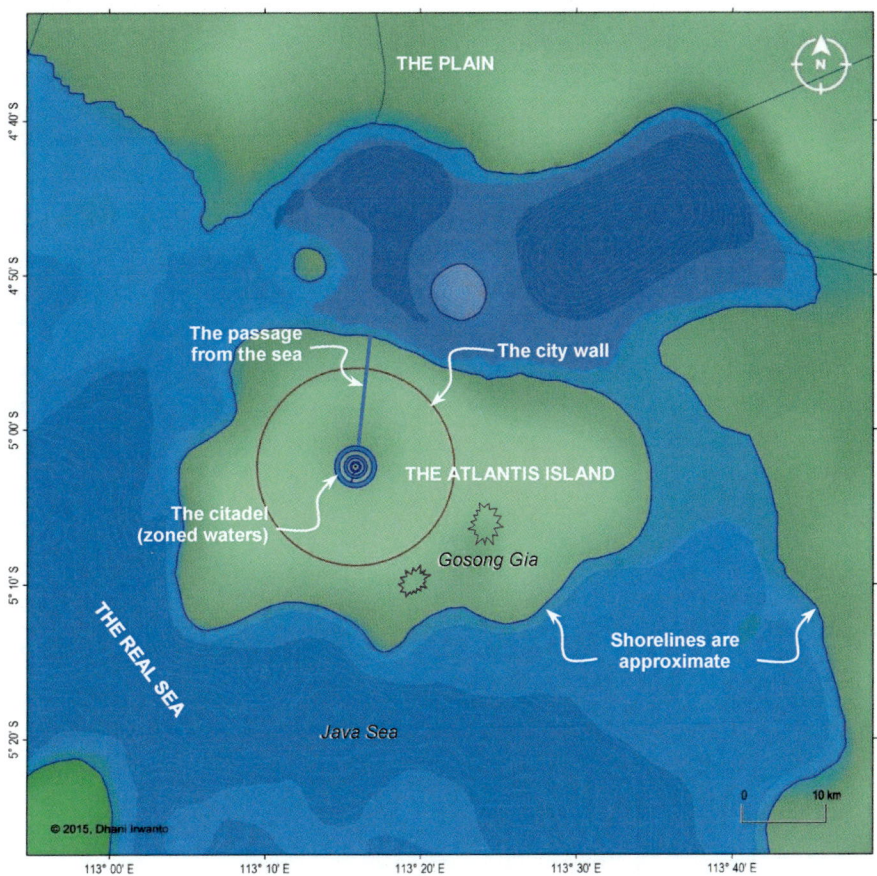

Figure 29 – Reconstruction of Atlantis Island and Atlantis City by the author based on
Plato's descriptions. The island, the shorelines and the rivers are reconstructed from the
GTOPO30 elevation grids published by the USGS. The sea level was around 60 meter below
the present-day sea level.

As stated in the previous section, it should be emphasized that the topography and
bathymetry do not reflect past conditions precisely, mainly due to the unknown processes of
sedimentation, scouring, littoral drift, limestone solution and tectonic movement over the
past 11,600 years. Limited data and measurement method of the bathymetric grids at the area
make the location coordinates and the land geography also not accurate.

From Plato's *Timaeus* Section 25d: "*For which reason the sea in those parts is
impassable and impenetrable, because there is a shoal of mud in the way; and this was
caused by the subsidence of the island.*"

"A shoal of mud" is the generally published translation of the Ancient Greek
phrase "πηλοῦ κάρτα βραχέος" written by Plato. "κάρτα βραχέος" is not

88923
122122232425262728293031323334353637383940

syntactically good and it is not found in any manuscript; "πηλός" is masculine and is the antecedent of the relative pronoun; "κατὰ βραχέος", for its turn, is adverbial. The simple meanings of the words are: πηλοῦ for "clay" or "mud", κάρτα for "very" and βραχέος for "shoal" or "reef". Other alternative translation is "the clay that exists in large quantity there and of the small depth" (Lopes, 2011).

The author translated πηλοῦ κάρτα βραχέος into "coral reef" for the reason that this sea formation is scarce in the Mediterranean so that the Greeks and the Egyptians did not own the term. The Mediterranean no longer shelters the great coral reefs that thrived 60 million years ago. This is due to millennia of climactic and oceanographic changes. Today, there are only a few species of colonial anthozoans that have the capacity to create the coral reefs. In 2010, the exploration vessel Nautilus has discovered for the first time an area of reefs with deep-sea corals in the Mediterranean, offshore of Israel. This area apparently stretches over a few kilometers, 700 meters under the surface and some 30 – 40 km off the coast.

In the above Plato's account, the citadel of Atlantis was impassable and impenetrable at the time of Solon (about 600 BC) because of the growth of a coral reef caused by sea level rise during the Ice Age ("subsidence of the island"). The present condition of the hypothesized site is that there is a coral reef identified by the sailors as Gosong Gia or Annie Florence Reef, a coral reef described as small in extent and dries at low water.

The Plato's description that *"they had fountains, one of cold and another of hot water, in gracious plenty flowing; and they were wonderfully adapted for use by reason of the pleasantness and excellence of their waters"* is noticeable. Bawean Island off in the Java Sea is a prototype of the Atlantis Island as it has the same environment, geological formation and tectonic processes, as well as situated close to Atlantis Island. There are several hot and cold springs in the island resulted from the tectonic activities in the region.

The description that *"the stone which was used in the work they quarried from underneath the center island, and from underneath the zones, on the outer as well as the inner side, one kind was white, another black, and a third red, and as they quarried, they at the same time hollowed out double docks, having roofs formed out of the native rock"* is also noticeable. The white, black and red colored stones mentioned by Plato are apparently similar to the igneous rock that is deposited in Bawean Island with white (acidic), black-grey (alkaline) and red (feroxide) colors. The igneous rock just like in the Bawean Island is hard and strong so that it has enough natural strength to stand as roofs of the hollowed out double docks.

The Java Sea depth at the time of Atlantis (11,600 BP) was around 20 – 30 meters so that it was sufficient to enable the navigation of large ships.

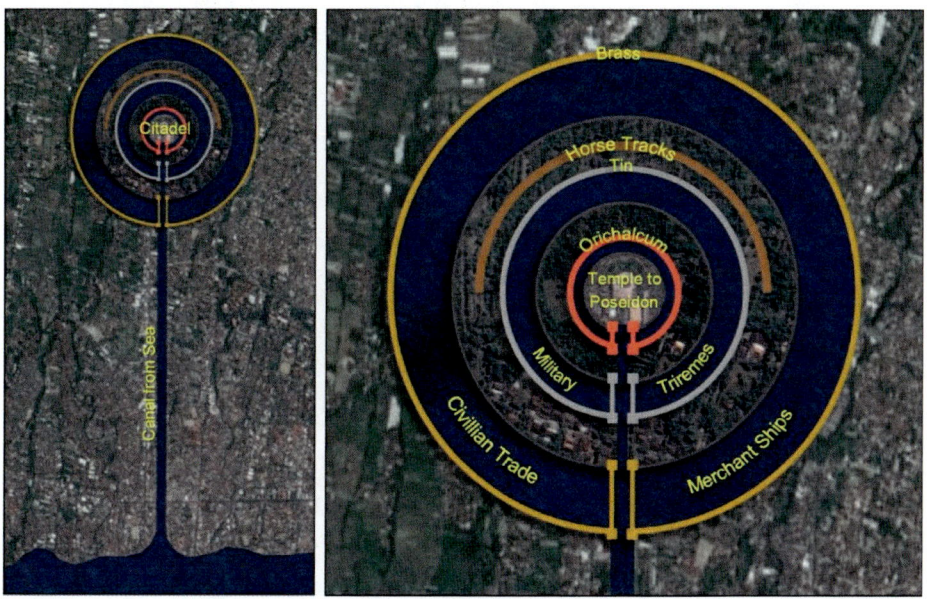

Figure 30 – Impression of the capital city of Atlantis

PLATO'S ATLANTIS PLAIN IS IN KALIMANTAN ISLAND

From Plato's *Critias* Sections 118a and 118b: "… *but the country immediately about and surrounding the city was a level plain, itself surrounded by mountains which descended towards the sea; it was smooth and even, and of an oblong shape, extending in one direction three thousand stadia, but across the center inland it was two thousand stadia. This part of the island looked towards the south, and was sheltered from the north. The surrounding mountains were celebrated for their number and size and beauty, far beyond any which still exist, having in them also many wealthy villages of country folk, and rivers, and lakes, and meadows supplying food enough for every animal, wild or tame, and much wood of various sorts, abundant for each and every kind of work.*"

From Plato's *Critias* Sections 118c to 118e: "*I will now describe the plain, as it was fashioned by nature and by the labours of many generations of kings through long ages. It was for the most part rectangular and oblong, and where falling out of the straight line followed the circular ditch. The depth, and width, and length of this ditch were incredible, and gave the impression that a work of such extent, in addition to so many others, could never have been artificial. Nevertheless I must say what I was told. It was excavated to the depth of a hundred, feet, and its breadth was a stadium everywhere; it was carried round the whole of the plain, and was ten thousand stadia in length. It received the streams which came down from the mountains, and winding round the plain and meeting at the city, was there let off into the sea. Further inland, likewise, straight canals of a hundred feet in width were cut from it through the plain, and again let off into the ditch leading to the sea: these canals were at intervals of a hundred stadia, and by them they brought down the wood from the mountains to the city, and conveyed the fruits of the earth in ships, cutting transverse passages from one canal into another, and to the city. Twice in the year they gathered the fruits of the earth-in winter having the benefit of the rains of heaven, and in summer the water which the land supplied by introducing streams from the canals."*

Plato describes the plain as a level plain, surrounded by mountains which descended towards the sea, smooth and even, rectangular and oblong shaped, three thousand stadia (about 555 kilometers) long, two thousand stadia (about 370 kilometers) wide, looked towards the south, sheltered from the north, surrounded by mountains celebrated for their number, size and beauty; and had wealthy villages of country folk, rivers, lakes, and meadows. These descriptions are exactly fit with the geographical conditions configured on map generated by the author (see Figure 31) as discussed below.

1. A level plain, smooth and even, descended towards the sea – The slope of the ground surface is mostly less than 1% declining southward towards the Java Sea and no visible mound on the whole plain. One may consider this as a very flat plain. The present-day conditions of the plain above the sea water level consist of swampy areas, tidal swamp irrigation practices, housing over water, water transportation, mangroves and peat land.

2. Surrounded by mountains celebrated for their number, size and beauty – There are two mountainous areas around the northern part of the plain, Muller-Schwaner and Meratus Mountains. The highest peak on the Muller-Schwaner Mountain* nearest to the plain is the Liangapran Hill with a height of 2,240 meters above the present day sea water level, while the one on the Meratus Mountain is the Mount Besar with a height of 1,890 meters. These mountains are mostly covered by primary forest, inhabited by enormous kinds of animals and as the inhabitations of the native Dayak tribes.

3. Looked towards the south and sheltered from the north – These are true that the plain is open on the south and sheltered by mountains on the north.

---

* The Muller-Schwaner Mountain is a name given by Adolf Frederik Molengraaff (*ca* 1860 – *ca* 1942 AD) for a mountain range in the central part of Kalimantan Island. The name was given to tribute the Dutch commander Major George Müller and the German adventurer Carl Schwaner.

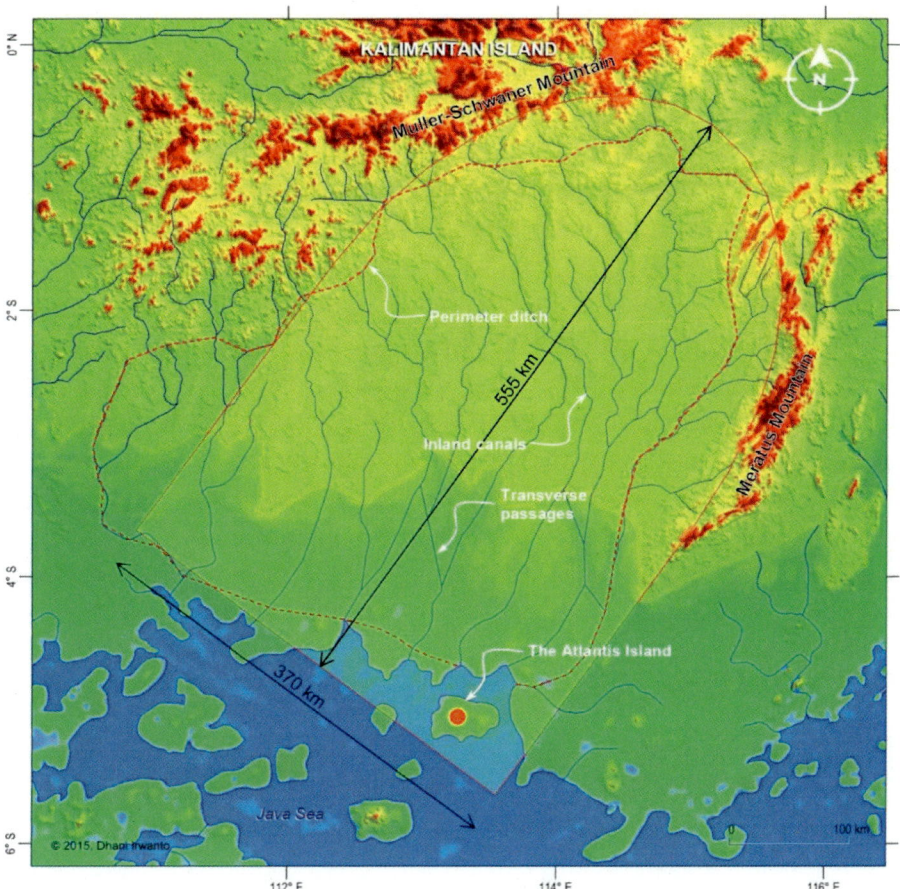

Figure 31 – The plain of Atlantis as described by Plato in *Critias*. The geography was generated using the same method as the previous map. The topography, bathymetry and streams layout do not reflect past conditions precisely, mainly due to the unknown processes of sedimentation, delta formation, river bed movement, meandering, scouring, littoral drift, limestone solution and tectonic movement over the past 11,600 years. However, the geography can be used to describe the general conditions of the plain during the Atlantis era.

4. Rectangular and oblong shaped, about 555 kilometers long and 370 kilometers wide – The shape of the plain is rectangular on the southern part and oblong (elliptical arc) on the northern part. The size is almost exactly 555 kilometers long and 370 kilometers wide. Of course, the nature never gives an exactly regular shape to the geography of the land so that Plato's descriptions are approximate to show the conditions in general.

5. Wealthy villages of country folk, rivers, lakes, and meadows – The area of the plain in present-day conditions is located in a tropical rain forest

117

region, has high precipitation rate over the year, has warm temperature over the year, mostly swampy and has many large rivers and tributaries so that the region is fertile and rich of food and daily necessity resources.

Concerning the water conveyor system on the plain, Plato describes that there were four kinds of channels: the circular (perimeter) ditch, the inland channels, the transverse passages and the irrigation streams. The perimeter ditch was artificial, 100 feet (about 30 meters) deep, 1 stadium (about 185 meters) wide, 10,000 stadia (about 1,850 kilometers) long, carried round the whole plain, received streams from the mountains, winding around the plain, meeting at the city and let off into the sea. The inland canals were straight, 100 feet (about 30 meters) wide, 100 stadia (about 18.5 kilometers) intervals, let off into the perimeter ditch and as means for transporting wood and products in ships. The transverse passages were cut from one inland canal into another. The irrigation streams tapping from the canals were meant to irrigate the land in the summer (dry season) while in the winter (rainy season) had the benefit of the rains. These descriptions are exactly fit with the present-day water conveyor system conditions on the plain as discussed below.

1. The perimeter ditch was artificial, about 30 meters deep and 185 meters wide – One of the river hypothesized as the perimeter ditch is the Barito River and probably the Negara River situated on the eastern side of the plain. Since this "ditch" had the nearest distance to the capital, the Egyptian was apparently passing it and reported. Barito River is the largest and the longest river in southern Kalimantan, which are about 1,000 kilometers long, 600 – 800 meters wide and an average of 8 meters deep. Floodings and sedimentations of the river on a very flat plain over the past 11,600 years have changed the regimes of the river but calculating the conveying capacity – area × velocity and assuming the same flow velocity because of the same gravitational energy slope – the cross section area of the flow (width × depth) as described by Plato is about 185 × 30 = 5,550 square meters while the area today is amazingly almost precise, 700 (average) × 8 = 5,600 square meters.

2. The perimeter ditch was about 1,850 kilometers long, winding around the plain, meeting at the city and let off into the sea – Measuring the length on the map (Figure 31) but considering the windingness factor from the topography, the resulted length is almost precisely the same as in Plato's *Critias*, ie 1,850 kilometers. While measuring the square and oblong shape of the plain, which is 555 kilometers long and 370 kilometers wide, a

perimeter length of 1,656 kilometers is obtained, also logically correct if the windingness factor is not considered. So, it is obvious that Plato is true.

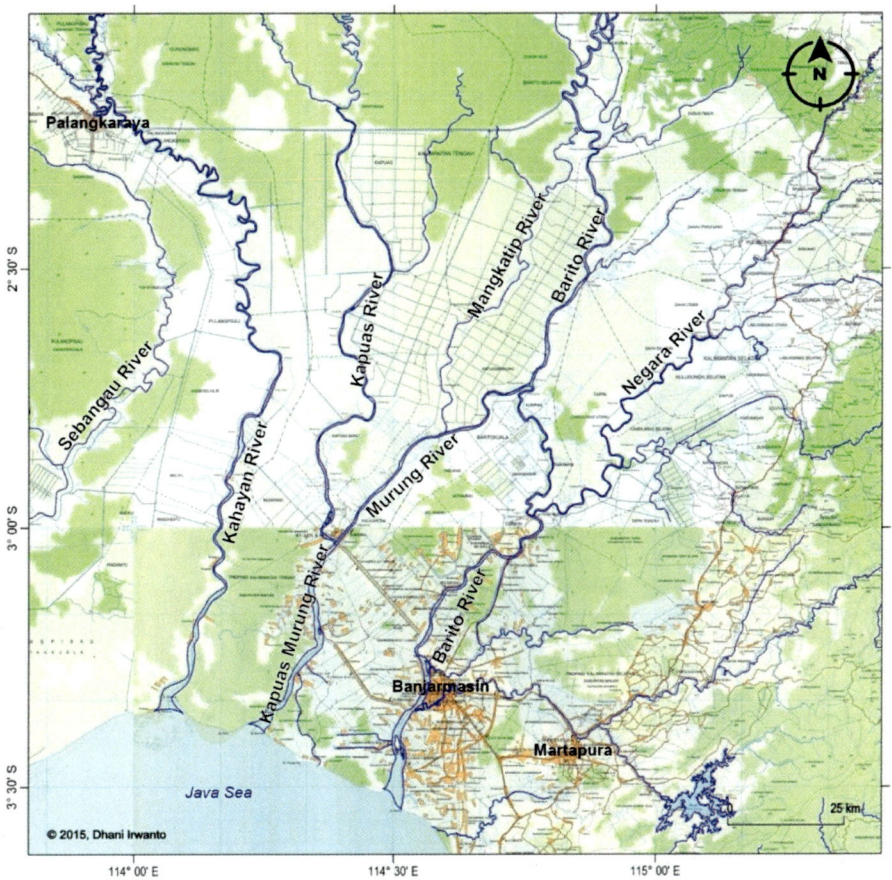

Figure 32 – Map showing the present-day water conveyor system on the plain described by Plato in *Critias*.

3. The perimeter ditch received streams from the mountains – This is true as the present-day rivers on the plain are originated from the Muller-Schwaner and Meratus Mountains.

4. The inland canals were straight, about 30 meters wide, 18.5 kilometers intervals and let off into the perimeter ditch – The present-day rivers represent the inland canals are the Kapuas, Murung, Kahayan, Upper Barito, Mangkatip and probably Sebangau Rivers. The regimes of these rivers should have been changed over the past 11,600 years due to any processes of flooding, sedimentation, river bed movement and

119

meandering on a very flat plain. Interchanges of flows and orders among the rivers might also occur. However, in general view the straightness and elongation of the rivers are preserved until today being parallel to each other and in the north-south direction, and in similar case as the Barito River, the widths have been widened. The average distance of these rivers is approximately 20 kilometers, also considered in close agreement to the Plato's figure of 18.5 kilometers.

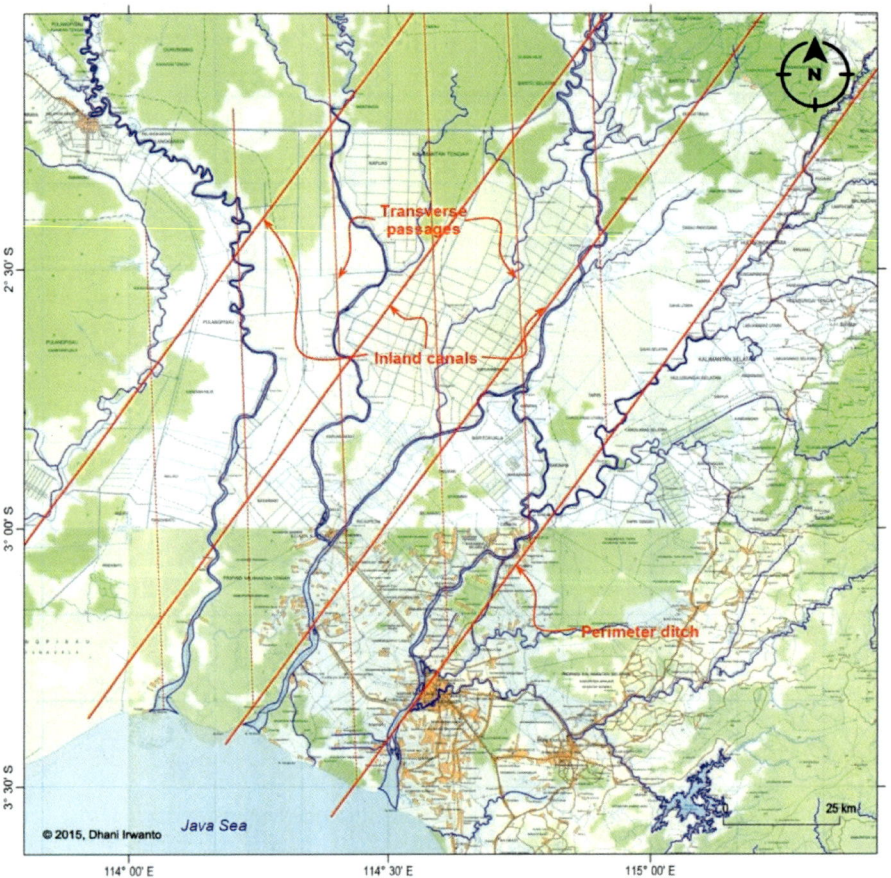

Figure 33 – Map showing reconstruction of canal system referred to the Plato's descriptions. The regimes of the rivers should have been changed over the past 11,600 years due to any processes of flooding, sedimentation, river bed movement and meandering on a very flat plain. Interchanges of flows and orders among the rivers might also occur. Here the author tries to reconstruct the canal system as described by Plato in *Critias*.

5. The inland canals were means for transporting wood and products in ships – This custom is alive until today. Rivers are an integral part of everyday life of people in this region. Most of the rivers in southern

Kalimantan are navigable. The traditional ship or vessel is locally known as "jukung" having many types or forms. These rivers and all their tributaries are a network of transportation system and become very important means for the people as every district is accessible by rivers. Since ancient times, the river network supports economic and social activities of the population of southern Kalimantan. Moreover, the river network has been the economic lifeblood of population because most of their economic activities are carried out through and in the rivers. Communications among regions in the hinterlands, the towns and ports in particular are also done via the river. The rivers become mainstays for the smooth distribution of goods and people from upstream to downstream and vice versa. Various types of forest, mining and agricultural products abundant in rural areas such as wood, rubber, gutta-percha, rattan, resin, "jelutung" (gum sap), wax, coal, gold, pepper, bird's nest, woven material, dried or salted fish, deer jerky, fruits and many others are transported to collection points or ports through the river network. Instead, a variety of daily necessities such as rice, sugar, salt, flour, corn, palm oil, tobacco, gambier, pottery, household appliances, copper wire, fabric (linen) and so on are also transported from the ports to various areas in the hinterlands through the river network.

Figure 34 – Kahayan River splitting the town of Palangkaraya, Central Kalimantan (*Source: Wikipedia®*)

Figure 35 – Floating market in the Barito River, Banjarmasin, South Kalimantan (*Source: Wikipedia®*)

Figure 36 – Water bus moors on a river quay in Palangkaraya, Central Kalimantan (*Source: Wikipedia®*)

6. The transverse passages were cut from one inland canal into another – This is exactly precise. Looking at the maps we can see numerous transverse passages exist in the region, some of them were built or rehabilitated in recent times. The passage is known locally as "anjir", a

canal linking two rivers as part of the transportation network. The canals are also used as primary tidal swamp irrigation canals supplying water to and draining from the cultivated lands.

Figure 37 – Anjir of Kalampan connecting Kahayan and Kapuas Rivers, Central Kalimantan
(*Source: Wikipedia*®)

Figure 38 – Anjir of Sarapat connecting Barito and Kapuas Rivers, Central Kalimantan
(*Source: Wikipedia*®)

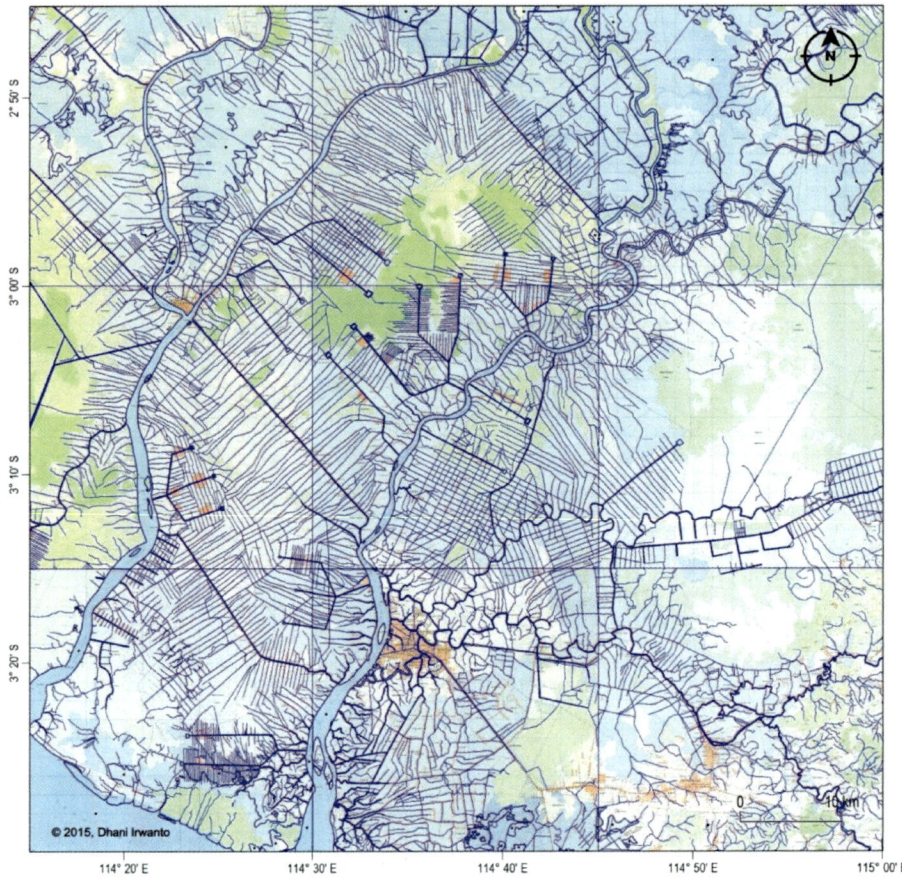

Figure 39 – Map showing *anjir* tidal swamp irrigation system in southern Kalimantan. Primary canals called "anjir" or "antasan" were constructed connecting two tidal rivers, also used as navigation purpose. Inland canals were built to irrigate and drain the fields from and to the *anjir*: secondary canals called "handil" or "tatah" and tertiary canals called "saka". During low tides, the canals drain the toxic water while during high tides fresh water enters the canals and conveyed to the fields.

7. The irrigation streams tapping from the canals supplied water to the land in dry season but rainfall in the rainy season yielding two crops in a year – This is also exactly precise. Today's practices of tidal swamp irrigation system in southern Kalimantan is traditionally known as "anjir system" where primary canals called "anjir" or "antasan" were constructed connecting two tidal rivers, also used as navigation purpose. Inland canals were built to irrigate and drain the fields from and to the *anjir*: secondary canals called "handil" or "tatah" and tertiary canals called "saka". During low tides, the canals drain the toxic water while during high tides fresh water enters the canals and conveyed to the fields. The system yields two

124

rice crops in a year. This system is also used to cultivate other crops or fish. Southern Kalimantan is today an exporter of rice to other regions.

Figure 40 – Anjir tidal swamp irrigation system in Central Kalimantan

The author concludes that the canal system described by Plato turns out precisely the present-day river transportation network and the "anjir" irrigation system in southern Kalimantan region.

THE KALIMANTAN ISLAND

In Plato's dialogues, the kingdom of Atlantis was founded by a god named Poseidon (Greek Ποσειδῶν) and the land was divided into ten portions given to his children. In the center of the citadel there was a holy temple dedicated to Poseidon and his wife, Cleito.

In the *Critias*, Solon while wrote his poem translated the god's name into "Poseidon". Poseidon is one of the twelve Olympian deities of the pantheon in Greek mythology. His main domain is the ocean, and he is called the "God of the Sea". Solon translated the name due to its similarity in the nature of the god.

The Greek Poseidon is equivalent to Baruna (Javanese ꦧꦫꦸꦤ) or Waruna* in the archipelago (Nusantara) which given the title of the Water God, the ruler of the seas and oceans. In pre-dharmic mythology, Baruna was considered as the

---

* Baruna or Waruna was in later time considered as a manifestation of Brahman in dharmic mythology.

125

almighty god against the others and the law founder of the world*. While in the Plato's dialogues it is said that the ten kings in his own division and in his own city are said to have the absolute control of the citizens, and, in most cases, of the laws; mutual relations of the kings were regulated by the commands of Poseidon which the law had handed down and were inscribed by the first kings on a pillar of *orichalcum*. Therefore, the author concludes that Poseidon and Baruna are identical evidenced that both of them were the gods of the seas/oceans and became the law founders.

The name of Baruna is still widely used in Nusantara nowadays as names of person, place, resort, ship, harbor, naval fleet, diving club and many others related to sea. Baruna Jaya I is the name of a survey vessel own by the Indonesian navy.

Each side of almost every temple, commonly found in classic Javanese temples, is adorned with carved Kalamakara. Kala or Batara Kala is a god of the underworld while Makara is a sea monster the vahana of sea god Baruna in ancient Javanese and Balinese mythology. Kala are carved above the gates while Makara are on both sides of the stairs of the gates.

Special attention is given to the island of Kalimantan (the English Borneo), an island formed after the rise of sea level during the Younger Dryas period, about 12,800 to 11,500 years ago. As hypothesized earlier, the plain of Plato's Atlantis was situated at the southern part of the island.

Besides some other classic names of the island like Hujung Tanah (the peninsula); Bakulapura, Tanjungpura or Tanjungnagara (the land of *tanjung* flowers); and Nusa Kencana (the island of gold); Kalimantan bore the name of Warunapura, means the land of Baruna or the land of the Sea God. Next, *Kakawin Nagarakretagama†* mentions an ancient state that was within the Majapahit spheres of influence called Baruné, later identified as Barunai, a kingdom of the modern Brunei. European sources further in the 16th century

---

* In dharmic mythology, Baruna continued to be considered as the god of all forms of water element, particularly the oceans.

† The *Nagarakretagama* or *Nagarakrtagama*, also known as *Desawarnana*, is an Old Javanese eulogy to Hayam Wuruk (*ca* 1334 – *ca* 1389 AD), a Javanese king and the fourth monarch of the Majapahit Empire (*ca* 1293 – *ca* 1500 AD). It was written on *lontar* (palm-leaf manuscripts) as a *kakawin* (long narrative poems composed in "Kawi" (Old Javanese) language and scripts) by Mpu Prapanca in *ca* 1365 AD (*ca* 1287 Saka). The *Nagarakretagama* contains detailed descriptions of the Majapahit Empire during its greatest extent.

AD showed the name of the island as Burné by Antonio Pigafetta* or Bornei by Duarte Barbosa†. The Dutch and British colonials named the island as Borneo. These changes are expressed in the following diagram.

Baruna ⟩ Barunai (Baruné) ⟩ Brunei ⟩ Burné (Bornei) ⟩ Borneo

This is another conclusion too that Kalimantan or Borneo is the island of Plato's Poseidon.

Kalimantan Island is first mentioned in Ptolemy's‡ *Guide to Geography* of about 150 AD. Roman trade beads and Indo-Javanese artifacts have been discovered that give evidence of a flourishing civilization dating to the 2nd or 3rd century BC. Three rough foundation stones with an inscription recording a gift to a Brahman priest dated from the early 5th century AD, found at Kutai, provide evidence of a dharmic kingdom in eastern Kalimantan. Brahmanic and Buddhist images in Gupta style have been found in the valleys of the Kapuas and other rivers in western Kalimantan. Later Kalimantan rulers were probably feudatories of the Majapahit Empire of eastern Java (*ca* 1293 – *ca* 1520 AD). With the arrival of Islam early in the 16th century, a number of Muslim kingdoms were founded, including the Banjarmasin, Sambas, Sukadana and Landak. The Sukadana rulers owed allegiance to the Muslim Mataram kingdom of Java.

---

* Antonio Pigafetta (*ca* 1491 – *ca* 1531 AD) was an Italian scholar and explorer from the Republic of Venice, traveled with the Portuguese explorer Ferdinand Magellan and his crew by order of the King Charles I of Spain on their voyage to the Indies. During the expedition, he served as Magellan's assistant and kept an accurate journal which later assisted him in translating the Cebuano language. It is the first recorded document concerning this language.

† Duarte Barbosa (*ca* 1480 – *ca* 1521 AD) was a Portuguese writer and Portuguese India officer between 1500 and 1516 – 1517, with the post of scrivener in Cannanore factory and sometimes interpreter of the local language (Malayalam). His *Book of Duarte Barbosa* (*Livro de Duarte Barbosa*) is one of the earliest examples of Portuguese travel literature, written in 1516, shortly after the arrival in the Indian Ocean. In 1519, Duarte Barbosa embarked on the first expedition to circumnavigate the world led by his brother-in-law Ferdinand Magellan; dying in 1521 at the feast of Rajah Humabon in Cebu at the Philippines.

‡ Claudius Ptolemy (*ca* 90 – *ca* 168 AD) was a Greco-Egyptian writer of Alexandria, known as a mathematician, astronomer, geographer, astrologer, and poet of a single epigram in the Greek Anthology. He lived in the city of Alexandria in the Roman province of Egypt, wrote in Greek, and held Roman citizenship.

The Dayak or Dyak or Dayuh are the native people of Kalimantan. It is a loose term for over 200 riverine and hill-dwelling ethnic subgroups, located principally in the interior of Kalimantan, each with its own dialect, customs, laws, territory and culture, although common distinguishing traits are readily identifiable. The Dayak indigenous religion has been given the name Kaharingan, and may be said to be a form of animism. The principal god is Ranying Hatalla Langit, popularly Hatalla, a male god, living in the highest domain. According to Kaharingan, their first ancestor was from an island named Pulau Batu Nindan Tarung. "Pulau batu" means the island of rock.

Figure 41 – Dayak in military clothing (1900 – 1940). (*Source: Wikipedia® attributed from Tropenmuseum of the Royal Tropical Institute (KIT), Nederland)*

The Dayak Iban people (also called Sea Dayak), possess an indigenous account of their history, in writing on *papan turai* (wooden records), in common cultural customary practices and in oral literature. This includes elaborate genealogical records, which usually go back about fifteen generations, although some purport to go back up to twenty-five.

The Barito languages are a score of Dayak languages (named after the Barito River). They are closely related to Malagasy languages spoken in Madagascar. Sama-Bajaw languages spoken by the Bajau ("Sea Gypsies") and Sama (Sinama) peoples of The Philippines and Malaysia, on Kalimantan and the Sulu Archipelago are also derived from the Barito lexical region.

Figure 42 – Example of *papan turai* in the Sarawak Museum at the exhibition "The Chosen 66" at Tun Abdul Razak Council, Kuching from 24 January to 28 February 2007. (*Source: Wikipedia®*)

RESOURCES OF MINERALS

From Plato's *Critias* Section 114e: "*In the first place, they dug out of the earth whatever was to be found there, solid as well as fusile, and that which is now only a name and was then something more than a name, <u>orichalcum</u>, was dug out of the earth* *in many parts of the island, being more precious in those days than anything except gold."*

From Plato's *Critias* Sections 116a and 116b: *"The stone which was used in the work they quarried from underneath the center island, and from underneath the zones, on the outer as well as the inner side. One kind was white, another black, and a third red, and as they quarried, they at the same time hollowed out double docks, having roofs formed out of the native rock."*

From Plato's *Critias* Sections 116b and 116c: *"The entire circuit of the wall, which went round the outermost zone, they covered with a coating of brass, and the circuit of the next wall they coated with tin, and the third, which encompassed the citadel, flashed with the red light of orichalcum."*

From Plato's *Critias* Section 116c: *"… in the center was a holy temple dedicated to Cleito and Poseidon, which remained inaccessible, and was surrounded by an enclosure of gold …"*

From Plato's *Critias* Sections 116d and 116e: *"All the outside of the temple, with the exception of the pinnacles, they covered with silver, and the pinnacles with gold. In the interior of the temple the roof was of ivory, curiously wrought everywhere with gold and silver and orichalcum; and all the other parts, the walls and pillars and floor, they coated with orichalcum. In the temple they placed statues of gold: there was the god himself standing in a chariot - the charioteer of six winged horses - and of such a size that he touched the roof of the building with his head; around him there were a hundred Nereids riding on dolphins, for such was thought to be the number of them by the men of those days. There were also in the interior of the temple other images which had been dedicated by private persons. And around the temple on the outside were placed statues of gold of all the descendants of the ten kings and of their wives …"*

Plato mentions that mining activity was part of the industry of Atlantis. They used a material he referred to as *orichalcum*. This material was more valuable in those days than anything other than gold.

In the Plato's *Critias*, the outermost circuits of wall of the Temple to Poseidon were coated with brass. The second circuits of walls were coated with tin. The third walls were covered, which encompassed the whole citadel, flashed with the red light of *orichalcum*. The interior walls, pillars and floors of the temple were completely covered in *orichalcum*, and the roof was variegated with gold, silver, and *orichalcum*. In the center of the temple stood a pillar of *orichalcum*, on which the laws of Poseidon and records of the first son princes of Poseidon were inscribed.

According to Plato's *Critias*, the Temple to Poseidon, which remained inaccessible, was surrounded by an enclosure of gold. The pinnacles outside the temple were covered with gold. All the outside of the temple, with the exception of the pinnacles, is covered with silver. The interior roof of the temple was of ivory, wrought everywhere with gold, silver and *orichalcum*. In the temple they placed a golden statue of Poseidon standing in a chariot with six winged-horses of such a size that he touched the roof of the building with his head. Around the temple on the outside were placed golden statues of all the descendants of the ten kings and of their wives.

The minerals were dug out from the earth in many parts of the island, including *orichalcum* that was abundant. Stones were quarried from underneath the center island and zones, on the outer and inner sides which had white, black and red colors. The roofs of the double docks were formed out of native rock.

In present day, the southern part of Kalimantan Island is rich of mineral resources. Gold and zircon* are abundant as these are the mainstay of the region at this time. A place named Gunungmas, means "golden hill", in the middle of Kahayan River is rich of minerals: gold, silver, copper, iron, zinc, tin, platinum and zircon. Heating to process the minerals is not a problem since Kalimantan Island also deposits coal abundantly.

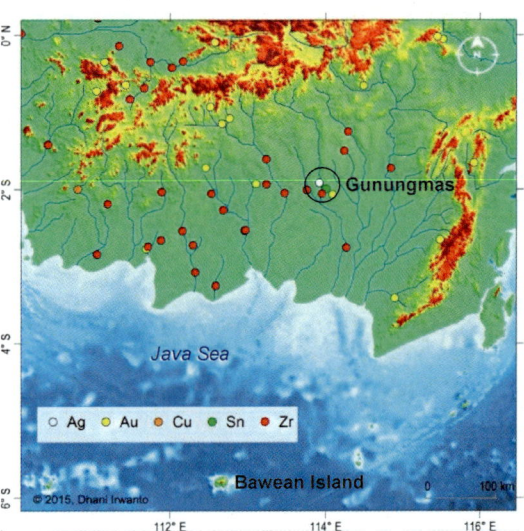

Figure 43 – Mineral resources in southern Kalimantan. Ag = silver, Au = gold, Cu = copper, Sn = tin and Zr = zircon.
(*Source: collected by the author*)

Besides some other classic names of the island, Kalimantan bore the name of Nusa Kencana meaning the island of gold. So, it is no doubt that the resources of gold in Atlantis were in Kalimantan Island, one of them was probably at Gunungmas as this site is easily accessible from the southern coast through Kahayan River. Today, the gold reserves in the area are approximately 45 million tons.

---

* Zircon (including *hyacinth* and yellow zircon) is a mineral belonging to the group of nesosilicates. Its chemical name is zirconium silicate and its corresponding chemical formula is $ZrSiO_4$. Zircon forms in silicate melts with large proportions of high field strength incompatible elements. The natural color of zircon varies between colorless, yellow-golden, red, brown, blue, and green.

130

Zircon is abundantly found along the alluvial deposits of inland rivers in southern and western Kalimantan, as a byproduct of gold mining activities. Zircon is found together with cassiterite (Sn) or *electrum* (Au, Ag) as the major minerals; sometimes also presents with ilmenite, magnesite, monazite, xenotime, pyrite, quartz and other sulfide minerals. Overall mineral deposits are generally derived from granite that has undergone weathering and transport. There is no definite record of the potential at this time. Production is estimated to ± 150,000 tons per year, mostly exported to China for industrial uses.

Orichalcum is composed from the Greek syllables *oros* (ὄρος, mountain) and *chalkos* (χαλκός, ore), simply means "mountain ore". We could speculate that the Plato's *orichalcum* is actually the zircon as this mineral can be "dug out of the earth in many parts of the island" or abundant in southern Kalimantan where the Atlantis plain is hypothesized, as shown on the above map. This material is

Figure 44 – *Hyacinth*, the red zircon

really valuable second to gold; it has gemstone quality and is popular as diamond simulant. Zircon ore requires to be processed through extraction, refinement and heating to bring out different colors of zircon products.

Plato mentions that the ring of wall of the Temple to Poseidon and Cleito was covered and flashed with the "red light" of *orichalcum*. No known metal or its alloy has a red color so that *orichalcum* is not a metal but is possibly the *hyacinth* (the red zircon). When finished, its nature is sparkling like diamond that metals do not posses, which why Plato describes it with the words "flashed" and "light", in particular.

In "being more precious in those days than anything except gold", Plato compares *orichalcum* with gold; while "zircon" derives from the Persian *zargun* (زرگون), meaning "golden-colored", corrupted into "jargoon", a term applied to light-colored zircons which the German adapt to *Zirkon*. Allegedly, Plato or Solon mistranslated *zargun*, the golden-colored material into *orichalcum* as there was no such word in Ancient Greek.

Amethyst or locally named "kecubung", a violet jewel, is also specifically found and renowned in southern Kalimantan. A place named Martapura located in the region is famous for its jewelry industry.

An island named Bawean (or Boyan) off in the Java Sea is a prototype of the Atlantis Island as it has the same environment, geological formation and tectonic processes, and situated close to Atlantis Island. Bawean and Atlantis Islands are both located on a geological arc identified by the geologists as Bawean Arc, spanning from the northern Java Island to the Meratus Mountain in Kalimantan Island. The island consists 85%

Figure 45 – Onyx stone

of igneous rock resulted from Quarternary volcanic activities; partly acidic with white color, partly alkaline with black to grey color and the other feroxide with red color. In addition, Bawean Island is distinguished for its onyx[*] stone resources.

If it similarly exists in the Atlantis Island, the white, black and red colored stones mentioned by Plato are apparently the onyx stone especially for the white and red colors, or igneous rocks for the three colors. Meanwhile, igneous rock has enough natural strength to stand as roofs of the hollowed out double docks.

***

---

[*] Onyx is a banded variety of chalcedony (a cryptocrystalline form of silica, composed of very fine intergrowths of the minerals quartz and moganite). The colors of its bands range from white to almost every color (save some shades, such as red, purple or blue). Commonly, specimens of onyx contain bands of black and/or white.

DISCUSSIONS

ATLANTIS STORY, BETWEEN FACT AND FICTION

Atlantis is within an allegory on the hubris of nations in Plato's works *Timaeus* and *Critias*, where it represents the antagonist naval power that besieges "Ancient Athens", the pseudo-historic embodiment of Plato's ideal state (as in *The Republic*). In the story, Athens was able to repel the Atlantean attack, unlike any other nation of the ("western") known world, supposedly giving testament to the superiority of Plato's concept of a state. At the end of the story, Atlantis eventually falls out of favor with the gods and famously submerges into the "Atlantic Ocean".

While present-day philologists and historians unanimously accept the story's fictional character, there is still debate on what served as its inspiration. The fact that Plato borrowed some of his allegories and metaphors – most notably the story of Gyges, a mythical magical artifact mentioned by Plato in Book 2 of his *Republic* – from older traditions has caused a number of scholars to investigate possible inspiration of Atlantis from Egyptian records of the Thera eruption, the Sea Peoples invasion, or the Trojan War. Others have rejected this chain of tradition as implausible and insist that Plato designed the story from scratch, drawing loose inspiration from contemporary events like the failed Athenian invasion of Sicily in 415 – 413 BC or the destruction of Helike in 373 BC.

Some ancient writers viewed Atlantis as fiction while others believed it was real. The philosopher Crantor (mid of 4th century BC – 276/5 BC) is often cited as an example of a writer who thought the story to be historical fact. His work, a commentary on Plato's *Timaeus*, is lost, but Proclus (*ca* 412 – *ca* 485 AD), a Neoplatonist of the 5th century AD, reports on it. The passage in question has been represented in the modern literature either as claiming that Crantor actually visited Egypt, had conversations with priests, and saw hieroglyphs confirming the story or as claiming that he learned about them from other visitors to Egypt. Other ancient historians and philosophers believing in the existence of Atlantis were Theophrastus (*ca* 371 – *ca* 287 BC), Posidonius (*ca* 135 – *ca* 51 BC) and Strabo (64/63 BC – *ca* 24 AD), though Strabo records Aristotle's joke about Plato's ability to conjure nations out of thin air and then destroy them.

Aristotle, as noted, thought little of Plato's ideas on Atlantis. He believed them to be little more than purely poetic imaginings, although, on close inspection, there are some contradictions even in Aristotle's comments on the lost continent. In a passage in the *Constitution of the Tegaeians*, he wrote that the natives of Arcadia had based an ancient claim to their land on the belief that they came from Atlantis and had inhabited their country "even before there had been a Moon in the heavens". However, Aristotle's general scoffing at the idea of Atlantis gained ground with later Greek and Roman writers who similarly doubted the theory. Thorwald C Franke in his book *Aristoteles und Atlantis* (2010) has carried out extensive research that brought him back to 1587 when a commentary on Strabo by Isaac Casaubon was published, which in turn was badly misinterpreted in 1816 by Jean Baptiste Joseph Delambre who attributed a critical comment by Aristotle regarding Homer's Achaean wall in the Illiad to be instead a reference to Plato's Atlantis. This had far-reaching consequences as Delambre's book was probably more generally available than Casaubon's, resulting in Delambre's error being widely disseminated and so in time his misinterpretation gained sufficient critical mass to become 'received wisdom'.

During the middle ages, Aristotle's influence remained strong and Atlantis was not even considered a serious subject for study. It was not until the Renaissance, with a rediscovery of the works of Plato, that an interest in Atlantis resurfaced. The possible existence of the lost continent of Atlantis has fired the imagination of writers, historians, geologists and archaeologists down the centuries.

Aside from Plato's original account, modern interpretations regarding Atlantis are an amalgamation of diverse, speculative movements that began in the 16th century. Contemporary perceptions of Atlantis share roots with Mayanism, which can be traced to the beginning of the Modern Age, when European imaginations were fueled by their initial encounters with the indigenous peoples of the New World. From this era sprang apocalyptic and utopian visions that would inspire many subsequent generations of theorists. Most of these interpretations are considered pseudohistory, pseudoscience, or pseudoarchaeology, as they have presented their works as academic or scientific, but lack the standards or criteria. As continental drift became more widely accepted during the 1960s, and the increased understanding of plate tectonics demonstrated the impossibility of a lost continent in the geologically recent past, most "Lost Continent" theories of Atlantis began to wane in popularity.

Plato was a member of an established Athenian family with political connections, through his stepfather, related to Pericles. As a young man Plato would have witnessed the downfall of Athens in 404 BC in the Peloponnesian war against the landlocked state of Sparta. Following Sparta's victory, Athens was plunged into chaos and tyranny. After eight months of enduring the tyrants, democracy was restored and the thirty oligarchs were either killed or driven out. The democracy, in settling old scores, had Socrates put to death on trumped up charges of corrupting the young, something that Plato never forgot or forgave. To Plato, Socrates' death meant a final disillusionment with contemporary politics. In the ten years following Socrates' execution Plato drifted away from politics towards philosophy.

Plato's seminal work, *The Republic*, outlines the ideology of Plato's perfect state, one in which the rulers are philosophers. It was written down in the early years of the academy which Plato had founded in *ca* 386 BC. This institution was his answer to his disgust with contemporary politics and was, in essence, to train the philosopher-rulers of a future Athenian state. The *Critias* dialogue is in direct response to Socrates demand to know how his ideal state will conduct itself in action. What Socrates means by this ideal state is of course the Plato's "republic". In essence, this story is to be an illustration of how the ideal state conducts itself in warfare against its neighbors. In considering the *Timaeus* and the *Critias*, which includes the story of Atlantis, it has to be read against the background of *The Republic*.

The story of Atlantis concerns the greatest and noblest action of Ancient Athens and the defeat of aggressive Atlantis. The story relates that this happened far back in history, so far indeed that the Greeks may not recollect it. There was no city of Athens in existence in 9,000 years before Solon. There may have been a small Neolithic settlement and the fine city of Athens simply did not exist. This account also has nothing to do with the archaeological evidence regarding Egypt in the Pre-dynastic Period. The Egyptians have their own creation myths and they have absolutely nothing to do with Athens.

The pre-history of Egypt* is known to the Neolithic period, beginning *ca* 6,000 BC or *ca* 8,000 BP. Yet, 9,000 years before Solon or 11,600 BP is beyond the historical span of Egypt. We could speculate that the ancient Egypt told by the priest is actually a primordial ethnic group and believed to be their ancestors prior the deluges and other catastrophes. The Egyptians were among the refugees and survivors of the catastrophes; then resettled on the land which is now called the Egypt. In the rescue, they brought records and registers, and

---

* The pre-history of Egypt spans the period of earliest human settlement to the beginning of the Early Dynastic Period of Egypt in *ca* 3,100 BC, starting with the first Pharaoh Narmer (also known as Menes). The Pre-dynastic Period is traditionally equivalent to the Neolithic period, beginning *ca* 6,000 BC and including the Proto-dynastic Period (Naqada III).

hereinafter preserved them in their temples. Linguistic and alphabet studies of the Rejang culture in southwestern Sumatera conducted by among others Sir Thomas Stamford Raffles (1817), J Park Harrison (1896), EEEG Schroder (1927) and MA Jaspen (1983) show some correlations to the ancient Phoenician and Egyptian. Indonesian has ancient knowledge of pyramid building just like the ancient Egyptian; the Gunung Padang pyramid in West Java, Indonesia dated 23,000 BC or earlier is claimed to be the earlier that those in the Egypt.

The story of Atlantis as told by the Egyptian priest is probably ever really existed but Plato had been distorting the facts in order to support his ideology of an ideal state as in *The Republic*, or he added some embellishments of his own or aspects drawn from other legends. He embodied Athens as part of the story to show the the greatest and noblest action of Ancient Athens, which was probably another state in the myth told by the Egyptian priest, created from records in their sacred registers preserved in their temples. The Egyptians were said to have preserved the most ancient records and traditions.

The existence of Atlantis is supported by the fact that it is described in great details, mainly in *Critias*. In additions, various conditions, events and goods like the two-season climate, flood (tsunami), *orichalcum*, geographical features, buffalo and produces unknown to Plato are also described in detailed and lengthy words. The recent knowledge of late glacial and postglacial sea level rise and land subsidence that occurred almost precisely at the time described by Plato also becomes strong evidence to the truth of the story.

SOLON USED EQUIVALENCY FOR NAMES

> In Plato's *Critias* Sections 113a and 113b, Critias told: *"Yet, before proceeding further in the narrative, I ought to warn you, that you must not be surprised if you should perhaps hear Hellenic names given to foreigners. I will tell you the reason of this: Solon, who was intending to use the tale for his poem, enquired into the meaning of the names, and found that the early Egyptians in writing them down had translated them into their own language, and he recovered the meaning of the several names and when copying them out again translated them into our language. My great-grandfather, Dropides, had the original writing, which is still in my possession, and was carefully studied by me when I was a child. Therefore if you hear names such as are used in this country, you must not be surprised, for I have told how they came to be introduced."*

Plato writes that the original writing about Atlantis was in early Egyptian that according to Critias, Dropides had the original writing which was in his possession. Solon, while wrote his poem, enquired into the meaning of the names and had translated them into their own language; when copying them out again translated them into Greek. Here, the names had been translated, *ie* from Egyptian into Greek. While the names were translated into each language of each ethnic group, the author presumes that they were translated from the native language of Atlantean into Egyptian then into Greek.

It can be implied from the statement that Plato's Atlantis was not located in or around the region where Critias domiciled, but being in a place that was not known. Solon translated the figures and place names based on their equivalences, so Plato's Atlantis was not in Egypt, Greece or their surrounding areas. None in the history records said that these regions were in contact with Atlantean except in the Plato's dialogues. Allegedly, characteristics of geographical features like the sea, the plain and the pillars were also translated based on their similarities.

Only the Greek names are known nowadays from the Plato's dialogues. The names were translated based on the personal natures of the figures or place names known by each ethnic group through similarities or equivalences. Biases might happen when translating them from one language into the others but the strong natures of each figure or place name were supposedly preserved. The names were most likely popular within societies that have been pass down from generations to generations, which could be revered figures, legends, myths, deities, gods, lords or sacred places.

EARTHQUAKES AND TSUNAMIS

In *Timaeus*, Plato mentioned that the island of Atlantis was beset by an earthquake and a flood, and sank into a muddy sea. Plato did not recognize "tsunami" so he equated it to "flood". The Greek historian Thucydides suggested in his late-5th century BC *History of the Peloponnesian War*, that tsunamis were related to submarine earthquakes, but the understanding of a tsunami's nature remained slim until the 20th century and much remains unknown. Also – it is speculated – the term "muddy sea" ("a shoal of mud" in *Timaeus*) was a condition of the sea after a volcano eruption.

A tsunami, also known as a seismic sea wave, is a series of water waves caused by the displacement of a large volume of a body of water, generally an ocean or a large lake. Earthquakes, volcanic eruptions and other underwater explosions, landslides, glacier calvings, meteorite impacts and other disturbances above or below water all have the potential to generate a tsunami. Tsunami waves do not resemble normal sea waves, because their wavelength is far longer. Rather than appearing as breaking waves, tsunamis may instead initially resemble rapidly rising tides, and for this reason they are often referred to as tidal waves.

BANDA ARC

The Banda Arc, a west facing horse-shoe shaped arc in eastern Indonesia situated west of Papua and in the easternmost extension of the Sunda subduction zone system, defines the locus of three converging and colliding major plates, the Indo-Australian Plate, the Pacific Plate and the Eurasian Plate, and reveals a characteristic bowl-shaped geometry in seismic tomographic images. Splinters of the Mesozoic southern Tethyan crust now form the base of the Banda Sea. On the surrounding islands, dismembered ophiolites can be found in high mountains. Recent studies in the metamorphic aureoles at the base of these ophiolites have revealed a new alternative for the explanation of the complex tectonic development of the arc, *ie* by invoking obduction as being the major mechanism in the emplacement of southern Tethyan crust onto the passive Australian continental margin.

The Banda Sea encircled by the Banda Arc occupies the main portion of the Banda Sea Plate. Frequent and significant earthquakes (see Figure 12), tsunamis (see Figure 13) and volcano eruptions (see Figure 14) took place in one of the most complex tectonic regions on Earth, in the general framework of the triple collision of continental Australia plate, oceanic Pacific plates and the southernmost tip of the Eurasian plate, called 'Sundaland'. The region is composed of a large number of geological provinces. In particular, the eastern termination of the Banda Sea features a number of strongly

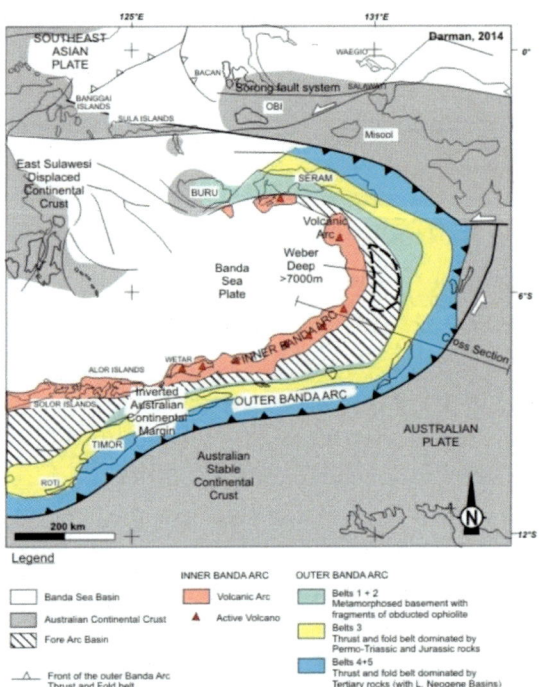

Figure 46 – Tectonic setting of the Banda Arc
(Darman, 2014; after Smet, 1999)
(*Source: Wikibooks®*)

curved, concentric tectonic provinces.

The USGS records of the largest earthquakes in the world since 1900 show that the earthquake in Banda Sea on February 1, 1938 with a magnitude of 8.5 is among them. Another at least 10 occurrences of large earthquakes in this region between 17th and 20th centuries are also known (Wichmann, 1918, 1923; Harris and Major, 2012). The NOAA records of the world's deadliest tsunamis from 1650 BC to 2010 AD cited from the National Geophysical Data Center show that 3 occurrences of deadliest tsunamis in the region are among them: in 1674, 1899 and 1992. Unfortunately, no investigation of deposits of ancient tsunamis is carried out in the region. Mount Tambora eruption in 1815 was the largest volcanic eruption in recorded history, caused global climate anomalies that included the phenomenon known as "volcanic winter": 1816 became known as the "year without a summer" because of the effect on North American and European weather. Crops failed and livestock died in much of the Northern Hemisphere, resulting in the worst famine of the 19th century.

DYNAMICS OF TSUNAMI

Tsunamis, like the ordinary wind waves, can undergo shoaling, refraction, reflection and diffraction. Most tsunami generated by large earthquakes travel in wave trains containing several large waves. In some cases, the waves in a tsunami wave train consist of an initial peak that then tapers off in height exponentially over 4 to 6 times. In other cases, the tsunami wave train consists of a maximum wave peak well back in the wave sequence.

The time it takes for a pair of wave crests to pass by a point is termed the wave period. This is a crucial parameter in defining the nature of any wave. Tsunamis typically have periods of 100 – 2,000 seconds (1.6 – 33 minutes), referred to as the *tsunami window*. Waves with this period travel at speeds of 600 – 900 km/hr (166 – 250 m/s) in the deepest part of the ocean, 100 – 300 km/hr (28 – 83 m/s) across the continental shelf, and 36 km/hr (10 m/s) at shore (Iida and Iwasaki, 1983). Because of the finite depth of the ocean and the mechanics of wave generation by earthquakes, a tsunami's wavelength – the distance between successive wave crests – lies between 10 and 500 kilometers. These long wavelengths make tsunami profoundly different from swell or storm waves.

The simplest form of ocean waves is sinusoidal in shape and oscillatory. Oscillatory waves are described for convenience by three parameters: their height (H), their wavelength (L), and their water depth (d). In deep water, the most significant factor is the ratio H/L, or wave steepness. In shallow water it is the ratio H/d, or relative height. For local tsunamis propagation in water depths greater than 50 meters, these ratios are much less than one. This implies that wave height relative to wavelength is very low – a feature characterizing tsunami in the open ocean.

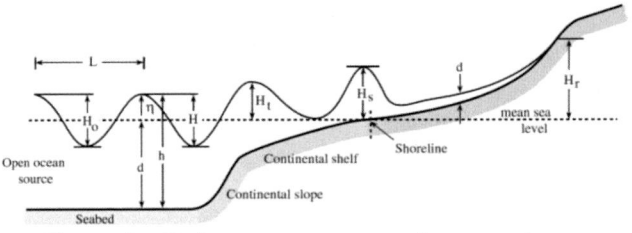

Figure 47 – Various terms to express the tsunami wave

Shallow water begins when the depth of water (d) is less than half the wavelength (L). As oceans are rarely more than 5 kilometers deep, the majority of tsunamis travel as shallow-water waves. In this case, the velocity of the wave is $C = (gd)^{0.5}$ and the wave length is $L = CT$; where g = gravitational acceleration (~9.8 m/s²) and T = wave period. The latter equation holds for linear, sinusoidal waves and is not appropriate for calculating the wavelength of a tsunami as it moves into shallow water. Linear theory can be used as a first approximation to calculate changes in tsunami wave height as the wave moves across an ocean and undergoes wave shoaling and refraction. The following formulae apply: $H_i = K_r K_s H_o$, $K_r = (b_o/b_i)^{0.5}$ and $K_s = (d_o/d_i)^{0.25}$; where K_r = refraction coefficient, K_s = shoaling coefficient, b = distance between wave orthogonals and d = water depth. Subscripts o and i denote at a source point and at any shoreward point, respectively. For a tsunami wave traveling from a distant source, the wave path or ray must also be corrected for geometrical spreading.

Tsunami are known for their dramatic run-up heights, which commonly are greater than the height of the tsunami approaching shore by a factor of 2 or more times. Tsunamis, having long periods of 100 – 2,000 seconds, can also be excited or amplified in height within harbors and bays if their period approximates some harmonic of the natural frequency of the basin – termed resonance. Here tsunami can oscillate back and forth for 24 hours or more. The oscillations are termed seiches. Seiches are independent of the forcing mechanism and are related simply to the 3-dimensional form of the bay. For a closed basin, $T_s = 2L_b(gd)^{-0.5}$ and for an open basin, $T_s = 4L_b(gd)^{-0.5}$; where L_b = length of a basin and T_s = wave period of seiching in a bay.

Say, there was an earthquake in the Flores Sea or Makassar Strait in Atlantis era causing an initial wave of 10 meter high. The sea depth was about 1,000 meters. The wave velocity was then C = $(9.8 \times 1,000)^{0.5} \approx 100$ m/s (360 km/hr). With an average Java Sea depth of 10 meters (in the era of Atlantis), assuming $K_r = (1/4)^{0.5} \approx 0.5$ and $K_s = (1,000/10)^{0.25} \approx 3.2$, by a simple calculation, the wave height was $H_i = 0.5 \times 3.2 \times 10 \approx 16$ meters in the ancient Java Sea. Approaching the shoreline with a depth of 2 meters (assuming $K_r = 1$ and $K_s = (10/2)^{0.25} \approx 1.5$), the wave height was $H_i = 1 \times 1.5 \times 16 \approx 24$ meters and the run-up could be twice. It was really a destructive wave and penetrated inland on a very flat plain. In fact, the recorded run-up of 1674 AD Banda Sea tsunami was much larger, 80 – 100 meters high on Ambon Island. Thus, we could speculate that the destruction of Atlantis was among others caused by a tsunami. It was due to the tsunami waves traveling in shallow water (ancient Java Sea) and penetrated inland on a very flat plain. The Meltwater Pulse 1A was probably also contributed the occurrence of earthquakes and tsunamis due to speedy increase of water burden on the Banda Sea Plate.

In Atlantis era, the Java Sea was forming a gulf with a rather narrow entrance and due to the many islands in it resonances and seiches might also occur, causing the wave became much higher and prolonged, and then aggravated its destructive nature.

PILLARS OF HERACLES

The Pillars of Heracles is the name given by Plato to describe the boundary marker of the Atlantis. According to his text, Atlantis lay just beyond this boundary. For centuries, the location of the Pillars of Heracles is debated by many. The Pillars are assumed by some to refer to the Rock of Gibraltar in Europe and to Mount Acha near Ceuta or Jebel Musain, which are west of Ceuta in Morocco. Others prefer to accept them as a physical pair of pillars set up outside a temple.

Classical writers frequently refer to the pillars without being in anyway specific regarding their location. The online encyclopedia Wikipedia notes that Pillars were, in earlier times, identified with the Strait of Sicily, but from the time of Erastosthenes (*ca* 250 BC) the term was used to refer to the Strait of Gibraltar, reflecting the expansion of the Greek maritime knowledge. However, the poet Pindar in the *Third Nemean Ode* would appear to have treated the pillars as a metaphor for the limit of established Greek geographical knowledge, a boundary that was never static.

In *Timaeus*, the Egyptian priest told Solon about the territorial boundary between Atlantis and its opponent as *"which are by you called the Pillars of Heracles"* to describe a state entrance or boundary markers which were situated in a strait. The words "by you" could mean that the markers were commonly known by the Athenian as "The Pillars of Heracles" but not necessarily the pillars as what the Athenian referred to. Plato does not call them 'pillars' but refers to them as *stélas* (στήλας, plural) and *stéle* (στήλη, singular) which is the Greek word for an upright stone slab or a pillar bearing an inscription or design and serving as a monument, marker, or the like. The author hypothesizes that the pillars are monuments built at places on state entrances or boundary line and could be anywhere at certain places along the boundary. The monument is locally known as "tugu", which has been the tradition in Indonesia until now to mark the boundary or entrances of a region, such as a village or a tribal area. Wars between peoples of the adjacent regions were quiet often in the past; the incidents were frequently at the boundaries.

The author makes a conjecture equating Heracles (Greek *Hēraklēs*, Ἡραχλῆς) to Kala or Batara Kala (Javanese ꦧꦛꦫꦑꦭ), a god of the underworld in ancient Javanese and Balinese mythology[*]. Kala is also named the creator of light and the earth, as well as the god of destruction who devours unlucky people. In mythology, he causes eclipses by trying to eat the Sun or the Moon.

According to the Javanese legend, Kala is the son of Batara Guru[†]. Batara Guru has a very beautiful wife named Dewi Uma. One day Batara Guru, in a fit of uncontrolled lust, forced himself on Dewi Uma. They had sexual intercourse on top of his Lembu Andini, a divine cow. This behavior was ashamed Dewi Uma who then cursed Batara Guru but Batara Guru cursed back Dewi Uma so she appeared as a fearsome and ugly ogre. This fierce form of Dewi Uma is also known in Javanese mythology as Batari Durga. From this relationship, Kala was born with the appearance of an ogre. Batara Guru then married off his consort Dewi Uma, after being cursed becoming Batari Durga, with their own son Batara Kala.

---

[*] Kala was later adopted in dharmic concept of *kala* meaning "time" or "black". It often used as one of the various names or forms of Yama in Indian Dharmism, while he is the son of Siwa (Shiva) in Javanese Dharmism.
[†] Batara Guru (also called Bathara Guru, Hyang Guru or Debata Guru) is the name of a supreme god in several Nusantara (archipelago) native mythologies. He was considered as a super god in the native beliefs of Austronesian people that inhabit the Nusantara. Batara Guru was then identified as Shiva after the adoption of Dharmism.

Batara Kala is described as having an insatiable appetite and being very rude. He was sent by the *dewa* to Earth to punish humans for their evil habits. However, Batara Kala was interested only in devouring humans to satisfy his appetite. Alarmed, the *dewa* then recalled Batara Kala from the Earth. He later became ruler of the underworld.

In comparison with the Greek mythology, Heracles (Romanized as Hercules) is the son of the affair Zeus had with the mortal woman Alcmene. Zeus seduced and made love to Alcmene after disguising himself as her husband, Amphitryon, king of Thebes. Zeus swore that the next son born of the Perseid house should become ruler of Greece, but by a trick of Zeus's jealous wife, Hera, another child, the sickly Eurystheus, was born first and became king. When Heracles grew up, he had to serve him and also suffer the vengeful persecution of Hera. Besides these Hera induced frenzies, Heracles was a very brutal character.

In spite of those, Heracles is a divine hero in Greek mythology. He is the greatest of the Greek heroes, a paragon of strength and masculinity, the ancestor of royal clans who claimed to be Heracleidae and a champion of the Olympian order against chthonic (underworld) monsters.

The similarity of Kala and Heracles is that each of them is a child of a supreme god, either Batara Guru or Zeus. Their births were outrageous; Kala was born from an uncontrolled lust of Batara Guru on Dewi Uma while Heracles was from a seduction of Zeus on Alcmene. They are having insatiable appetites and being very rude, brutal, and violent in their whole lives.

Traditionally, Javanese people try to obtain the Kala favor to prevent misfortune, especially to children. Exorcism ceremonies, called *ruwatan*, are held for children born under "unlucky" circumstances, such as being born feet-first. This is to prevent such children from being devoured by Batara Kala. This ceremony usually includes a *wayang* (Javanese shadow-puppets) performance and a *selamatan* feast.

Batara Kala is a god in the traditional Balinese mythology. He mastered the underworld along with the goddess Setesuyara. He was also named as the creator of the earth and light.

From the ancient until present day, gargoyle-like faces of Kala are often found at temple entrances, boundary pillars, welcome monuments, gates, doorway, niches, furniture, wall hangings and traditional musical instruments; ubiquitous

143

in Java and Bali. Similar figures are also found at Dayak houses. Mythologically, Kala face represents the threshold between everyday and divine worlds or as an evil spirits repellent. In common, it becomes architectural style of buildings and artistical ornaments.

Figure 48 – Various forms of Kala face

We could speculate that the state entrances or boundary of Atlantis were marked by some monuments decorated with Kala faces or alike as traditionally exist today. In Atlantis time, sea transportation afforded greater mobility than travel over land to reach one place from another and to cross the border; and certainly markers are installed at the boundary line such as at a strait. These markers were told by the Egyptian priest to Solon those were something like the "Pillars of Heracles" which was known to the Athenians. Tanahlot and Uluwatu

144

temples in Bali known as have been built from the Megalithic Age (the present temples are dharmic), and Balekambang temple in East Java are examples of those marine markers.

Figure 49 – Bajangratu gate, a relict of Majapahit Empire built in the 14th century is a typical monument decorated with Kala faces. Similar monuments are ubiquitous in Java and Bali, allegedly what the Egyptian priest told to Solon those were called the "Pillars of Heracles" by the Athenians.

Figure 50 – Tanahlot (left), Uluwatu (middle) and Balekambang (right) temples with Kala faces

TRACES OF ATLANTIS

HYANG CONCEPT

Hyang or personified as Sang Hyang (Kawi, Javanese, Sundanese and Balinese) is an unseen spiritual entity that has supernatural power in ancient Nusantara mythology. This spirit can be either divine or ancestral. In modern Nusantara this term tends to be associated with gods, *dewata* or God, widely associated with Indonesian Dharmism developed in ancient Java and Bali for more than a millennium ago. However this term actually has an older origin, it has its root in indigenous animism and dynamism beliefs of Austronesian people that inhabit the Nusantara archipelago. The Hyang concept is indigenously developed in archipelago and considered not originated from Indian dharmic religions.

Before the adoption of Dharmism, Buddhism and Islam, the natives of Nusantara archipelago believe in the powerful but unseen spiritual entity that can be either benevolent or malevolent. They also believe that the deceased ancestors are not gone away or disappear completely. The ancestral spirit may gain god-like spiritual power and still involved in their offspring's worldly affairs. That is why the veneration and reverence to honor ancestor is an important element in the belief system of native ethnic groups, such as Nias, Dayak, Batak, Toraja, Papuan, as well as many other ethnic groups in Nusantara.

The etymology of Hyang is alive in modern affairs. *Sanghyang* and *rahyang* refer to gods. *Dahyang, danyang* or *dayang* refers to the guardian spirits of certain sacred or haunted places. The Javanese word *tiyang* means "person" is believed to be derived from the words *ti* and *hyang* means the descendant of Hyang. *Parahyangan* or *priangan* means the abode of the noble Hyangs. *Mojang Priangan* refers to a girl from Priangan. Dieng Plateau in Central Java is composed from combined words of *di-hyang* means Hyang's place in a height. Gunung Padang in West Java is from *pada-hyang* means the sacred place of Hyangs. The word *sembahyang*, a synonym with Islamic *shalat* ritual is originated from combined words *sembah-hyang* means worship the Hyang. Some Javanese people believe that the word *wayang*, an antiquity theater, was derived from the words *ma* and *hyang* means towards the Hyang. Some figures of gods and deities in the *wayang* story have their noble titles beginning with Sang Hyang. The term Negeri Kahyangan means the Land of Hyangs or the heaven land. Sangeang Api (or Sanghyang Api), an active volcano complex in Nusatenggara Islands, was found in 14th century Majapahit script of *Nagarakretagama*.

Kahyangan (from *ka-hyang-an*, a place for the Hyangs), in another term is *swarga* or *surga* means heaven, is somewhere in the realm that is trusted by the adherents of some beliefs as the abode of the Hyangs. The term Kahyangan is popular in Java, Bali and Lombok in their doctrines of

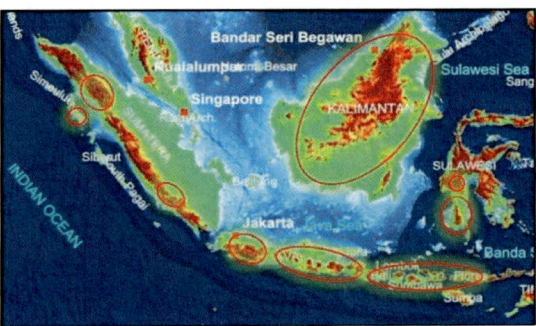

Figure 51 – Spreads of Hyang concept

Kejawen, Sunda Wiwitan and Balinese Dharmism as well as in their antiquity story of the *wayang*. Kahyangan is similar to Banua Ginjang in the Batak and Kaharingan in the Dayak mythologies.

JAVA

In central and eastern Javanese mythology, Hyang is an unseen spiritual entity that has supernatural power associated with gods. Batara Guru (Javanese ꦲꦸꦠꦫꦒꦸꦫꦸ) is a Hyang that rules Kahyangan (from *ka-hyang-an*, the realm of the Hyangs). He gives revelations, gifts and abilities. Batara Guru has a consort named Dewi Uma and begat some children. In *wayang kulit* (the antiquity shadow-puppet), Batara Guru is the only character whose feet face forward, with four hands, pointed canine teeth, a blue neck and paralyzed legs. He always rides Lembu Andini the divine cow, and is also known by several names including Sang Hyang Manikmaya, Sang Hyang Caturbuja, Sang Hyang Otipati, Sang Hyang Jagadnata, Sang Hyang Nilakanta, Sang Hyang Trinetra and Sang Hyang Girinata. Batara Guru has two brothers, Sang Hyang Maha Punggung and Sang Hyang Ismaya. Their parents are Sang Hyang Tunggal and Dewi Rekatawati. Batara Guru is the father of Dewi Sri, the Rice Goddess in native Javanese mythology.

Figure 52 – Batara Guru

SUNDA

For the Sunda Wiwitan beliefs of the Sundanese (western Java), a supreme god named Sang Hyang Kersa created the universe and also other gods such as mother goddess Batari Sunan Ambu and Batara Guru. Batara Guru rules the Kahyangan or *swargaloka* as the king of gods, while Sang Hyang Kersa remains unseen. According to Sundanese legends, the Parahyangan (from *pa-ra-hyang-an*, the place for the noble Hyangs) highland, also known as Priangan, was magically created when the Hyangs (gods) are happy and smiling. To fill the land, Sang Hyang Kersa created animals and demons, while the myth of Sang Hyang Sri (also known as Nyai Pohaci Sanghyang Asri) explains the origin of rice and plants on earth as told in *Wawacan Sulanjana*, an ancient Sundanese manuscript contains the Sundanese mythology. According to the Sundanese legend, the Priangan Plateau was primordially a lake called Danau Hyang ("Hyang Lake").

BALI

In Balinese Dharmism perspective, the supreme god is known as Sang Hyang Widhi Wasa (also known as Acintya or Sang Hyang Tunggal), which means the Almighty God. Sang Hyang Widhi Wasa is associated with the concept of Brahman, that their religion had a single god, though there are various manifestations. Three well known manifestations of Sang Hyang Widhi Wasa, namely Brahma, Wisnu and Siwa, which are named as Tri Murti; Brahma is the creator (*utpatti*), Wisnu is the caretaker (*sthiti*) and Siwa is the destroyer (*praline*). Other noted manifestation is Dewi Sri, the goddess of rice.

Figure 53 – Sanggah Pamerajan, a set of shrines in Balinese culture

Balinese Dharmism adherers believe that all the creations of Sang Hyang Widhi Wasa will face the cycle of birth, life and death. The essence of power of Sang Hyang Widhi Wasa is expressed in a set of shrines called Sanggah Pemerajan at outside of every dharmic house. The empty seat (*palinggih*) at the top of the Padmasana, the main seat, is for Sang Hyang Widhi Wasa.

DAYAK

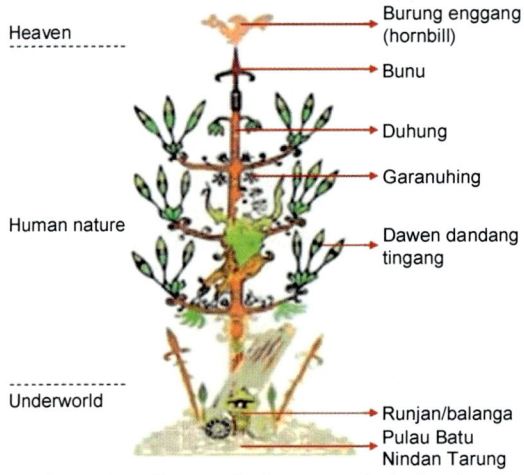

Figure 54 – Batang Garing, a symbol of universe

In Kaharingan, a folk religion professed by many Dayaks in Kalimantan, their supreme God is called Ranying Hatalla Langit, their ancestral spirits (divine man) Sangiang, their ancient language Sangen and their ancestors Tato-hiang. In addition, Kaharingan has ritual offerings called Tiwah, place of worship called Balai Basarah or Balai Kaharingan and holy books called Panaturan, Talatah Basarah (group of prayers) and Tawar (a guide to seek God's help by giving rice). The main festival of Kaharingan is the Tiwah festival, which lasts for thirty days, and involves the sacrifice of many animals like buffalos, cows, pigs, and chickens as offerings to the Supreme God.

In their religion, the universe is divided into three divisions of life: underworld, human nature and heaven, as symbolized in a tree called Batang Garing.

Among the many tribes of Dayaks in Kalimantan, those living in the upper reaches of the rivers in the province of Central Kalimantan are the Dayak Ngaju, the Lawangan, the Ma'anyan and the Ot Danum, known as the Barito Dayaks, named after the large Barito river. Among these, the most dominant are the Ngaju, who inhabit the Kahayan river basin by the present city of

Palangkaraya. In practice the Ngaju focus on the supernatural world of spirits, including ancestral spirits.

The Kaharingan religion is correlated to the Hyang concept. The names Ranying, Sangiang, Sangen, Tato-hiang and Kahayan are phonetically in close resemblance to and derived from the words "hyang", "ra-hyang", "sang-hyang" and "ka-hyang-an".

BUGIS

The Buginese (southern Sulawesi) developed an extraordinary creation myth called Galigo (Buginese ᨕᨘᨁᨗ). According to *Sure' Galigo* (an epic of creation myth of the Bugis), Datu Patoto' is the supreme god; with his wife Datu Palinge' begat Batara Guru who was sent to earth to cultivate it as human being. His divine name was La Toge' Langi'. He had at least ten children from his five concubines, but only one son from his beloved consort, We Nyili' Timo'. He is the father of Batara Lattu' and grand father of Sawerigading, the main characters in the Buginese *Sure' Galigo*. He is also the father of Sangiang Serri, the goddess of rice and fertility in Buginese mythology. However, mankind does not descend from them but from their servants and the servants of other divine rulers.

The present of Batara Guru and Sangiang Serri in the Buginese mythology at least shows its correlation to the Hyang concept.

TORAJA

In the Torajan (central Sulawesi) mythology, their ancestors came down from heaven using stairs, which were then used by the Torajans as a communication medium with Puang Matua, the creator and supreme god. The cosmos, according to *aluk* (the way), is divided into the upper world (heaven), the world of man (earth), and the underworld. At first, heaven and earth were married, and then there was darkness, a separation, and finally the light. Animals live in the underworld, which is represented by rectangular space enclosed by pillars, the earth is for mankind, and the heaven world is located above, covered with a saddle-shaped roof. Other Torajan gods include Pong Banggai di Rante (god of Earth), Indo' Ongon-Ongon (a goddess who can cause earthquakes), Pong Lalondong (god of death), and Indo' Belo Tumbang (goddess of medicine); and there are many more.

BATAK

In Batak (northern Sumatera) mythology, the universe is divided into three worlds, namely the upper world called Banua Ginjang, the middle world called

Banua Tonga and the underworld called Banua Toru. The middle world, where humans live, is also an intermediary between the upper world and the underworld. The upper world is the abode of the gods, while the underworld is the abode of demons and spirits of the earth and fertility. Colors commonly used by the Batak people for household appliances, Hauduk, Ulos cloth and wood carvings are white, red and black are symbols of the three-world.

The creator of the world in the Batak mythology is Mulajadi na Bolon, assisted by a series of other deities which are divided into seven levels in the upper world. Mulajadi na Bolon has three children namely Debata Guru, Debata Soripada and Debata Mangala Bulan; they are known as Debata Sitolu Sada (three gods in one) or Debata na Tolu (three gods). The three gods are under the control of the supreme god Mulajadi na Bolon. It was told that Mulajadi na Bolon sent his daughter Tapionda to earth at the foot of Pusuk Buhit mountain. Tapionda later became the mother of the first king of Batak.

Other noted gods are Debata Idup (the god of life) and Pane na Bolon who rules the middle world. Many other gods are associated with the dharmic gods; among others are Boraspati ni Nato and Boru Saniang Naga. In addition, there are spirits that abode lakes, rivers and mountains.

The term *debata* is identical to *dewata* or *hyang* and there is single supreme god so that the Batak mythology is correlated to the Hyang concept. The present of Debata Guru in the Batak mythology at least shows its correlation to the concept.

REJANG

Rejangese is one of the oldest ethnic groups in Sumatera living mainly on the southwest coast of the island, on the cool-weather slopes of the Barisan mountain range, in the province of Bengkulu, Indonesia. Most of the Rejangese inhabit the regions of Rejang Lebong, Kepahiang, Central Bengkulu, North Bengkulu and Lebong Regencies. Megalithic sites are ubiquitous in this area influenced by the Basemah culture in southwestern Sumatera.

The Rejangese called them Hejang (Rejangese ᨆᨿ). Rejangese language is not obviously close to other Malayo-Polynesian languages. Rejangese have their script, known as the Rejang Kaganga alphabet, somewhat similar to Phoenician alphabet. There is no connection to the Dayak Rejang inhabiting eastern and northern Kalimantan.

In their culture, rituals are performed on the occasion of the opening of forest land for slash-and-burn farming (a ritual called *kedurai agung*) and during the rest of the cycle of rice cultivation. The most important ritual, *kedurai mundang biniak*, is performed just before the sowing of rice. On this occasion the rice goddess, Nyang Serai, leave the rice and the village and goes to heaven in order to take care of the rainfall. The festivities include a dance performed every evening by seven boys and seven girls from different clans as an expression of clan exogamy. *Mundang biniak* is held over seven days, and use to be performed only once every three to seven years. In other years seed is blessed by a smaller ritual, *membasuh biniak*. The ritual cycle ends at the harvest, when Nyang Serai returns to the village and ensures that the rice spirit will not leave the rice being stored in the barns.

The Rejang culture is correlated to the Hyang concept that in the rituals they worship the rice goddess, Nyang Serai, identical to Sanghyang Sri, Sangiang Serri and Dewi Sri in other cultures. Some people believe that Rejang is derived from the words *ra* and *hyang*, meaning the noble Hyang. A region named Kepahiang as well as Hiang (in the neighboring Kerinci region) having the same pre-historic age also can be correlated.

NIAS

Nias is an island off the western coast of Sumatera. In their mythology, the universe is made of three superposed worlds. The upper world, Tetehöli Ana'a, is the model, the place of origin of the gods, in the sky, in the clouds and long ago near the earth. That world has several villages with different people who are often opposed to each other. Lowalangi is the god of this upper world. Silewe Nazarata, his sister and/or wife, gave knowledge to humans: she taught them how to cultivate fields, build houses and carve statues. The underworld is dark, sometimes identified with a cave or a large hole peopled with evil spirits. From it come earthquakes. It is the home of Lature Danö, the elder brother of Lowalangi. The middle world, or world of humans, was created by the gods or in certain versions by one of them by means of their skin scales.

RICE CULTIVATION

In the book *Eden in the East* (1998), Stephen Oppenheimer claims that the domestication of rice was not in China but in the Malay Peninsula, *ca* 9,000 years ago. Here grains of rice were found from the eras between 7,000 and 5,000 BC on the Malay Peninsula. This time period is several years older than the arrival of the Austronesian people from Taiwan who were thought to have brought farming technologies to Southeast Asia.

Evidence of wild rice on the island of Sulawesi dates back from *ca* 3,000 BC. In the Philippines, the evidence of rice cultivation can be found in the 2,000 to 3,000-year old Banaue rice terraces that were carved into the mountains by ancestors of the Batad indigenous people. Evidence for the earliest cultivation, however, comes from eighth-century stone inscriptions from the central island of Java, which show kings levied taxes in rice. The images of rice cultivation, rice barn, and mouse pest investing a rice field are evident in Karmawibhangga bas-reliefs of Borobudur. Divisions of labor between men, women, and animals that are still in place in Indonesian rice cultivation, were carved into relief

Figure 55 – Bas-relief of Borobudur Temple showing rice field ploughing

friezes on the ninth-century Prambanan temples in Central Java: a water buffalo attached to a plough; women planting seedlings and pounding grain; and a man carrying sheaves of rice on each end of a pole across his shoulders (*pikulan*). In the sixteenth century, Europeans visiting the Indonesian islands saw rice as a new prestige food served to the aristocracy during ceremonies and feasts.

Rice production in Southeast Asia history is linked to the development of iron tools and the domestication of wild Asian water buffalo for cultivation of fields and manure for fertilizer. Rice production requires exposure to the sun. Once covered in dense forest, much of the landscape had been gradually cleared for permanent fields and settlements as rice cultivation developed over the last 1,500 years.

Rice is a staple for all classes in contemporary Indonesia, and it holds the central place in Indonesian culture and Indonesian cuisine: it shapes the landscape; is sold at markets; and is served in most meals both as a savory and a sweet food. Dewi Sri (Javanese and Balinese), Sang Hyang Sri (Sundanese), Sangiang Serri (Buginese) and Nyang Serai (Rejangese) are the Nusantara pre-dharmic era goddess of rice and fertility, still widely worshipped on the islands. Despite her mythology is native to the Nusantara, after the adoption of Dharmism as early as first century, the goddess is associated with the dharmic goddess Lakshmi as both are attributed to wealth and family prosperity.

152

Initially the economy of Java relied heavily on rice agriculture. Ancient kingdoms such as the Tarumanagara, Medang, Sunda, Galih, Mataram and Majapahit were dependent on rice yields and tax. Java was famous for rice surpluses and rice export since ancient times, and rice agriculture contributed to the population growth of the island. Agriculture, especially traditional rice cultivation, has become the main way of life of traditional Javanese and Sundanese people. Note that *java* means "rice" in Sanskrit.

In Bali, Subak is the name of irrigation system for rice fields which was developed more than 1,000 years ago. For Balinese, irrigation is not simply providing water for the plant's roots, but water is used to construct a complex, pulsed artificial ecosystem. Rice fields in Bali were built around water temples. The water managements is under the authority of the priests in water temples, who practice Tri Hita Karana philosophy comprises five sets of rice terraces and associated water temples, a self-described relationship among humans, the earth and the gods. Subak is a traditional ecologically sustainable irrigation system that binds Balinese agrarian society together within the village's Bale Banjar community center and Balinese temples. In June 2012, Subak was enlisted as a UNESCO world heritage site.

Rice has been cultivated for many millennia in South Sulawesi. Once the center of maritime commerce on the Southeast Asian seas, and still the home of a robust ship-building industry, South Sulawesi has long exported rice grown in the fields inland from the port of Makassar. Rice cultivation dominates the province's agriculture.

Southern Kalimantan has been known for their specific "anjir system" for irrigation of rice field where primary canals called "anjir" or "antasan" were constructed connecting two tidal rivers, also used as navigation purpose. Inland canals were built to irrigate and drain the fields from and to the *anjir*: secondary canals called "handil" or "tatah" and tertiary canals called "saka". During low tides, the canals drain the toxic water while during high tides fresh water enters the canals and conveyed to the fields. The system yields two rice crops in a year. This system is also used to cultivate other crops or fish. Southern Kalimantan is today an exporter of rice to other regions.

TEMPLE AND PYRAMID BUILDING

A temple is a structure reserved for religious or spiritual activities, such as prayer and sacrifice, or analogous rites. Ancient temples in Nusantara have mortuary function as well as attributed with the afterlife. Temples of ancient Java also used to store the ashes of cremated deceased kings or royalties.

A pyramid is a structure whose outer surfaces are triangular and converge to a single point at the top, making the shape roughly a pyramid in the geometric sense. A step pyramid is an architectural structure that uses flat platforms, or steps, receding from the ground up, to achieve a completed shape similar to a geometric pyramid. Step pyramids are structures which characterized several cultures throughout history, in several locations throughout the world. These pyramids are typically large and made of several layers of stone. The term refers to pyramids of similar design that emerged separately from one another, as there are no firmly established connections between the different civilizations that built them.

As well as menhirs, stone tables, and stone statues, Austronesian megalithic culture in Nusantara also featured earth and stone step pyramid structure, referred to as *punden berundak*, regarded as one of the characteristics of the original culture of the archipelago. These structures have been found and spread throughout Nusantara as far as Polynesia, although in the latter are not always in the form of steps, as in structures known as *marae* in the Maori culture. Among them are found in Hyang-Argapura Mountains, Lebak Sibedug, Basemah, Pangguyangan, Cisolok and Gunung Padang; the latter of which is the biggest and the oldest Megalithic Site in Southeast Asia dated *ca* 23,000 BC or older (Natawidjaja, 2013). The Sukuh and Cetho temples in Central Java (dates are debated) show the Austronesian indigenous elements of step pyramid that somewhat resemble Mesoamerican pyramids. The construction of stone pyramids was based on the native belief that mountains and other high places are the abode of the spirits of the ancestors, or Hyangs.

As said in Plato's *Critias*, the temple to Poseidon and Cleito was built in the center island which was a hill, encircled by rings of waters. To reach the temple from the innermost ring of water, steps on the hill slope were definitely required. This could mean that the temple is featuring an earth-and-stone step pyramid structure, characterizes the original culture of Nusantara that is referred to as *punden berundak*.

The step pyramid is the basic design of the 8th or 9th century Borobudur buddhist temple in Central Java. The later temples built in Java were influenced by Indian dharmic architecture, as displayed by the towering spires of Prambanan temple.

Most of Southeast Asia's great temples were built by the 13th century. The royal temple, which dominated Southeast Asian culture, typically stood on a terraced plinth, upon which towered shrines could multiply. Construction was ideally of stone but could be brick sculpted with stucco. Exteriors displayed carved rhythmic moldings and figures.

In about 770 AD the Javanese Selendra dynasty began its series of superb stone cut monuments, culminating in the huge mahayana buddhist Borobudur and the dharmic Prambanan (*ca* 900 – 930 AD). In about 800 AD the Cambodian king Jayavarman II built a brick mountain for a temple group. This plan was furthered when foundations were laid for Angkor, a scheme based on a grid of reservoirs and canals. Successive kings built more temple mountains there, culminating in Angkor Wat.

Among Southeast Asia's most impressive sites is the city of Pagan in Myanmar, with many brick and stucco buddhist temples and stupas built in 1056 – 1287 AD. Burmese stupas (*eg* Shwe Dagon Pagoda) typically have a spreading, bell-shaped base topped by a dome and pointed spire. The many monasteries of Myanmar and Thailand, like those of Laos and Vietnam, have been repeatedly enlarged and rebuilt. The architecture of the dharmism in Bali is vigorously fantastical, with gilt paint and colored glass.

BOAT AND SHIP BUILDING

In the Ice Age, landbridges between islands and continents were created (see Figure 7). The western islands on the Sunda Shelf – Sumatera, Java, Bali and Kalimantan – were joined to each other and to the Asian mainland. The eastern islands – Sulawesi, Lombok, Flores, Timor, Maluku and the Philippines – have never been linked by landbridges to either the Sunda Shelf or Australia, or to each other.

The *Homo erectus* originated from Africa spread out to mainland Southeast Asia as far as Bali by tracking the landbridges. Earliest *Homo erectus* in Indonesia was first on Java and has been dated to 1.51 – 1.02 million years BP. However, stone tools dated to around 840,000 years BP have been found on the island of Flores, midway between Java and Australia. This suggests that this ancient human might have been able to cross a series of water gaps in the Nusatenggara chain of islands in order to land on the island of Flores. In 2004, a most remarkable discovery of a new human-like species, *Homo floresiensis*, was reported from Flores. Some bones were found together with stone tools, the bones of the Komodo dragon and an extinct dwarf elephant known as *stegodon*. This new humanoid was present on the island until at least 18,000 years ago.

Migration beyond Bali to Flores required sea crossings and could not have occurred by accident so that *Homo erectus* could have the ability to build seaworthy craft some 600,000 years before the first *Homo sapiens* appeared on earth. How they crossed is unclear, as no boat remain have been found. Tools suitable for hollowing out logs were not yet invented, but giant *bambu*, ideal for rafts, grows in the region and people at this time had good cutting tools to build the rafts.

The earliest known evidences of maritime activities in Austronesia are found as cave paintings in the islands of Muna (Southeast Sulawesi), Seram (Maluku) and Arguni (Papua) dated back some 10,000 years BC, those are fully decorated by sailboat paintings. Similarities of prehistorical remains found in Java and Australian Aborigines show that ancient maritime activities had been made between them. Long distance sailing technology in the region must have appeared much earlier, with the peopling of Australia through Southeast Asia some 40,000 years ago (Green, 2006). *Jukung*, a type of boat used by the people of southern Kalimantan is found similarly in Madagascar, as well as their languages are closely similar.

Archaeologists have revealed ample evidence of the active maritime networks in the Southeast Asia region that existed from at least 5,000 years ago, at the beginning of the Austronesian migration that spread throughout all of insular Southeast Asia and most of the Pacific (Bellwood, 1985, 1991, 1995; Bellwood and Dizon, 2005; Horridge, 1995; Reid, 1988; Ronquillo, 1998; Scott, 1994; Solheim, 1988, 2006). As pointed out by linguists, archaeologists, and anthropologists, shared cultural traits such as language, agriculture, animal husbandry and pottery-making are evidence of the Austronesian maritime connection. Likewise a boatbuilding tradition emerged out of Southeast Asian islands but scarcely addressed in archaeology and history subjects.

The oldest remain of Southeast Asian boat in the archaeological record was discovered in Pontian in the Malay Peninsula carbon dated to 260 – 430 AD. Remains of sewn-plank boats were found in Payapasir, North Sumatera dated to 12th – 14th century AD, Sambirejo in South Sumatera carbon dated to 610 – 775 AD, Kolam Pinisi in South Sumatera carbon dated to 434 – 631 AD and Punjulharjo in Central Java carbon dated to 660 – 780 AD. Boat remains in the Philippines were found in Butuan, southern Philippines carbon dated to 320,

1250 and 1215 AD (Peralta, 1976 in Lacsina, undated) and in Gujangan Island dated to 15th to 16th century AD (Cuevas *et al*, undated in Lacsina, undated).

Similarities between boat-building technology in the Austronesian and in the Indian Ocean about 5,000 years ago were observed. Wooden boards added on the canoe hulls and sewn-plank boats spread across the archipelago were also observed on the boats in Egypt, Mesopotamia and the Indus River Valley. However, Horridge (2006) claimed that it is not appropriate to correlate them seeing that the Austronesian linguistic speakers spread over the archipelago long before they were influenced by boat-building technology in the Indian Ocean or even Egypt. He shows that the Austronesian boats were developed using a triangular-shaped sail since about 200 BC demonstrated by the spread of bronze kettle which is one of the artifacts of the Dong Son culture, but this sail type was developed in the Indian Ocean more recently about 200 AD and was adopted by the Portuguese sailors a thousand years later.

Austronesian boats on its development have unique characteristics with a triangular sail and single outrigger. The outrigger is made of *bambu* trunks with transverse connectors at the top of the hull, while the triangular sail is formed using *bambu* sticks supported by a slanting mast (Horridge, 2006).

Cloves and cinnamon were allegedly trade commodities brought by Austronesian linguistic speaker sailors towards India and Sri Lanka, and perhaps also towards the east coast of Africa by outrigged boats. They left trails of influences such as boat design, boat building techniques, outriggers, fishing techniques and so on as evidenced in the Greek literatures (Christie, 1957 in Horridge, 2006). Hornel (1928 in Horridge, 2006) supported this argument that the boat shape in Bantu tribe in Victoria Nyanza, Uganda in East Africa is similar to those in Indonesia.

BOROBUDUR SHIP

A Borobudur ship is the 8th-century wooden double outrigger, sailed vessel of Nusantara archipelago depicted in some bas reliefs of the Borobudur Buddhist temple in Central Java, Indonesia. This has been designated as a World Heritage Site by UNESCO. The ships depicted on Borobudur were most likely the type of vessels used for inter-insular trades and naval campaigns by the Selendran and Sriwijayan thalassocracy empires that ruled the region around the 7th to the 13th century. The function of the outrigger was to stabilize the ship; a single or double outrigger canoe is the typical feature of the seafaring Austronesian vessels. It is considered by scholars to have been the most likely type of vessel used for their voyages and exploration across Southeast Asia, Oceania and the Indian Ocean.

In the late 20th century, Philip Beale, a British sailor, became interested in depictions of the ship at Borobudur and decided to reconstruct one. Aided by government and international bodies, he organized an expedition team that constructed

Figure 56 – The image of a ship on Borobudur temple bas relief

the ship and, from 2003 to 2004, sailed it from Indonesia to Madagascar and to Ghana, proving that long-distance trade had occurred. The Samudraraksa Museum was constructed at Borobudur Archeological Park to house the ship, opening in 2005, and provides other displays to interpret the ancient maritime history of Indonesia.

PINISI

Pinisi (variously spelled *phinisi, pinissi* or *pinisi'*) is a masterpiece traditional two-masted sailing ship. It was mainly built by the Konjo tribe, a sub-ethnic group of Bugis-Makassar mostly residents at the Bulukumba regency of South Sulawesi but was, and still is used widely by the Buginese and Makassarese, mostly for inter-insular transportation, cargo and fishing purposes within Indonesian archipelago. Traditional Buginese *lontara* manuscripts and stories document the use of *pinisi* by Buginese for transport, as a sailing boat, and a warship.

Figure 57 – Drawing of a *pinisi* of *lamba* type by Xavier Romero-Frias.
(*Source: Wikipedia*®)

In its original form, the *pinisi* is a double ended hull type, having sharply raked stem and stern post. There was not a centerline rudder, instead most often made use of twin rudders, one on each aft quarter. The large mainsails are reefed towards the mast, much like a curtain, thus allowing the gaff to be used as deck crane in the harbor. The lower part of the mast itself may resemble a tripod or is made of two poles. *Pinisi* may be

20 to 35 meters long and 350 tons in size. The masts may reach to 30 meters above the deck.

There are two general types of *pinisi*: *lamba* or *lambo* – a long and slender built, having a straight stern, is the one currently surviving in its motorized version; and *palari* – older type with a curved stern and keel, usually smaller than the *lamba*.

Pinisi has proved to sail from Muarabaru, South Sulawesi to Vancouver, Canada through Pacific Ocean, a distance of about 11,000 kilometers, in the 1986 Nusantara Pinisi Expedition to participate the Vancouver Expo.

PADEWAKANG

Padewakang (variously spelled *paduwakang* or *paduakan*) is a traditional sailing ship widely employed for far-distance fishing and trade in South Sulawesi until the early 20th century. *Padewakang* were the biggest craft of the trading and war fleets of the famed South Sulawesian kingdoms, used by Mandar, Makassar and Bugis traders and warriors for hundreds of years in their plying the seas between western Papua, the southern parts of the Philippines, and the Malay Peninsula. Between the end of the 16th to the early 20th centuries they routinely sailed for the coasts of northern Australia in search of *tripang* (sea cucumber).

Padewakang is the most remarkable boats equipped with Indonesian traditional rectangular sails called *tanjak* or *tanja'*. Sources since the earliest times of Chinese, Arabian and European describe *tanjak* as the typical sail of what they called the "Islands below the Wind".

From the beginning of the 20th century, *padewakang* was gradually replaced by the *pinisi*.

WATER BUFFALO SACRIFICE

In Plato's *Critias* Sections 119d to 120a: "*There were bulls who had the range of the temple of Poseidon; and the ten kings, being left alone in the temple, after they had offered prayers to the god that they might capture the victim which was acceptable to him, hunted the bulls, without weapons but with staves and nooses; and the bull which they caught they led up to the pillar and cut its throat over the top of it so that the blood fell upon the sacred inscription. Now on the pillar, besides the laws, there was inscribed an oath invoking mighty curses on the disobedient. When therefore, after slaying the bull in the accustomed manner, they had burnt its limbs, they filled a bowl of wine and cast in a clot of blood for each of them; the rest of the victim they put in the fire, after having purified the column all round.*"

Plato did not recognize "water buffalo" so he equated it to "bull" (Greek *távros*, ταύϱως; plural form *távron*, ταύϱων) in the *Critias*.

Figure 58 – Bull (left) and water buffalo (right)

Water buffalo (Indonesian and Malaysian *kerbau*), also called Asian buffalo and Asiatic buffalo, is a large bovine native to Southeast Asia and the Indian Subcontinent. The water buffalo is one of the animals of greatest economic and religious value used as a sacrificial victim in the Southeast Asia, Indian sub-continent and southern China. In these monsoon regions of Asia, the buffalos are offered in sacrifice to divinities or divine spirits by populations adhering to Dharmism or Buddhism, and by tribal groups adhering to Hyang concept. Water buffalos are also commonly used to plough the rice fields, to prepare the soil for planting with handmade wooden plows, since the ancient time in Southeast Asia.

The role as the carrier of dead souls to the world beyond and/or of zoomorphic symbol of the ancestors is attributed to the water buffalo sacrifice by a series of Asian tribal populations of various ethnic and religious belief affiliations inhabiting a region extending from Middle India to the Indonesian archipelago across Upper Myanmar, South China and the Indo-Chinese highlands. Such a conception of the buffalo as the "vehicle" used by the souls of the departed to reach the afterworld is prominent, in particular, among the Gadaba, Saara, Bondo and Kondh tribes of Orissa (central-eastern India); the Naga and Kuki (or Chin) tribes of the Indo-Myanmarese border; the Jingpo, Wa, Akha (or Hani), Lamet and Black Tai ethnic minorities of Upper Indo-China; the Miao (or Hmong), Dai and Zhuang ethnic minorities of southern China; the Jarai ethnic group of central Vietnam; and the Dayak, Toraja, Batak and Sumbanese tribes of Indonesia (Brighenti, 2005). Many of these human groups, notably those inhabiting the mountain areas of South China and Upper Indo-China, felt but marginally the effects of Indian cultural influence (mainly through the spread of Buddhism).

A characteristic of Southeast Asian houses is the forked horn on the roof, which is considered to be a symbol of the buffalo, regarded throughout the region as a link between heaven and this world. The most famous stilt houses of Indonesia are those of the Dayak in Kalimantan, the Minangkabau and Batak in Sumatera, and the Toraja in Sulawesi.

DAYAK

The main festival of Kaharingan, a folk religion professed by many Dayaks in Kalimantan, is the Tiwah demise festival, to honor and to lead the soul of the deceased towards the afterworld (Lewu Tatau, the heaven). The Tiwah festival, particularly by the Iban and Ngaju Dayaks, lasts for thirty days and involves the sacrifice of buffalos as offerings to the Supreme God (Ranying Hatalla Langit). Singing and dancing rituals are held around the remains of the dead in the night participated by all people, whether men or women, old or young. The festival reaches its most dramatic climax at the buffalo sacrifice. If only one buffalo is slaughtered, it is done a day before the cremation, but for several, the sacrifice can be done either at once, a day before or one after one before the cremation takes place. The buffalos are slaughtered using spears, alternately by some people. They are tied to poles, called *sapundu*, while the executioners aim their spears at the heads and bodies. The person who has the obligation to throw the first spear is the brother of the deceased. If he is indisposed, he can be represented by his cousin.

After the buffalo sacrifice, members of the family trample on the carcasses and share the meat. Commonly, the cremation ceremony is held a day after the buffalo sacrifice festival. A purifying ceremony is held three to seven days after the Tiwah festival to drive all the evil spirits away. All the utensils used in the Tiwah are discarded as they are considered to be attached to those evil spirits. The purifying ceremony is led by a *balian* (shaman).

TORAJA

In Toraja society, a funeral ritual called Rambu Solo is the most elaborate and expensive event. The richer and more powerful the individual, the more expensive is the funeral. In the Aluk religion adhered by the Torajan, only nobles have the right to have an extensive death feast. The death feast of a nobleman is usually attended by thousands and lasts for several days. A ceremonial site, called *rante*, is usually prepared in a large, grassy field where shelters for audiences, rice barns, and other ceremonial funeral structures are specially made by the deceased family. The ceremony is often held weeks, months, or years after the death so that the deceased's family can raise the significant funds needed to cover funeral expenses. A funeral ritual of the noble Ne' Gandeng died in 1994 lasted for 9 years with slaughtering of more than 500 water buffalos.

One component of the ritual is the slaughter of water buffalos called *mantunu*. The more powerful the person who died, the more buffalos are slaughtered at the death feast. Buffalo carcasses, including their heads, are usually lined up on a field waiting for their owner, who is in the "sleeping stage". Torajans believe that the deceased will need the buffalo to make the journey and that they will be quicker to arrive at Puya (the land of souls, or afterlife) if they have many buffalos. Slaughtering tens of water buffalos and hundreds of pigs using a machete is the climax of the elaborate death feast, with dancing and music and young boys who catch spurting blood in long *bambu* tubes. Some of the slaughtered animals are given by guests as "gifts", which are carefully noted because they will be considered debts of the deceased's family. However, a cockfight, known as *bulangan londong*, is an integral part of the ceremony. As with the sacrifice of the buffalos and the pigs, the cockfight is considered sacred because it involves the spilling of blood on the earth. In particular, the tradition requires the sacrifice of at least three chickens. However, it is common for at least 25 pairs of chickens to be set against each other in the context of the ceremony.

Buffalo horns hung in a vertical array on the front gable are a sign of prestige and are customarily used to signify the wealth of the household. Furthermore, a buffalo head made from painted wood and buffalo-dung, but crowned with real horns, is mounted on the façades.

SUMBA

Sumba is an island that has been cut off from the rest of the world for so long that its ancient animistic traditions survive to this day. Throughout the year the island is the site of many fascinating rituals, the most spectacular of them all are the Pasola ceremonies that take place during the months of February and March at selected locations along the west coast of the island. The Pasola are wild and martial events involving hundreds of charging horsemen battling with spears on a large playing field. Serious injuries are common and there are occasional deaths of horses and even riders. In fact a Pasola is not considered successful without a proper amount of bloodletting. In Sumba, blood on the ground is necessary to make it fertile, and one of the aims of the Pasola is to make the conditions right for the rice harvests that take place in the months of April and May.

The funerary rituals of Sumba continue to this day. Huge blocks of stone are cut and dragged great distances to the mortuary ground to construct mausoleums for the rich and the nobility. An average sized stone can weigh in the range of

162

six tons, and larger stones weigh more than twenty. Until recently, particularly at the funerals of noblemen, literally hundreds of water buffalos, horses, pigs and dogs were slaughtered to accompany the departed soul to the afterlife. The number of animals dispatched was, and still is, prestige enhancing. Funerals can be quite expensive and in some cases may require hundreds of pigs, horses, and water buffalos for sacrifice. In Sumba it is believed that the more animals that are sacrificed, the more respect is given to the dead who can then rest in peace in the world of the ancestors.

The front porches of many traditional houses are often decorated with huge buffalo horns and pig jawbones from sacrificed animals during the ritual ceremonies of the years gone by.

BATAK

In the religious world of the Toba and Karo Bataks, the gods and the creation of mankind are far less significant than the complex concepts connected with the "life-soul" (*tendi*, Karo or *tondi*, Toba) and the "death-soul" (*begu*). A person receives his "life-soul" from Mulajadi na Bolon (the creator) before his birth.

Traditional Batak beliefs hold that the dead occupy a hierarchical status similar to the social position they held in life. This means that a rich and powerful individual remains influential after death; and this status can be elevated if the family holds a reburial ceremony. A rich descendant can advance a *begu* to the status of a *sumangot* (noble, honorable and dignified ancestral spirit) by means of a great ceremony and a Horja feast which can last up to seven days. In antiquity a vast number of pigs, cattle or water buffalos were slaughtered at such festivals.

Mangalahat Horbo is a festival of slaughters of water buffalos as the voice of thanksgiving to the Mulajadi na Bolon for the result of the earth and the welfare of the people. The festival invites all leaders of the regions. After the buffalos are slaughtered, the meat is shared among the leaders to celebrate the solidarity and gratitude to the Mulajadi na Bolon.

Ornamentation is very important in Karo houses, with buffalo horns an essential decoration of the traditional houses, and two white-painted horns are mounted on each end of the roof (the mounting is done in the night, so nobody sees), using both male and female buffalos. Ornaments in Karo houses served traditionally to protect the residents from evil spirits, and to demonstrate the status of the owner. With the fading of traditional religious beliefs, they are now largely decorative and a reminder of past cultural traditions.

MODERN PRACTICE

A practice of burying a water buffalo head to bring good luck and to keep off misfortune is one of the traditions of people in Nusantara. The modern practice is particularly found in a ceremony called "placing first stone" before starting the construction of a house, a building, a monument or a bridge. Such a ceremony is held in a belief that the construction will run successfully and nothing worse will occur to the tenant.

The buffalo head burying has actually long been practiced from primitive time but continues to this day, even by modern and educated people, in the construction of advanced technological buildings in modern cities. When building a house, some people believe that finding a good day, providing offerings (*sesaji*) and burying a buffalo head are mandatory requirements and considered as a way to strengthen the building.

To the environment, some people are practicing *ruwatan* (exorcism) rituals to provide magical power to prevent negative auras by burying buffalo heads. This is particularly done in areas where natural hazards exist like volcano eruption, earthquake or flood. Along the coastal area of Java, a tradition by fishermen communities to give offerings to the sea (*larung*) is still in practice; such offerings contain buffalo heads, various kinds of traditional snacks, vegetables and so on.

KALIMANTAN ELEPHANT

In *Critias*, Plato mentioned that there were abundance of animals, including elephants in Atlantis and the roof of the temple to Poseidon was made of ivory.

The Kalimantan elephant, commonly called Kalimantan pygmy elephant (*Elephas maximus borneensis*) is the smallest elephant sub-species in the world. The males may only grow to less than 2.5 meters, while other Asian elephants grow up to 3 meters. They have babyish faces, larger ears, longer tails that reach almost to the ground and are more rotund; also less aggressive than other Asian elephants. The indigenous people of Dayak Agabag in Tulin Onsoi give this remarkable species a nickname, "Nenek". According to them, elephant is a sacred animal and should not be disturbed.

Until recently the Kalimantan pygmy elephants were believed to be a remnant population of a domesticated herd abandoned on the island by the Sultan of

Sulu in the 17th century. However, DNA studies by WWF* and Columbia University in 2003 recognized that the elephants are likely an indigenous sub-species which were split from the other sub-species in Pleistocene Age some 300,000 years ago. When the sea level rise in the Last Glacial Age separated the Kalimantan Island from the Asian mainland, the elephants were isolated in the island from their cousins on mainland Asia and Sumatera and later evolved to become a distinct Asian elephant sub-species.

WWF estimates that there may be fewer than 1,500 pygmy elephants on Kalimantan, although no population surveys have been conducted yet. In 2007 – 2012, a joint research of WWF Indonesia and Nature Conservation Agency predicted that the pygmy elephant population in East Kalimantan is around 20 – 80 individuals only. A study by Raymond Alfred *et al* in 2010 estimated the number in Sabah about 2,040. The Kalimantan pygmy elephant has been classified as endangered species by the IUCN Red List†.

Figure 59 – Kalimantan pygmy elephants
(*Source: WWF Indonesia*)

The loss of Kalimantan elephant's habitat and home range has pushed the species into conflict with human. WWF Indonesia's data shows from 2005 – 2007 approximately 16,000 palm oil trees owned by community and palm oil plantation companies were damaged by elephants. Furthermore, monitoring result from 2005 until 2009 shows 11 villages in Nunukan District, East Kalimantan were prone to human-elephant conflict. In the Lower Kinabatangan Wildlife Sanctuary in Sabah, it is estimated that 20 percent of resident elephants

---

* The World Wide Fund for Nature (WWF) is an international non-governmental organization founded on April 29, 1961, and is working on issues regarding the conservation, research and restoration of the environment. It was formerly named the World Wildlife Fund, which remains its official name in Canada and the United States.
† The IUCN Red List of Threatened Species (also known as the IUCN Red List or Red Data List), founded in 1964, is the world's most comprehensive inventory of the global conservation status of biological species. The International Union for the Conservation of Nature (IUCN) is the world's main authority on the conservation status of species.

have sustained injuries from illegal snares set by some people from the new palm plantations.

The now extinct Java pigmy elephants (*Elephas maximus sondaicus*) those once inhabited Java are identical to the Kalimantan pigmy elephants.

BAWEAN ISLAND

Bawean Island (or Boyan Island) is an island located approximately 150 km north of Surabaya in the Java Sea, off the coast of Java. It is administered by Gresik Regency of East Java province. It is approximately 15 km in diameter and is circumnavigated by a single narrow road. Bawean is dominated by an extinct volcano at its center that rises to 655 m above sea level. Its population as at the 2010 Census is about 70,000 people, but more than 26,000 of them (that is about 70% of the male population) were temporarily living outside, working in other parts of Indonesia, Singapore and Malaysia. As a result, females constituted about 77% of the actual population of the island, which is thus often referred to as "The Princess Island" (Indonesian *pulau putri*). The island has rich nature with many endemic species, such as Bawean Deer (*Hyelaphus kuhlii*) which is only found on the island and is included in the IUCN Red List.

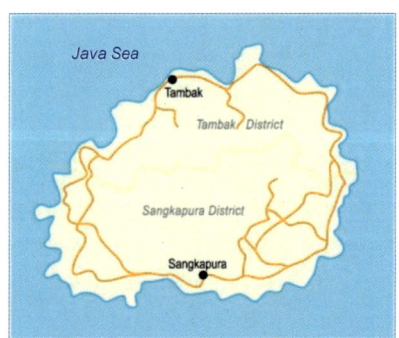

Figure 60 – Bawean Island

The highest point (655 m) is at Gunung Tinggi ("high hill"). Here are a few caldera lakes, the largest being the Lake Kastoba. It has an area of about 0.3 km², depth of 140 meters, and is located at an altitude of about 300 meters. There are several small rivers and waterfalls, the highest being Laccar and Patarselamat, as well as hot springs such as Kebundaya and Taubat. Igneous rocks make about 85% of its surface with occasional limestone, sandstone and dolomite. The island has deposits of coal and onyx which are being mined from the early 2000s. There are several large underwater petroleum and gas fields around the island.

Bawean is an island that is known in the archipelago to have the most ancient and enormous mystical and occult myths and these are generally associated to the jinns.

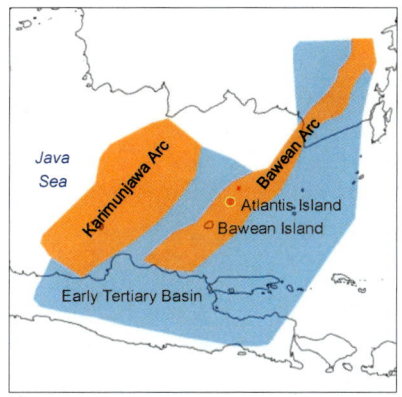

Figure 61 – Both Bawean and Atlantis Islands are located on Bawean Arc.

Bawean Island is a prototype of the Atlantis Island as it has the same environment, geological formation and tectonic activities, as well as situated close to Atlantis Island. Bawean and Atlantis Islands are both located on a geological arc identified by the geologists as Bawean Arc, spanning from the northern Java Island to the Meratus Mountain in Kalimantan Island, formed in the Paleogene and Neogene periods through tectonic processes caused by extensional faulting in the Java Sea that separated Java and Kalimantan. Bawean Arc is flanked by Western and Eastern Bawean basins.

The author previously makes a conjuncture that the white, black and red colored stones mentioned by Plato are apparently the igneous rock that might also deposited in the Atlantis Island. There are hot and cold springs, also mentioned by Plato. In addition, the igneous rock just like in the Bawean Island is strong enough to stand as roofs of the hollowed out double docks in Atlantis Island.

LEGEND OF AJISAKA

Ajisaka is a Javanese legend that tells the story about how civilization came to Java, brought by legendary first king of Java named Ajisaka, and the mythical story of Javanese script origin.

As told by the legend, Ajisaka came from a place called Bhumi Majethi. Javanese interpretation holds that his name came from Javanese words of *aji* means king and *saka* means pillar, foundation or essential. The myth has been described as the tale of a hero that brought civilization and order to Java by defeating an evil giant king Dewatacengkar that once ruled the island under the kingdom of Medang Kamulan. The legend also hold that king Ajisaka was the inventor of the Saka year, or at least the first king that initiated the adoption of calendar system in Java. The kingdom of Medang Kamulan was probably linked to the primordial (*kamulan* means "primordial") of the actual historical Medang kingdom (*ca* 732 – *ca* 1006 AD).

One day Ajisaka told his two servants, by the names of Dora and Sembada, that he was going to Java. He told them that while he was away, both of them have to guard his *pusaka* (heirloom) and no one except Ajisaka himself was allowed to take the *pusaka*. After arriving in Java, Ajisaka moved inland to the kingdom of Medang Kamulan. In a big battle, Ajisaka could successfully push king Dewatacengkar to fall to the Java Southern Sea (Indian Ocean). Ajisaka then became a ruler of the Medang Kamulan kingdom.

Meanwhile, after becoming ruler of the Medang Kamulan kingdom, Ajisaka sent a messenger back home to inform his faithful servants Dora and Sembada, to bring the *pusaka* to Java and send them to Ajisaka. Then Dora came to Sembada and told Ajisaka's order. Sembada refused since he clearly remembered Ajisaka previous order: no one except Ajisaka himself was allowed to take the *pusaka*. Dora and Sembada each felt suspicious towards another, and suspecting each other tried to steal the *pusaka*. So they fought each other to death. Ajisaka that was curious of why it is taken so long for the two to come to Java, finally came home himself only to discover the body of his two faithful servants and the terrible misunderstanding among them. To remember the faithful acts of his two servants, Ajisaka composed a poem that later become the origin of Hanacaraka Javanese script. The Javanese alphabet itself forms a poem, and a perfect pangram, of which the line-by-line translation is as follows.

ꦲꦤꦕꦫꦏ
ha na ca ra ka
There [were two] messengers.

ꦢꦠꦱꦮꦭ
da ta sa wa la
[They] had animosity [between each other].

ꦥꦝꦗꦪꦚ
pa dha ja ya nya
[They were] equally powerful [in fight].

ꦩꦒꦧꦛꦔ
ma ga ba tha nga
Here are the corpses.

Javanese script was added to the Unicode Standard* in October 2009 with the release of version 5.2. The Unicode block is U+A980 – U+A9DF, consists of 91 codepoints: 53 letters, 19 punctuation marks, 10 numbers and 9 vowels.

The script was widely used by the court scribes of Java and the Lesser Sunda Islands. They are used also to write historical accounts (*babad*), stories (*serat*), ancient verses (*kakawin*) and divination guides (*primbon*) among many others, with the most popular being copied and rewritten over the centuries. Today use

---

* Unicode is a computing industry standard for the consistent encoding, representation and handling of text expressed in most of the world's writing systems. It is Developed in conjunction with the *Universal Character Set* standard and published as *The Unicode Standard*, the latest version of Unicode contains a repertoire of more than 110,000 characters covering 100 scripts and multiple symbol sets. As of June 2014, the most recent version is Unicode 7.0. The standard is maintained by the Unicode Consortium.

is encouraged by the Yogyakarta and Central Java governments in road signs and public signage alongside Bahasa Indonesia, as administered in the 2012 local legislation.

Ajisaka came from a place called Bhumi Majethi. A similar word of *majethi* in Sanskrit is *majjati* meaning sunken, submerged or drawn. Hence, we could speculate that the legendary Ajisaka was from a sunken island, somewhere in the Java Sea. According to another Javanese legend, the original name of Bawean Island was Majethi and correlates the legend of Ajisaka to this island. One of the two sub-districts in the island is named Sangkapura; a variant of Sakapura means the town of [Aji]Saka. Another legend says that the island was primordially under the rule of Babileono kingdom. After the conversion of the islanders to Islam around 17th century AD, the name was associated to *majdi*, in Arabic means coin.

It is said that in 1950s there was found an inscription made by Ajisaka to commemorate Dora and Sembada. The inscription was found at Tinggen site in Tanjunganyar village, written on a large rock in Javanese script with Ajisaka's left foot stamp. To prevent idolatrous by the local community, the village head instructed to destroy the rock; the fragments were then used to build the foundations of a bridge at Muara village. A grave named Makam Panjang ("long grave") at Tinggen site is believed by the local people where the *pusaka* of Ajisaka was buried.

JAMU AND BUMBU

> From Plato's *Critias* Section 115a: "*Also whatever fragrant things there now are in the earth, whether roots, or herbage, or woods, or essences which distil from fruit and flower, grew and thrived in that land; ...*"

Indonesia and Malaysia are famous for their specific herbal medicines called "jamu" and flavorings or spices called "bumbu"; both are using similar plant materials.

JAMU

Jamu is traditional medicine in Indonesia, predominantly herbal medicine made from natural materials, such as plant's roots, tubers, bark, flowers, seeds, leaves and fruits. Materials from livestock such as honey, milk, domestic chicken eggs and animal's biles are also often used.

169

Plants have been used for medicinal purposes in Nusantara since pre-historic time. The origin and development of *jamu* is not completely known, claimed to have originated in the Medang Kingdom dated back to the eighth century. Beneath a *kalpataru** tree as shown at a bas-relief on the wall of Borobudur temple in Central Java, people crushed the ingredients for the preparation of *jamu*. Similar bas-reliefs are also found at Prambanan (Central Java), Penataran (East Java) and Tegalwangi (East Java) temples. Eighth and ninth century manuscripts about formulation and extraction of herbs from the plants written on *lontar* were found, as in *Lontar Usada* in Bali and *Lontar Pabbura* in South Sulawesi. Knowledge about the herb formulations of natural ingredients has also been recorded, as in *Kawruh bab Jampi Jawi* (*Knowledge of Javanese Herbs*) by the Surakarta Kingdom published in 1858 consisting of 1734 formulations.

One of the first European physicians to study *jamu* was Jacobus Bontius (Jacob de Bondt), who was a physician in Batavia (today's Jakarta) in the early seventeenth century. His writings, *De Medicina Indorum* in 1642, contain information about indigenous medicine. A comprehensive book on indigenous herbal medicine in the Indies was published by Georgius Everardus Rumphius, who worked in Ambon during the early eighteenth century. He published a book called *Herbaria Amboinesis* (*The Ambonese Spice Book*). During the nineteenth century, European physicians had a keen interest in *jamu*, as they often did not know how to treat the diseases they encountered in their patients in the Indies. The German physician Carl Waitz published on *jamu* in 1829, *Praktische waarnemingen over eenige Javaansche geneesmiddelen* (*Practical observations on a number of Javanese medications*). In the 1880s and 1890s, AG Vorderman published extensive accounts on *jamu* as well. Pharmacological research on herbal medicine was undertaken by M Greshoff and WG Boorsma at the pharmacological laboratory at the Bogor Botanical Garden in West Java. A *jamu* handbook, *Wenken en Raadgevingen Betreffende het Gebruik Van Indische Planten, Vruchten Enz* (*Guidance and Advice Regarding the Use of Indies Plants, Fruits, Etc*), was published by Kloppenburg-Versteegh in 1911. An Irish journalist Susan Jane-Beers' opus *Jamu: The Ancient Indonesian Art of Herbal Healing* published in 2001 remains the only definitive English guide on the subject and also the most widely read outside Indonesia since *Herbaria Amboinesis*.

---

* *Kalpataru*, also known as *kalpavriksha*, *kalpadruma* or *kalpapādapa*, is a wish-fulfilling divine tree in dharmic mythology.

In the second conference of the Indonesian
Association of Physicians held in Surakarta, Central
Java, in March 1940, two presentations on the *jamu*
were given. During the Japanese occupation,
Indonesian Jamu Committee was formed in 1944.
During the following decades, the popularity of
jamu increased, although physicians had rather
ambivalent opinions about it. Today, *jamu*
producers are associated in Association of Jamu
and Medicine Entrepreneurs of Indonesia.

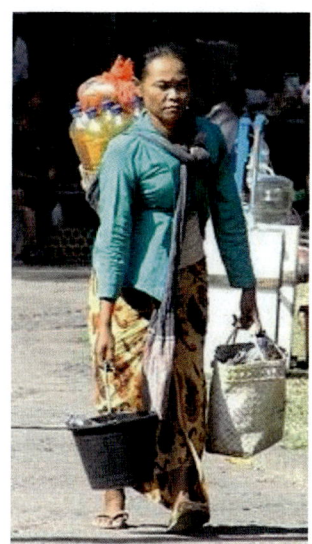

Nusantara is rich in its various medicinal plants. A
survey by the Indonesian Ministry of Health
showed that Indonesia has more than 7,000 species
of medicinal plants, where about a thousand of
them have been used by the people for medicinal
purposes. Though heavily influenced by Ayurveda
from India, Indonesia is a vast archipelago with
numerous indigenous plants not found in India,

Figure 62 – A woman
carrying a *bambu* basket on
her back roaming the street to
sell *jamu*, a common view in
Indonesia

and includes plants similarly found in Australia beyond the Wallace Line. *Jamu*
may vary from region to region, the different *jamu* prescriptions are not written
down but handed down between the generations.

Jamu can be found throughout Indonesia and Malaysia; however it is most
prevalent in Java. *Jamu* is often distributed in the form of powder, pills, capsules
and drinking liquid. *Jamu* shops, which sell only ingredients or prepare the *jamu*
on spot as required by buyers, as well as women carrying *bambu* basket on her
back roaming the street to sell *jamu*, are commonly seen ways to distribute *jamu*
in Indonesia. Nowadays, *jamu* is also mass manufactured and exported.

Some examples of herbs for *jamu* prescriptions are as follow.

1. Rhizomes: *bengle* (*Zingiber brevifolium*), *jahe* (ginger, *Zingiber officinale*), *kencur*
   (aromatic galangal, *Kaempferia galanga*), *kunyit* (turmeric, *Curcuma domestica*),
   lempuyang (*Zingiber zerumbet* or *Zingiber aromaticum*), *lengkuas* or *laos* (greater
   galangal, *Alpinia galanga*), *temulawak* (*Curcuma xanthorrhiza*)
2. Leaves: *brotowali* or *bratawali* (*Tinospora crispa* or *Tinospora tuberculata
   rumphii*), *sambang darah* (*Excoecaria cochinchinensis* or *Excoecaria bicolor*), *secang*
   (*Caesalpinia sappan*)
3. Seeds: *adas* (*Foeniculum vulgare*)

4. Fruits: *ceplukan* (cutleaf groundcherry, *Physalis angulata*), *jeruk nipis* (key lime, *Citrus aurantifolia*), *nyamplung* or *kosambi* (*Calophyllum inophyllum*)
5. Barks: *kayu manis* (cinnamon, *Cinnamomum burmannii*)
6. Flowers: *ilang-ilang* (*Cananga odorata*), *melati* (jasmine, *Jasminum sambac*), *alang-alang* (*Gramineae*)

BUMBU

Bumbu is the Indonesian and Malaysian word for spices mixture or seasoning, and it commonly appears in the names of certain spice mixtures, sauces and seasoning pastes. It is commonly found in Indonesian cuisine, which includes its regional variants such as Balinese, Javanese, Sundanese, Padang, Batak and Manado cuisines. It is spread over various meats, poultries, seafoods and vegetables; used in stews, soups, barbecue, *soto*, *gulai*, and also as a common addition to Indonesian-style instant noodles.

Known throughout the world as the "Spice Islands", the Indonesian islands of Maluku contributed to the introduction of its native spices to the world cuisine. Spices such as *pala* (nutmeg/mace), *cengkeh* (clove), *daun pandan* (pandan leaves), *kluwek* (*Pangium edule*) and *laos* (galangal) are native to Indonesia. It is likely that *lada hitam* (black pepper), *kunyit* (turmeric), *sereh* (lemongrass), *salam koja* (curry leaf), *bawang merah* (shallot), *kayu manis* (cinnamon), *kemiri* (candlenut), *ketumbar* (coriander), and *asam jawa* (Javanese tamarind) were introduced from India, while *jahe* (ginger), *daun bawang* (scallions) and *bawang putih* (garlic) were introduced from China. Those spices from mainland Asia were introduced early, in ancient times, thus they became integral ingredients in Indonesian cuisine. While the New World spices such as chili pepper and tomato were introduced by Portuguese and Spanish traders during the age of exploration in the 16th century.

TAPAI OR TAPE

From Plato's *Critias* Section 115b: "... *and are fruits which spoil with keeping, with which we console ourselves after dinner ...*"

Tapai or *tape* is a traditional fermented food as a dessert indigenous and popular throughout Southeast Asia. It is a sweet or sour alcoholic paste and can be used directly as a food or in traditional recipes. *Tapai* can be made from a variety of carbohydrate sources, but typically from cassava (*Manihot esculenta*), white rice (*Oryza sativa*) or glutinous rice (*Oryza sativa glotinosa*). Fermentation is performed by a variety of moulds by inoculating a carbohydrate source with the required

Figure 63 – *Tapai* or *tape* made from cassava
(left) and glutinous rice (right)

microorganisms in a starter culture, locally known as *ragi*, including *Aspergillus oryzae*, *Rhizopus oryzae*, *Amylomyces rouxii* or *Mucor* species, and yeasts including *Saccharomyces cerevisiae*, *Saccharomycopsis fibuliger*, *Endomycopsis burtonii* and others, along with bacteria. *Tapai* is also used to make alcoholic beverages locally known as *arak* or *brem*.

Tapai or *tape* is known in different names, in Indonesia as *tape* or *tapai*, Java as *tapé*, Sunda (western Java) as *peuyeum*, Malaysia and Brunei as *tapai*, Thailand as *khao-mak*, Cambodia as *chao* or *tapai*, and the Philippines as *tapay* or *binuburang*. Glutinous rice *tapé ketan* is a noted regale in Java during the *idul fitri* festival.

COCONUT

> In Plato *Critias* Section 115b: "… *and the fruits having a hard rind, affording drinks and meats and ointments …*"

Coconut (*Cocos nucifera*) provides a nutritious source of meat, juice, milk, and oil that has fed and nourished populations around the world for generations. On many islands coconut is a staple in the diet and provides the majority of the food eaten. Nearly one third of the world's population depends on coconut to some degree for their food and their economy. Among these cultures the coconut has a long and respected history.

Figure 64 – Coconut

Coconut is highly nutritious and rich in fiber, vitamins, and minerals. It is classified as a "functional food" because it provides many health benefits beyond its nutritional content. Coconut oil is of special interest because it possesses healing properties far beyond that of any other dietary oil and is extensively used in traditional medicine among Asian and Pacific populations. Pacific islanders consider coconut oil to be the cure for all illness. The coconut palm is so highly valued by them as both a source of food and medicine that it is called "the tree of life". Only recently has modern medical science unlocked the secret to coconut's amazing healing powers.

Coconut oil is edible oil that has been consumed in tropical places for thousands of years. Studies done on native diets high in coconut oil consumption show that these populations are generally in good health, and don't suffer as much from many of the modern diseases of western nations where coconut oil is seldom consumed anymore. Coconut oil is an excellent massage oil and smoothener for the skin. In the tropical parts of the world, natives commonly spread coconut oil on their skin, as they believe that it protects from the sun's harmful rays. So this natural oil, without any chemical or additives, can protect the skin in some of the hottest and sunniest places on earth better than the processed and artificial sun creams.

The nutrient-rich coconut sap comes right out of the inflorescence of the tree is naturally abundant in 17 amino acids (the building blocks of protein), broad-spectrum B vitamins (especially rich in inositol, known for its effectiveness on depression, high cholesterol, inflammation, and diabetes), vitamin C, minerals (high in potassium, essential for electrolyte balance, regulating high blood pressure, and sugar metabolism), as well as FOS (*fructooligosaccharide*, a prebiotic that promotes digestive health). Coconut tree sap produces a multitude of delicious products, including coconut vinegar, coconut amino seasoning sauce, coconut nectar, coconut sugar and coconut alcoholic beverage, all made through raw methods of either aging the sap for up to 1 year, or evaporating it at low temperature after it is collected.

Coconut sugar is produced by tapping the sap from the tree and boiling it down to produce syrup, which is then sold as is, or allowed to crystallize into various shapes and sizes. Coconut sugar is known in different names, in Indonesia as *gula merah* or *gula jawa* (Javanese sugar), Myanmar as *htanyet*, Cambodia as *skor tnot*, the Philippines as *pakaskas*, Malaysia as *gula anau*, Laos and Thailand as *nam tan pip* and Vietnam as *đường thốt nốt*.

Coconut milk is a very popular food ingredient used in Southeast Asia, South Asia, Southern China and the Caribbean. Traditionally, coconut milk is acquired through the grating of a brown coconut, mixing the resulting substance with a small amount of water to dissolve the fat present in the grated meat. The squeezed coconut meat is then soaked in water and squeezed further to produce thin coconut milk. Thick milk is mainly used to make desserts as well as rich and dry sauces. Thin milk is used for soups and general cooking. Unlike cow's milk, coconut milk is lactose free so can be used as a milk substitute by those with lactose intolerance. It is a popular choice with vegans and makes a great base for smoothies, milkshakes or as a dairy alternative in baking.

Coconut water is the watery liquid that usually comes from the young, still immature green coconut, although mature coconuts also have coconut water. Coconut water is high in many vitamins and minerals, especially potassium. Because it contains electrolytes, it is considered one of the best natural rehydrating drinks in the tropics. The still jelly-like coconut meat is often added to coconut water to make a tropical drink. Coconut water has received a great deal of attention for it's perceived health benefits, and is an important treatment for acute diarrhoea in the developing world. Research suggests the clear liquid has the same electrolyte balance found in isotonic drinks, proving useful for rehydration or after long periods of intensive exercise.

Coconut vinegar is similar to other fermented vinegars such as apple cider and balsamic vinegars. It can either be made with coconut water or from the sap of the coconut tree, left in the open air to ferment, where it eventually turns into a vinegar. Coconut vinegar is a staple condiment in Southeast Asia, and is also used in some regions of India. Coconut vinegar is white and cloudy with a very pungent acidic taste and a hint of yeast. As with apple cider vinegar, coconut vinegar includes the "mother", or culture of organisms that caused the fermentation. Coconut vinegar is a food appropriate for diabetic patients, as it is very low on the glycemic index, coming in at only 35 on the scale.

Indonesian and Malaysian *tuak* or *lambanóg* in the Philippines is a distilled alcoholic drink made from fermented sap of coconut flowers. The clear distillate may be blended, aged in wooden barrels, or repeatedly distilled and filtered depending upon the taste and color objectives of the manufacturer.

DNA analysis of more than 1,300 coconuts from around the world reveals that the coconut was brought under cultivation in two separate locations, one in the Pacific basin and the other in the Indian Ocean basin. What's more, coconut genetics also preserve a record of prehistoric trade routes and of the colonization of the Americas. In the Pacific, coconuts were likely first cultivated in island Southeast Asia, meaning the Philippines, Malaysia, Indonesia, and perhaps the continent as well. In the Indian Ocean the likely center of cultivation was the southern periphery of India, including Sri Lanka, the Maldives, and the Laccadives. The Pacific coconuts were introduced to the Indian Ocean a couple of thousand years ago by ancient Austronesians establishing trade routes connecting Southeast Asia to Madagascar and coastal east Africa (Olsen *et al*, 2011).

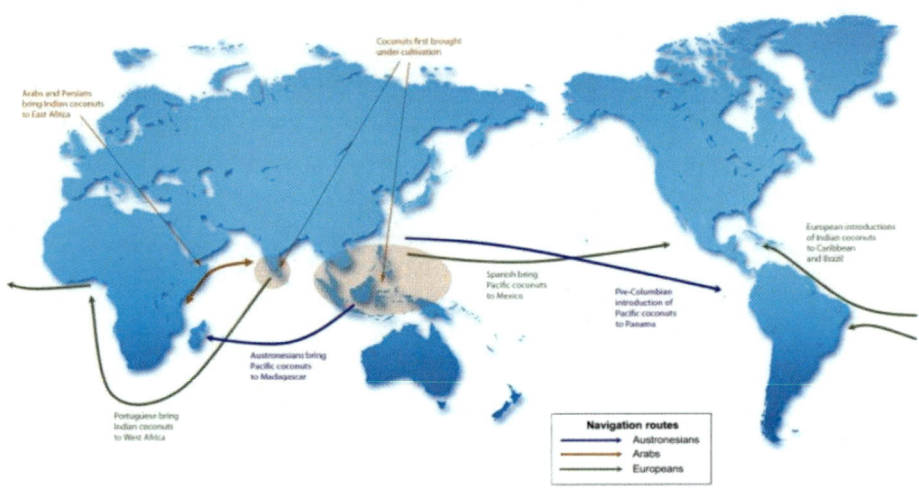

Figure 65 – Analysis of coconut DNA revealed much more structure than scientists expected given the long history of coconut exploitation by people. Written in the DNA are two origins of cultivation and many journeys of exploration and colonization. (*Source: Olsen et al, 2011*)

CORRELATED OR JUST COINCIDENCE?

In Kaharingan, a folk religion professed by many Dayak tribes in southern Kalimantan, their supreme god and their creator of universe is called Ranying Hatalla Langit or simply Hatalla. Hatalla (means "god") or sometimes pronounced as "atala". Is Hatalla connected to Atlas or Atlantis?

At the estuary area of Barito River in southern Kalimantan, the present-day nearest place to the hypothesized location of Atlantis Island, there are villages named Sungai Telan Besar, Sungai Telan Kecil and Sungai Telan Muara. *Sungai, besar, kecil* and *muara* mean "river", "large", "small" and "estuary", respectively. "Telan" is in close resemblance with Atlas or Atlantis. Does Sungai Telan mean "the river of Atlantis"?

The Kenyah Dayak people in northern Kalimantan mostly inhabit the forest and are spiritually connected to it. They call the forest Tala Olen. They have strict cultural rules about cutting down the trees in the forest or damaging it in any way. Does "tala" have a connection to Atlas or Atlantis?

In a legend of the Aztec, indigenous peoples of central Mexico, Aztlán was their ancestral home. Aztecah is the Nahuatl (the language of Nahua Aztec people) word for "people from Aztlán". In Nahuatl, "atl" means "water" and their water god is also named Atl. Similar legend is found in the K'iche' Maya tradition, in their epic *Popul Vuh*, the first people created are gathered at Tollan, the place of seven caves, where they receive their languages and their gods. Aztlán and Tollan are in close resemblance with Atlas or Atlantis. Sukuh and Cetho temples in Central Java are respected somewhat resemble the Mesoamerican pyramids. The "tree of life" concept of the Dayak is well described in the tomb of Mayan king Pakal, existence probably goes back to the Olmec time. Were there any connections among those civilizations?

A legend of the islanders of Bawean Island says that the island was primordially ruled by Babileono kingdom. The author is inspired and speculates to correlate Babileono to Babylon, a significant city in ancient Mesopotamia. According to the myth, Babylon and Akkad were post-deluge civilizations. The Greek form *Babylon* (Βαβυλών) is adapted from Akkadian *Babili*. In the Hebrew Bible, the name appears as בָּבֶל (*Bavel*), Tiberian as בָּבֶל (*Bāvel*) and Syriac as ܒܳܒܶܠ (*Bāwēl*). Ernst Emil Herzfeld (1879 – 1948 AD), a German archeologist, philologist, and polyhistorian of ancient Near East and Iran, wrote about *Bawer* in Ancient Iran, and the name *Babil* could refer to *Bawer*. *Bavel*, *Bawel* and *Bawer* are in close resemblance with Bawean. Moreover, Akkad and Saka are also in close resemblance. Were Mesopotamian civilization post-deluge refugees of Atlantis and the origin place names retained?

A more speculation, Akkad was also written as Agade in the Sumerian list of kings. The precise archaeological site of the city-state of Akkad has not yet been found. Agade is in close resemblance with Gades, the land controlled by Gadeirus, one of the kings of Atlantis in Plato's *Critias*. Also, Crantor commentary to Plato's work mentions that one of the islands around Atlantis was sacred to Hades. Are Agade, Gades and Hades identical? Is the island sacred to Hades is the Bawean Island?

ATHENS AND AUSTRONESIAN CONNECTION

Plato used the word "island" (Greek *nêsos*, νῆσος) to describe the sunken Atlantis. When we search a word of the same meaning in today's Austronesia, we could find a word *nusa*; phonetically in a very close resemblance with the word "nêsos". *Nusa* and its variant *nuswa* meaning "island" are used by people inhabiting the Austronesian archipelago nowadays.

There are so many islands named using *nusa*, such as in Nusadua, Nusapenida, Nusakambangan, Nusatenggara (Lesser Sunda Islands), Nusalembongan, Nusaceningan, Nusabarong, Nusalaut, Nusabesar and Nusadolong in Indonesia; Nusakuya and Nusatengah in Malaysia; and Nusa Islands, Tanusa, Kanhanusa, Bihintinusa, Bulinusa, Laminusa and Nusabuani in the Philippines.

The Nusantara concept is still in use until today – came from the word *nusa* and a suffix *-ntara* – was taken from an oath by the prime minister Gajah Mada (*ca* 1290 – *ca* 1364 AD) in the Majapahit Empire in *ca* 1336 AD as written on *kakawin Pararaton* and *Nagarakretagama*, and consisted the regions in the archipelago which are today's Indonesia, Malaysia, southern Thailand, Brunei Darussalam, the Philippines, Timor Leste and Papua New Guinea. The Nusantara concept was also used before by Kertanegara, a king of Singasari kingdom, in 1275 AD as *Cakrawala Mandala Dwipantara*. *Dwipa* means "island" in Sanskrit. The suffix *-ntara* means "space" or "covers a vast area" and is not the Sanskrit *antara* or Latin *inter* meaning "between" but is close to the Greek *terra* meaning "earth" or "land"; similar uses like *dirgantara* (*dirga-ntara*) means "aerospace" and *belantara* (*bala-ntara*) means "vast area full of dangers". A word *bangsa* is derived from the words *ba-nusa* means "nation" or "the people inhabiting the island and their descendants".

Inspired from the above, we could find some words used by Austronesian and ancient Greek people which have the same meaning and phonetically similar, such as *ika* (Greek *ekeî*, ἐκεῖ) for "there", *soma* (Greek *sôma*, σῶμα) for "body", *kepala* (Greek *kephalḗ*, κεφαλή) for "head", *agra* or *arga* (Greek *akra*, ἄκρα) for "hill" or "hill-top", *pohon* (Greek *phutón*, φυτόν) for "tree", *bulan* or *wulan* (Greek *selḗnē*, σελήνη) for "moon" or "month", *ikan* (Greek *ikhthús*, ἰχθύς) for "fish", *waluya* (Greek *euexía*, εὐεξία) for "good health", *rukh* (Greek *psukhḗ*, ψυχή) for "soul" or "spirit", *hati* (Greek *páthos*, πάθος) for "heart" or "emotion" and *asmara* (Greek *hímeros*, ἵμερος) for "love" or "desire".

In Egypt mythology, the island of Nesisi or Neserser, "the island of flames" where Thoth came from, is often mentioned in the myths, also in close resemblance with the words *nusa* or *nêsos*. "Island" in Egyptian hieroglyph is written as  (Gardiner code *N18:Z1*N23*, transliterated *iw*).

Origins of post-deluge civilizations

The author conjectures the origins of post-deluge civilizations of Atlantis as shown on Figure 66. What did they bring?

1. Civilization – As written by many authors, humanity was first flourished in Sundaland where ideal climatic conditions for development were found, and it was there that they invented farming, agriculture, trading and civilization.

2. Language – Scholastic belief by etymologists and linguists are positive that all world languages sprang from a common source. Paleo-Sanskrit is one of the theories that it is the ancestor of Sanskrit, Indo-Iranian, Indo-European, Mesoamerican, Sino-Tibetan, Austronesian and all other languages of the world.

3. Myths and doctrines – All the gods and goddesses of various world religions are parallel. Similar myths of great floods, creation and heaven are found all over the world. Brahma, Abram, Avram, Abraham and Ibrahim are believed by some as the same person.

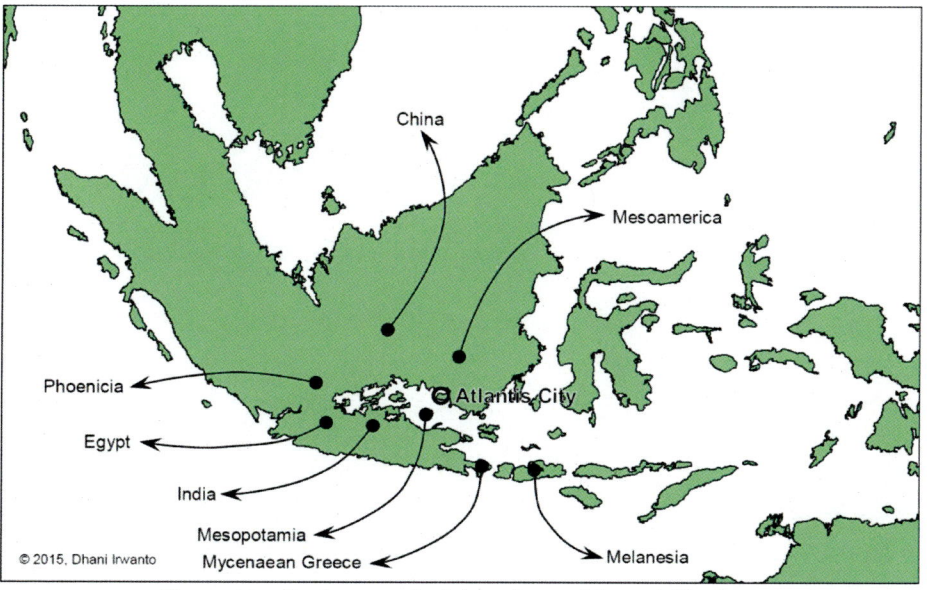

Figure 66 – Conjecture of origins of post-deluge civilizations

4. Pyramid building – There are hundreds of pyramids still standing all over the world. Cultures separated by oceans, who supposedly never discovered each other's existence, built these giant triangular structures, aligned them to cardinal directions, encoded within them sacred geometry/math, and used them as sepultures. The Gunung Padang pyramid in West Java, Indonesia dated 23,000 BC or earlier is claimed to be the earliest one.

5. Boat and ship building – Boat and ship have been the instrumental in the development of civilization, affording humanity greater mobility than travel over land, whether for trade, transport or warfare, and the capacity for fishing. Similarities among boat and ship building technology in the Austronesian and other parts of the world were observed. The earliest seaworthy boats may have been developed as early as 40,000 years ago, according to one hypothesis explaining the habitation of Melanesia and Australia.

6. And so on.

***

CHECKLIST

Phrases or names in double quotes are, wherever possible translated into English, as given by Plato, either Greek translation from the original account or terms not found in Greek. Phrases in parenthesis are interpretations by the author.

No	Phenotype	Plato's account		Evidence
		Section in *Timaeus*	Section in *Critias*	
A	**THE COUNTRY**			
1	At a distant point in the "Atlantic Ocean" (ancient Greek understanding)	24e		✓
2	Larger than "Libya" and "Asia" (Asia Minor) combined (ancient Greek understanding)	24e	108e	✓
3	The way to other islands	24e		✓
4	Might pass to opposite continent encompasses true ocean	24e		✓
5	Landscape of the whole country, at the region on the side of the ocean, was very lofty and precipitous		118a	✓
6	A small hill and a vast level plain near the sea, accessible by ships, vessels and boats from the sea; waterways on the plain discharge to the sea		113c, 113e, 118d	✓
7	Beyond bordering monuments, the Greek call monuments of "Heracles"	24e, 25c	108e, 114b	✓
8	In front of a strait	24e, 25a		✓
9	A sea surrounded by a boundless continent	25a		✓
10	Some islands in the sea	24e	114c	✓
11	Two-season climate – "summer" (dry) and "winter" (wet)		112d, 118e	✓
12	Hot and cold springs		113e, 117a	✓
13	Abundant of water benefit of the annual rainfall		111c	✓
14	Excellently attempered climate		111e, 112d	✓
15	Fertile, best soil for agriculture and farming		111e, 113c	✓

181

No	Phenotype	Plato's account		Evidence
		Section in *Timaeus*	Section in *Critias*	
16	Vast diversity of flora and fauna		114e, 115a, 115b	✓
17	Elephant, horse, "bull" and dolphin		114e, 116e, 117c to 117e, 119b, 119d to 120a	✓
18	Abundant of food to sustain a civilization and to create an army (about 20 million people)		111e, 118e, 119a	✓
19	Advanced civilization in the era	24e, 25a		✓
20	Earthquakes and "floods" from the sea (tsunami)	25c, 25d	108e, 111a, 112a	✓
21	Sunken ceaselessly (post-glacial sea level rise)		111b, 111c	✓
22	The sea at the Atlantis capital "is now" (Solon's time) impassable and impenetrable because of a "reef of clay" (coral reef), caused by "subsidence" of the island (sea level rise)	25d		✓
23	The "Atlantis City" is now under the sea	25d		✓
B	**PRODUCES ("FRUITS")**			
24	Two harvests each year, in "winter" fed by rains and in "summer" by irrigation from the canals		118e	✓
25	Roots, herbage, woods and essences distilled from "fruit" and flower		115a	✓
26	Cultivated "fruit", dried, for nourishment and any other, used for food – common name pulse		115a	✓
27	"Fruits" having a hard rind, affording drinks and meats and ointments		115b	✓
28	Chestnuts and the like, which furnish pleasure and amusement		115b	✓
29	"Fruits" which spoil with keeping, consoled after dinner		115b	✓
30	Wondrous and in infinite abundance		115b	✓

No	Phenotype	Plato's account		Evidence
		Section in *Timaeus*	Section in *Critias*	
C	**VAST PLAIN NEAR THE CAPITAL**			
31	Immediately about and surrounding the city was a level plain		118a	✓
32	Surrounded by mountains which descended towards the sea		118a	✓
33	Smooth and even		118a	✓
34	General shape was rectangular and oblong		118a, 118c	✓
35	Extending in one direction 3,000 stadia (± 555 km), across the center inland 2,000 stadia (±370 km)		118a	✓
36	Looked towards the south, sheltered from the north		118b	✓
37	Surrounded by mountains celebrated their number, size and beauty, there were many wealthy villages of country folk		118b	✓
38	Rivers, lakes and meadows – abundant food supply for every animal, wild or tame		118b	✓
39	Plenty of wood of various sorts – abundant for each and every kind of work		118b	✓
D	**WATERWAYS ON THE PLAIN**			
	Perimeter ditch			
40	1. Incredible in size, unexpected that they were artificial		118c	✓
41	2. 100 ft (±30 m) deep, 1 stadium (±185 m) wide, 10,000 stadia (±1,850 km) long		118c	✓
42	3. received streams from the mountains		118d	✓
	Inland canals and transverse passages			
43	1. Inland canals were straight, about 100 ft (±30 m) wide, 100 stadia (18.5 km) intervals and let off into the perimeter ditch		118d	✓
44	2. Transverse passages were cut from one inland canal into another		118e	✓
45	3. Means for transporting wood and products in ships		118e	✓

No	Phenotype	Plato's account		Evidence
		Section in *Timaeus*	Section in *Critias*	
	Irrigation streams			
46	1. Tapping from the canals		118e	✓
47	2. Supplied water to the land in "summer" (dry) but rainfall in the "winter" (rainy) yielding two crops in a year		118e	✓
E	**MINERALS AND ROCKS**			
48	"Brass"/"bronze" (copper, tin and zinc)		116b, 116c	✓
49	Tin		116b, 116c	✓
50	"Orichalcum", more precious mineral than anything except gold, flashing, red color, abundant resources		114e, 116c, 116d	✓
51	Gold		114e, 116c, 116d, 116e	✓
52	Silver		116d, 116e	✓
53	White, black and red stones		116a, 116b	✓
54	Hollowed out rock for double docks		116a, 116b	✓
F	**MYTHS AND CUSTOMS**			
55	"Poseidon" (sea or water god, law founder)		113c to 113e, 116c, 116d, 117b, 119c, 119d	✓
56	"Heracles" (son of a supreme god, outrageous birth, has insatiable appetites and being very rude, brutal and violent)	24e, 25c	108e, 114b	✓
57	"Bull" sacrifice		119d to 120c	✓
58	Temple or pyramid		116c, 116d, 116e, 117c, 119c	✓

184

No	Phenotype	Plato's account		Evidence
		Section in *Timaeus*	Section in *Critias*	
59	Maritime activities		114d, 115c to 116a, 117d, 117e, 119b	✓
60	Transportation by waterways		118e	✓

***

REFERENCES

PLATO'S TEXTS

1. http://classics.mit.edu/Plato/timaeus.html – *Timaeus by Plato, Written 360 BCE*, Translated by Benjamin Jowett
2. http://classics.mit.edu/Plato/critias.html – *Critias by Plato, Written 360 BCE*, Translated by Benjamin Jowett
3. http://classics.mit.edu/Plato/republic.html – *The Republic by Plato, Written 360 BCE*, Translated by Benjamin Jowett
4. http://www.perseus.tufts.edu/hopper/text?doc=plat.+tim.+* – Perseus Digital Library, Gregory R Crane, Editor-in-Chief, Tufts University. * is the section number. *Plato. Plato in Twelve Volumes, Vol. 9* translated by WRM Lamb, Cambridge, MA, Harvard University Press; London, William Heinemann Ltd, 1925
5. http://www.perseus.tufts.edu/hopper/text?doc=plat.+criti.+* – Perseus Digital Library, Gregory R Crane, Editor-in-Chief, Tufts University. * is the section number. *Plato. Plato in Twelve Volumes, Vol. 9* translated by WRM Lamb, Cambridge, MA, Harvard University Press; London, William Heinemann Ltd, 1925
6. http://www.perseus.tufts.edu/hopper/text?doc=plat.+rep.+*.* – Perseus Digital Library, Gregory R Crane, Editor-in-Chief, Tufts University. *.* is the book.section numbers. *Plato. Plato in Twelve Volumes, Vols 5 & 6* translated by Paul Shorey, Cambridge, MA, Harvard University Press; London, William Heinemann Ltd, 1969

CITED THEORIES

1. Arysio Nunes dos Santos, *Atlantis: The Lost Continent Finally Found, The Definitive Localization of Plato's Lost Civilization*, Atlantis Publications, June 2005
2. http://www.atlan.org – *Atlantis - the Lost Continent Finally Found*
3. Stephen Oppenheimer, *Eden in the East: The Drowned Continent of Southeast Asia*, Weidenfeld and Nicolson, 1998
4. http://www.bradshawfoundation.com/books/eden_in_the_east.php – Bradshaw Foundation, The Book Review, *Eden in the East: The Drowned Continent of Southeast Asia* by Stephen Oppenheimer
5. http://www.bradshawfoundation.com/stephenoppenheimer/index.php – Bradshaw Foundation, Professor Stephen Oppenheimer, *Journey of Mankind, The Peopling of The World*

6. http://www.bradshawfoundation.com/journey – Journey of Mankind, The Peopling of The World
7. Wilhelm G Solheim, David Bulbeck, *Archaeology and Culture In Southeast Asia: Unraveling The Nusantao*, University of Hawaii Press, 2007
8. http://www.grahamhancock.com/archive/underworld/DrSunilAtlantis.php – *Where was Atlantis? Sundaland fits the bill, surely!* by Dr Sunil Prasannan
9. Danny Hilman Natawidjaja, *Plato Never Lied: Atlantis Is in Indonesia*, Booknesia, 2013

DIGITAL DATA SOURCES

1. https://lta.cr.usgs.gov/GTOPO30 – USGS, *Global 30 Arc-Second Elevation (GTOPO30)*
2. http://www.gebco.net/data_and_products/gridded_bathymetry_data – GEBCO, *Gridded bathymetry data*
3. http://www.ngdc.noaa.gov/mgg/global/global.html – NOAA, *ETOPO1 Global Relief Model*
4. http://earthquake.usgs.gov/data/centennial – USGS, *Centennial Earthquake Catalog*
5. http://earthquake.usgs.gov/earthquakes/world/10_largest_world.php – USGS, *Largest Earthquakes in the World Since 1900*
6. http://www.ngdc.noaa.gov/hazard/tsu.shtml – NOAA NGDC, *Tsunami Data and Information*
7. http://www.ngdc.noaa.gov/hazard/earthqk.shtml – NOAA NGDC, *Earthquake Data and Information*
8. http://www.ngdc.noaa.gov/hazard/volcano.shtml – NOAA NGDC, *Volcano Data and Information*
9. http://www.worldclim.org – WorldClim, *Global Climate Data*
10. http://pubs.usgs.gov/of/2010/1254 - USGS, *Mineral Facilities of Asia and the Pacific*
11. http://www.bakosurtanal.go.id/peta-rupabumi – Badan Informasi Geospasial, *Peta Rupabumi*

WIKIPEDIA® AND WIKIBOOKS® BY THE WIKIMEDIA FOUNDATION

The Wikimedia Foundation is the non-profit organization that operates Wikipedia and other free knowledge projects. The Wikimedia Foundation is a 501(c)(3) tax-exempt non-profit organization with offices in San Francisco, California, USA.

1. http://en.wikipedia.org/wiki/Atlantis – Wikipedia, *Atlantis*
2. http://en.wikipedia.org/wiki/Plato – Wikipedia, *Plato*

3. http://en.wikipedia.org/wiki/Timaeus_(dialogue) – Wikipedia, *Timaeus (dialogue)*

4. http://en.wikipedia.org/wiki/Critias_(dialogue) – Wikipedia, *Critias (dialogue)*

5. http://en.wikipedia.org/wiki/The_Republic_(Plato) – Wikipedia, *The Republic (Plato)*

6. http://en.wikipedia.org/wiki/Location_hypotheses_of_Atlantis – Wikipedia, *Location hypotheses of Atlantis*

7. http://en.wikipedia.org/wiki/Benjamin_Jowett – Wikipedia, *Benjamin Jowett*

8. http://en.wikipedia.org/wiki/Proclus – Wikipedia, *Proclus*

9. http://id.wikipedia.org/wiki/Atlantis,_The_Lost_Continent_Finally_Found – Wikipedia, *Atlantis, The Lost Continent Finally Found*

10. http://en.wikipedia.org/wiki/Stephen_Oppenheimer – Wikipedia, *Stephen Oppenheimer*

11. http://en.wikipedia.org/wiki/Nusantao_Maritime_Trading_and_Communication_Network – Wikipedia, *Nusantao Maritime Trading and Communication Network*

12. http://en.wikipedia.org/wiki/Wilhelm_Solheim – Wikipedia, *Wilhelm Solheim*

13. http://en.wikipedia.org/wiki/Athens – Wikipedia, *Athens*

14. http://en.wikipedia.org/wiki/Sundaland – Wikipedia, *Sundaland*

15. http://id.wikipedia.org/wiki/Paparan_Sunda – Wikipedia, *Paparan Sunda*

16. http://en.wikibooks.org/wiki/The_Geology_of_Indonesia – Wikibooks, *The Geology of Indonesia*

17. http://en.wikipedia.org/wiki/Glaciology – Wikipedia, *Glaciology*

18. http://en.wikipedia.org/wiki/Ice_age – Wikipedia, *Ice age*

19. http://en.wikipedia.org/wiki/Last_Glacial_Maximum – Wikipedia, *Last Glacial Maximum*

20. http://en.wikipedia.org/wiki/Younger_Dryas – Wikipedia, *Younger Dryas*

21. http://en.wikipedia.org/wiki/Java_Sea – Wikipedia, *Java Sea*

22. http://en.wikipedia.org/wiki/Δ18O – Wikipedia, $\delta^{18}O$

23. http://en.wikipedia.org/wiki/Meltwater_pulse_1A – Wikipedia, *Meltwater pulse 1A*

24. http://en.wikibooks.org/wiki/The_Geology_of_Indonesia/Java_%26_Java_Sea – Wikibooks, *The Geology of Indonesia/Java & Java Sea*

25. http://en.wikibooks.org/wiki/The_Geology_of_Indonesia/Kalimantan – Wikibooks, *The Geology of Indonesia/Kalimantan*

26. http://en.wikibooks.org/wiki/The_Geology_of_Indonesia/Banda_Arc – Wikibooks, *The Geology of Indonesia/Banda Arc*

27. http://en.wikibooks.org/wiki/The_Geology_of_Indonesia/The_lesser_Sunda_Islands – Wikibooks, *The Geology of Indonesia/The lesser Sunda Islands*

28. http://en.wikipedia.org/wiki/Köppen_climate_classification – Wikipedia, *Köppen climate classification*

29. http://en.wikipedia.org/wiki/Hadley_cell – Wikipedia, *Hadley cell*

30. http://en.wikipedia.org/wiki/Agriculture – Wikipedia, *Agriculture*

31. http://id.wikipedia.org/wiki/Irigasi – Wikipedia, *Irigasi*

32. http://en.wikipedia.org/wiki/Wallace_Line – Wikipedia, *Wallace Line*

33. http://id.wikipedia.org/wiki/Garis_Wallace – Wikipedia, *Garis Wallace*

34. http://en.wikipedia.org/wiki/Flora_of_Indonesia – Wikipedia, *Flora of Indonesia*

35. http://id.wikipedia.org/wiki/Daftar_flora_identitas_provinsi_di_Indonesia – Wikipedia, *Daftar flora identitas provinsi di Indonesia*

36. http://en.wikipedia.org/wiki/Fauna_of_Indonesia – Wikipedia, *Fauna of Indonesia*

37. http://id.wikipedia.org/wiki/Fauna_Indonesia – Wikipedia, *Fauna Indonesia*

38. http://en.wikipedia.org/wiki/Plate_tectonics – Wikipedia, *Plate tectonics*

39. http://en.wikipedia.org/wiki/Earthquake – Wikipedia, *Earthquake*

40. http://en.wikipedia.org/wiki/Tsunami – Wikipedia, *Tsunami*

41. http://en.wikipedia.org/wiki/Volcano – Wikipedia, *Volcano*

42. http://id.wikipedia.org/wiki/Daftar_gunung_di_Indonesia_menurut_lokasi – Wikipedia, *Daftar gunung di Indonesia menurut lokasi*

43. http://en.wikipedia.org/wiki/New_World – Wikipedia, *New World*

44. http://en.wikipedia.org/wiki/Mineral – Wikipedia, *Mineral*

45. http://en.wikipedia.org/wiki/Brass – Wikipedia, *Brass*

46. http://en.wikipedia.org/wiki/Orichalcum – Wikipedia, *Orichalcum*

47. http://en.wikipedia.org/wiki/Zircon – Wikipedia, *Zircon*

48. http://en.wikipedia.org/wiki/Onyx – Wikipedia, *Onyx*

49. http://id.wikipedia.org/wiki/Sungai_Barito – Wikipedia, *Sungai Barito*

50. http://id.wikipedia.org/wiki/Sungai_Kahayan – Wikipedia, *Sungai Kahayan*

51. http://id.wikipedia.org/wiki/Anjir – Wikipedia, *Anjir*

52. http://en.wikipedia.org/wiki/Nagarakretagama – Wikipedia, *Nagarakretagama*

53. http://en.wikipedia.org/wiki/Antonio_Pigafetta – Wikipedia, *Antonio Pigafetta*

54. http://en.wikipedia.org/wiki/Duarte_Barbosa – Wikipedia, *Duarte Barbosa*

55. http://en.wikipedia.org/wiki/Ptolemy – Wikipedia, *Ptolemy*

56. http://en.wikipedia.org/wiki/Dayak_people – Wikipedia, *Dayak people*

57. http://id.wikipedia.org/wiki/Suku_Dayak – Wikipedia, *Suku Dayak*

58. http://en.wikipedia.org/wiki/Barito_Languages – Wikipedia, *Barito languages*

59. http://en.wikipedia.org/wiki/Banjar_people – Wikipedia, *Banjar people*

60. http://id.wikipedia.org/wiki/Suku_Banjar – Wikipedia, *Suku Banjar*

61. http://en.wikipedia.org/wiki/Batak – Wikipedia, *Batak*

62. http://id.wikipedia.org/wiki/Suku_Batak – Wikipedia, *Suku Batak*

63. http://en.wikipedia.org/wiki/Toraja – Wikipedia, *Toraja*

64. http://id.wikipedia.org/wiki/Suku_Toraja – Wikipedia, *Suku Toraja*

65. http://en.wikipedia.org/wiki/Bugis – Wikipedia, *Bugis*

66. http://id.wikipedia.org/wiki/Suku_Bugis – Wikipedia, *Suku Bugis*

67. http://en.wikipedia.org/wiki/Sumba – Wikipedia, *Sumba*

68. http://id.wikipedia.org/wiki/Suku_Sumba – Wikipedia, *Suku Sumba*

69. http://en.wikipedia.org/wiki/Rejangese_people – Wikipedia, *Rejangese pople*

70. http://id.wikipedia.org/wiki/Suku_Rejang – Wikipedia, *Suku Rejang*

71. http://en.wikipedia.org/wiki/Rejangese_alphabet – Wikipedia, *Rejangese alphabet*

72. http://id.wikipedia.org/wiki/Aksara_Kaganga – Wikipedia, *Aksara Kaganga*

73. http://id.wikipedia.org/wiki/Megalit_Basemah – Wikipedia, *Megalit Basemah*

74. http://en.wikipedia.org/wiki/Nias – Wikipedia, *Nias*

75. http://id.wikipedia.org/wiki/Suku_Nias – Wikipedia, *Suku Nias*

76. http://en.wikipedia.org/wiki/Javanese_people – Wikipedia, *Javanese people*

77. http://id.wikipedia.org/wiki/Suku_Jawa – Wikipedia, *Suku Jawa*

78. http://en.wikipedia.org/wiki/Sundanese_people – Wikipedia, *Sundanese people*

79. http://id.wikipedia.org/wiki/Suku_Sunda – Wikipedia, *Suku Sunda*

80. http://en.wikipedia.org/wiki/Balinese_people – Wikipedia, *Balinese people*

81. http://id.wikipedia.org/wiki/Suku_Bali – Wikipedia, *Suku Bali*

82. http://en.wikipedia.org/wiki/Malay_race – Wikipedia, *Malay race*

83. http://id.wikipedia.org/wiki/Suku_Melayu – Wikipedia, *Suku Melayu*

84. http://id.wikipedia.org/wiki/Polynesia – Wikipedia, *Polynesia*

85. http://en.wikipedia.org/wiki/Kebatinan – Wikipedia, *Kebatinan*

86. http://id.wikipedia.org/wiki/Kejawen – Wikipedia, *Kejawen*

87. http://en.wikipedia.org/wiki/Sunda_Wiwitan – Wikipedia, *Sunda Wiwitan*

88. http://id.wikipedia.org/wiki/Sunda_Wiwitan – Wikipedia, *Sunda Wiwitan*

89. http://id.wikipedia.org/wiki/Wawacan_Sulanjana – Wikipedia, *Wawacan Sulanjana*

90. http://en.wikipedia.org/wiki/Parahyangan – Wikipedia, *Parahyangan*

91. http://id.wikipedia.org/wiki/Parahyangan – Wikipedia, *Parahyangan*

92. http://en.wikipedia.org/wiki/Hinduism_in_Indonesia – Wikipedia, *Hinduism in Indonesia*

93. http://id.wikipedia.org/wiki/Agama_Hindu – Wikipedia, *Agama Hindu*

94. http://en.wikipedia.org/wiki/Kaharingan – Wikipedia, *Kaharingan*

95. http://id.wikipedia.org/wiki/Kaharingan – Wikipedia, *Kaharingan*

96. http://en.wikipedia.org/wiki/Hyang – Wikipedia, *Hyang*

97. http://id.wikipedia.org/wiki/Hyang – Wikipedia, *Hyang*

98. http://en.wikipedia.org/wiki/Sureq_Galigo – Wikipedia, *Sureq Galigo*

99. http://id.wikipedia.org/wiki/Sureq_Galigo – Wikipedia, *Sureq Galigo*

100. http://en.wikipedia.org/wiki/Batara_Guru – Wikipedia, *Batara Guru*

101. http://id.wikipedia.org/wiki/Batara_Guru – Wikipedia, *Batara Guru*

102. http://en.wikipedia.org/wiki/Batara_Kala – Wikipedia, *Batara Kala*

103. http://id.wikipedia.org/wiki/Batara_Kala – Wikipedia, *Batara Kala*

104. http://id.wikipedia.org/wiki/Rara_Jonggrang – Wikipedia, *Rara Jonggrang*

105. http://id.wikipedia.org/wiki/Sri – Wikipedia, *Sri*

106. http://en.wikipedia.org/wiki/Wayang – Wikipedia, *Wayang*

107. http://id.wikipedia.org/wiki/Wayang – Wikipedia, *Wayang*

108. http://id.wikipedia.org/wiki/Arsitektur_Jawa – Wikipedia, *Arsitektur Jawa*

109. http://id.wikipedia.org/wiki/Arsitektur_Bali – Wikipedia, *Arsitektur Bali*

110. http://en.wikipedia.org/wiki/Poseidon – Wikipedia, *Poseidon*

111. http://en.wikipedia.org/wiki/Atlas_(mythology) – Wikipedia, *Atlas (mythology)*

112. http://en.wikipedia.org/wiki/Heracles – Wikipedia, *Heracles*

113. http://en.wikipedia.org/wiki/History_of_Egypt – Wikipedia, *History of Egypt*

114. http://en.wikipedia.org/wiki/History_of_ Athens – Wikipedia, *History of Athens*

115. http://en.wikipedia.org/wiki/Anatolia – Wikipedia, *Anatolia*

116. http://id.wikipedia.org/wiki/Gajah_kalimantan – Wikipedia, *Gajah kalimantan*

117. http://en.wikipedia.org/wiki/Rice – Wikipedia, *Rice*

118. http://id.wikipedia.org/wiki/Padi – Wikipedia, *Padi*

119. http://id.wikipedia.org/wiki/Subak_(irigasi) – Wikipedia, *Subak (irigasi)*

120. http://en.wikipedia.org/wiki/Temple – Wikipedia, *Temple*

121. http://en.wikipedia.org/wiki/Candi_of_indonesia – Wikipedia, *Candi of Indonesia*

122. http://id.wikipedia.org/wiki/Candi – Wikipedia, *Candi*

123. http://en.wikipedia.org/wiki/Temple – Wikipedia, *Temple*

124. http://en.wikipedia.org/wiki/Borobudur – Wikipedia, *Borobudur*

125. http://en.wikipedia.org/wiki/Step_pyramid – Wikipedia, *Step pyramid*

126. http://id.wikipedia.org/wiki/Punden_berundak – Wikipedia, *Punden berundak*

127. http://en.wikipedia.org/wiki/Gunung_Padang_Megalithic_Site – Wikipedia, *Gunung Padang Megalithic Site*

128. http://id.wikipedia.org/wiki/Situs_Gunung_Padang – Wikipedia, *Situs Gunung Padang*

129. http://en.wikipedia.org/wiki/Borobudur_ship – Wikipedia, *Borobudur ship*

130. http://en.wikipedia.org/wiki/Pinisi – Wikipedia, *Pinisi*

131. http://en.wikipedia.org/wiki/Bawean – Wikipedia, *Bawean*

132. http://id.wikipedia.org/wiki/Pulau_Bawean – Wikipedia, *Pulau Bawean*

133. http://en.wikipedia.org/wiki/Aji_Saka – Wikipedia, *Aji Saka*

134. http://id.wikipedia.org/wiki/Aji_Saka – Wikipedia, *Aji Saka*

135. http://en.wikipedia.org/wiki/Javanese_script – Wikipedia, *Javanese script*

136. http://id.wikipedia.org/wiki/Aksara_Jawa – Wikipedia, *Aksara Jawa*

137. http://id.wikipedia.org/wiki/Aksara_Bali – Wikipedia, *Aksara Bali*

138. http://id.wikipedia.org/wiki/Aksara_Sunda_Baku – Wikipedia, *Aksara Sunda Baku*

139. http://en.wikipedia.org/wiki/IUCN_Red_List – Wikipedia, *IUCN Red List*

140. http://en.wikipedia.org/wiki/Bawean_deer – Wikipedia, *Bawean deer*

141. http://en.wikipedia.org/wiki/Unicode – Wikipedia, *Unicode*

142. http://en.wikipedia.org/wiki/Jamu – Wikipedia, *Jamu*

143. http://en.wikipedia.org/wiki/Bumbu_(seasoning) – Wikipedia, *Bumbu (seasoning)*

144. http://en.wikipedia.org/wiki/Tapai – Wikipedia, *Tapai*

145. http://en.wikipedia.org/wiki/Aztlán – Wikipedia, *Aztlán*

146. http://en.wikipedia.org/wiki/Popol_Vuh – Wikipedia, *Popol Vuh*

147. http://en.wikipedia.org/wiki/Tollan – Wikipedia, *Tollan*

148. http://en.wikipedia.org/wiki/Babylonia – Wikipedia, *Babylonia*

MISCELLANEOUS

1. –, *The Dialogues of Plato translated into English with Analyses and Introductions by B Jowett, MA in Five Volumes*, 3rd edition revised and corrected, Oxford University Press, 1892

2. Edlic Sathiamurthy and Harold K Voris, *Maps of Holocene Sea Level Transgression and Submerged Lakes on the Sunda Shelf*, The Natural History Journal of Chulalongkorn University, Supplement 2: 1-43, August 2006

3. Virginia Matheson Hooker, *A Short History of Malaysia: Linking East and West*, Allen & Unwin, 2003

4. Jean-Michel Chazine, *Rock Art, Burials, and Habitations: Caves in East Kalimantan*, Asian Perspectives, Vol 44, No 1, University of Hawai'i Press, 2005

5. Jean-Michel Chazine and Jean-George Ferrié, *Recent Archaeological Discoveries in East Kalimantan, Indonesia*, IPPA Bulletin 28, 2008, pp 16 – 22

6. Anggraeni and Sunarningsih, *The Prehistoric Settlement at Jambu Hilir, South Kalimantan Province, Indonesia*, IPPA Bulletin 28, 2008, pp 120 – 26

7. Ki Suryo Saputro, *Serat Pustakaraja Parwa* (translated), 1983

8. Christian Heine, Leonardo Quevedo, Hamish McKay, R Dietmar Müller, *Plate Tectonic Consequences of competing models for the origin and history of the Banda Sea subducted oceanic lithosphere*, EarthByte Group, School of Geosciences, The University of Sydney, NSW, Australia

9. A Krabbenhoeft, RW Weinrebe, H Kopp, ER Flueh, S Ladage, C Papenberg, L Planert, and Y Djajadihardja, *Bathymetry of the Indonesian Sunda margin-relating morphological features of the upper plate slopes to the location and extent of the seismogenic zone*, Natural Hazards and Earth System Sciences, 10, 1899–1911, 2010

10. Catherine T Flessen, *Bellwood and Solheim: Models of Neolithic movements of people in Southeast Asia and the Pacific*, Norwegian University of Science and Technology, 2006

11. Kurt Lambeck, Hélène Rouby, Anthony Purcell, Yiying Sun, and Malcolm Sambridge, *Sea level and global ice volumes from the Last Glacial Maximum to the Holocene*, Proceedings of the National Academy of Sciences of the United States of America, Vol 111, No 43, October 28, 2014

12. Peter U Clark, Alan C Mix, *Ice sheets and sea level of the Last Glacial Maximum*, Elsevier Science Ltd, 2001

13. M Siddall, EJ Rohling, A Almogi-Labin, Ch Hemleben, D Meischner, I Schmelzer & DA Smeed, *Sea-level fluctuations during the last glacial cycle*, Nature PublishingGroup, NATURE Vol 423, No 19 June 2003

14. Michael K Gagan, Erica J Hendy, Simon G Haberle, Wahyoe S. Hantoro, *Post-glacial evolution of the Indo-Pacific Warm Pool and El Niño-Southern oscillation*, Elsevier Ltd and INQUA, Quaternary International 118–119, 2004, pp 127 – 143

15. Ian Metcalfe, *Tectonic framework and Phanerozoic evolution of Sundaland*, International Association for Gondwana Research, Gondwana Research 19, 2011, pp 3 – 21

16. –, *Key Indicator of Indonesia Energy and Mineral Resources*, Center for Data and Information on Energy and Mineral Resources, Ministry of Energy and Mineral Resources, Indonesia, 2011

17. Chin S Kuo, *The Mineral Industry of Indonesia*, US Department of the Interior, US Geological Survey, 2013

18. Pui-Kwan Tse, *The Mineral Industry of Malaysia*, US Department of the Interior, US Geological Survey, 2013

19. –, *Sailing Directions (Enrute): Borneo, Jawa, Sulawesi, and Nusa Tenggara*, National Geospatial-Intelligence Agency, Publication No 63, Eleventh Edition, 2009

20. Jürg Schneider, *The making of "new seed": ritual, politics and rice seed production in Indonesia*, 1998

21. Narifumi Maeda, *Agricultural Rites in South Sulawesi*, Southeast Asian Studies, Vol. 28, No 4, March 1991

22. Suwido H Limin, Jentha and Yunsiska Ermiasi, *History of the Development of Tropical Peatland in Central Kalimantan, Indonesia*, TROPICS Vol 16 (3), Issued May 31, 2007

23. Francesco Brighenti, *Buffalo sacrifice and mortuary ritual in tribal cultures of Monsoon Asia*, Bubalus bubalis 1, 2005

24. Robert Hall, *The SE Asian Gateway: History and Tectonics of the Australia-Asia Collision, Australia-SE Asia collision: plate tectonics and crustal flow*, Geological Society, London, Special Publications, 355, pp 75 – 109

25. E Bryant, *Tsunami, Chapter 2 – Tsunami Dynamics*, Springer International Publishing Switzerland, 2014, pp 19 – 32

26. Finn Løvholt, Daniela Kühn, Hilmar Bungum, Carl B Harbitz and Sylfest Glimsdal, *Historical tsunamis and present tsunami hazard in eastern Indonesia and the southern Philippines*, Journal of Geophysical Research, Vol 117, 2012,

27. Indrabakti Sangalang, Endang Titi Sunarti Darjosanjoto, Muhammad Faqih, *Understanding Space Based on The Symbol of Batang Garing on Dayak Ngaju House*

28. Ligaya SP Lacsina, *Traditional island Southeast Asian watercraft in Philippine archaeological sites*, National Museum of the Philippines

29. Raymond Alfred, A Christy Williams, Jan Vertefeuille, John Payne, Patrick Andau, Laurentius Ambu, Symphorosa Sipangkui, Angela Lim, *Satellite Tracking of Borneo's Pygmy Elephants June 2005 – June 2006*, WWF, 2006

30. Raymond Alfred, Abd Hamid Ahmad, John Payne, Christy William, Laurentius Ambu, *Density and Population Estimation of the Bornean Elephants (Elephas maximus borneensis) in Sabah*, Online Journal of Biological Sciences 10 (2): 92-102, 2010

31. Prithiviraj Fernando, TNC Vidya, John Payne, Michael Stuewe, Geoffrey Davison, Raymond J Alfred, Patrick Andau, Edwin Bosi, Annelisa Kilbourn, Don J Melnick, *DNA Analysis Indicates That Asian Elephants Are Native to Borneo and Are Therefore a High Priority for Conservation*, PLoS Biology, Volume 1, Issue 1, 2003, pp 110 – 115

32. Soedarsono Riswan and Harini Sangat-Roemantyo, *Jamu as Traditional Medicine in Java, Indonesia*, South Pacific Study Vol 23, No 1, 2002

33. Susan Jane-Beers, *Jamu: The Ancient Indonesian Art of Herbal Healing*, Tuttle Publishing, 2001

34. Washington University in St Louis, *Deep history of coconuts decoded: Origins of cultivation, ancient trade routes, and colonization of the Americas*, ScienceDaily, 24 June 2011

35. SC Woodhouse MA, *English – Greek Dictionary, A Vocabulary of The Attic Language*, George Routledge & Sons, Limited, London, 1910

36. http://www.activemind.com/Mysterious/Topics/Atlantis – Active Mind, *Atlantis*

37. http://www.lost-civilizations.net/atlantis.html – Lost Civilizations, *Atlantis*

38. http://atlantipedia.ie/samples – Atlantipedia

39. http://www.naturalhistorymag.com/picks-from-the-past/12467/lost-continents – Natural History, *Lost Continents*

40. http://www.ncca.gov.ph/about-culture-and-arts/articles-on-c-n-a/article.php?subcat=13&i=364 – National Commission for Culture and The Arts, *The Austronesian Expansion – a Reaction to "Paths of Origin"*

41. http://www.greek-gods.info – Gods and Goddesses of Ancient Greek

42. http://neon.mems.cmu.edu/cramb/Processing/history.html – *A Short History of Metals* by Alan W Cramb

43. http://www.kastenmarine.com/phinisi_history.htm – Michael Kasten, *The Indonesian Phinisi*

44. http://www.iucnredlist.org – IUCN, *The IUCN Red List of Threatened Species*™

45. http://www.worldwildlife.org/species/borneo-pygmy-elephant – WWF, *Borneo Pygmy Elephant*

46. http://wwf.panda.org/what_we_do/endangered_species/elephants/asian_elephants/borneo_pygmy_elephant – WWF, *Borneo Pygmy Elephant*

47. http://www.wwf.or.id/en/news_facts/press_release/?27422/habitat-gajah-kerdil-kalimantan-terancam-dirusak-oleh--dua-perusahaan-hti – WWF, *The Habitat of Borneo Pygmy Elephants Threatened by Two Industrial Plantation Companies*

48. https://sites.google.com/site/jawaunicode/main-page – *Fonta Unicode Aksara Jawa*

49. http://content.time.com/time/world/article/0,8599,2107489,00.html – Time, *Jamu: Why Isn't Indonesia's Ancient System of Herbal Healing Better Known?* By Ian Lloyd Neubauer

50. https://evrinasp.wordpress.com/2013/09/08/pengembangan-jamu-sebagai-warisan-budaya – Evrina SP, *Pengembangan Jamu Sebagai Warisan Budaya*

***

INDEX

***

Made in the USA
Monee, IL
09 August 2022

11238576R10124